DISCOVER[ING]
MEN

Feminism has put the critical study of men and masculinities firmly on to the academic agenda. In *Discovering Men* David Morgan explores key issues in this field of study, looking at the theoretical, practical and political difficulties that arise when men begin to study themselves, and considering the deep assumptions that underlie this area of enquiry.

David Morgan investigates the various strategies that may be adopted in exploring men and masculinities, drawing constantly on feminist critique of men's theoretical and everyday practice. He recommends a critical re-reading of classic sociological texts in order to bring out the 'hidden' stories about masculinities that they tell, and re-examines well-documented areas within sociology, focusing on studies of men at work. He analyses situations where masculinity may be problematic, such as male unemployment, shifts in the gender balance in the workplace, and, historically, the suffrage movement. He also discusses the limitations of using autobiography and personal experience.

Discovering Men is one of the first books in the field to focus on issues of methodology and epistemology and to explore the difficulties of men studying men in a patriarchal society. It will be essential reading for courses dealing with gender issues, and will also be of interest to students of women's studies, social history, social policy and research methodology.

David Morgan is Senior Lecturer in Sociology at the University of Manchester. He has written extensively on issues of gender and the family, and is co-editor of two books, *Gender, Class and Work* and *Men, Masculinities and Social Theory*.

Critical studies on men and masculinities

Jeff Hearn and David H.J. Morgan (editors)
Men, Masculinities and Social Theory

David Jackson
Unmasking Masculinity
A critical autobiography

Jeff Hearn
Men in the Public Eye

Arthur Brittan
The Competitive Self (forthcoming)

Tim Edwards
Erotic Politics (forthcoming)

Editorial advisory board

Harry Brod (*Kenyon College, Ohio*)
Cynthia Cockburn (*City University, London*)
Bob Connell (*University of California, Santa Cruz*)
Paul Gilroy (*University of Essex*)
Jalna Hanmer (*University of Bradford*)
Jeff Hearn (*University of Bradford*)
Michael Kimmel (*State University of New York*)
Marianne Krüll (*University of Bonn*)
David Morgan (*University of Manchester*)
Mary O'Brien (*Ontario Institute of Studies in Education*)
Pratibha Parmar (*Writer and Film-maker*)
Ken Plummer (*University of Essex*)
Rosemary Pringle (*Macquarie University, Sydney*)
Lynne Segal (*Middlesex Polytechnic*)
Victor Seidler (*Goldsmiths' College, London*)
Elizabeth Stanko (*Brunel University, London*)
Jeffrey Weeks (*Bristol Polytechnic*)
Sue Wise (*University of Lancaster*)

DISCOVERING
MEN

David H. J. Morgan

London and New York

First published in 1992
by Routledge
11 New Fetter Lane, London EC4P 4EE

Simultaneously published in the USA and Canada
by Routledge
a division of Routledge, Chapman and Hall Inc.
29 West 35th Street, New York, NY 10001

British Library Cataloguing in Publication Data
A catalogue record for this book is available from the British Library

Library of Congress Cataloging in Publication Data
A catalog record for this book is available on request

ISBN 0–415–07621–8
        0–415–07622–6 (pbk)

Typeset in Bembo by LaserScript, Mitcham, Surrey
Printed and bound in Great Britain by
Biddles Ltd, Guildford and King's Lynn

Contents

Figures

Series editor's preface

Gender is one of the most pervasive and taken-for-granted features of our lives. It figures strongly in the make-up of all societies. Yet it is easy to see that gender may also create problems – in terms of power, oppression, inequality, identity and self-doubt.

The growth of modern feminism and the associated development of women's studies have brought a deep questioning of women's social position. At the same time feminism and women's studies have provided continuing critical analyses of men and masculinities. In a rather different way the rise of gay liberation and gay scholarship has shown that previously accepted notions of sexuality and gender are no longer just 'natural'. This has led to a recognition that the dominant forms of men and masculinities are themselves not merely 'natural' and unchangeable. In addition, inspired particularly by important research in women's studies and the need for a positive response to feminism, some men have in recent years turned their attention to the critical study of men. These various focuses on men are clearly very different from the traditional concern with men that has characterized the social sciences, where in the worst cases men have been equated with people in general. Thus men and masculinities are not seen as unproblematic, but as social constructions which need to be explored, analysed, and indeed in certain respects, such as the use of violence, changed.

This series aims to promote critical studies, by women and men, on men and masculinities. It brings together scholarship that deals in detail with the social and political construction of particular aspects of men and masculinities. This will include studies of the changing forms of men and masculinities, as well as the broader historical and comparative studies. Furthermore, because men have been dominant in the writing of social science and production of malestream theory, one area of special interest for critical assessment is the relationship of men and masculinities to social science itself. This applies to both the content and 'results' of previous social research, and to the understanding of social theory in all its various guises – epistemology, ideology, methodology, and so forth.

Each book in the series will approach its specific topic in the light of feminist theory and practice, and where relevant, gay liberation and gay scholarship. The task of the series is thus the critique of men and masculinities, and not the critique of feminism by men. As such the series is pro-feminist and gay affirmative. However, this critical stance does not mean that men are simply to be seen or understood negatively. On the contrary, an important part of an accurate study of men and masculinity is an appreciation of the positive features of men's lives, and especially the variety of men's lived experiences. The series includes a wide range of disciplines – sociology, history, politics, psychoanalysis, cultural studies – as well as encouraging interdisciplinarity where appropriate. Overall, the attempt will be made to produce a series of studies of men and masculinities that are anti-sexist and anti-patriarchal in orientation.

Finally, while this series is primarily an academic development it will also at times necessarily draw on practical initiatives outside academia. Likewise, it will attempt to speak to changing patterns of men's practice both within and beyond academic study. Just as one of the most exciting aspects of feminism is the strong interrelation of theory and practice, so too must the critical study of men and masculinities and the change in men's practice against patriarchy develop in a close association.

Jeff Hearn

Acknowledgements

This list could be very long indeed, overlapping with and extending the various exercises in autobiography to be found in the following pages. However, I shall restrain myself, mentioning only the following: Jeff Hearn, editor of this series, for his constant friendly support and encouragement: Gordon Smith, at Unwin Hyman during the course of this project, for his sympathetic support, despite delays on my part; Liz Stanley and Sue Wise, colleagues and friends, whose influence may be noted on many of these pages even where it is not formally acknowledged; Janet Finch, who read the whole of the manuscript in draft and made numerous supportive comments and suggestions; Pat Robinson, who typed the final manuscript.

To Janet with love

Introduction

From time to time, in the morning assembly, the school would sing a hymn by George Herbert:

> A man that looks on glass,
> On it may stay his eye;
> Or if he pleaseth, through it pass,
> And then the heaven espy.

For some years I would puzzle over these words. Gradually two possible interpretations emerged. In the first place, I assumed, the glass of Herbert's time was full of imperfections and that it was all too easy to concentrate on the irregular surface of the window and to fail to look beyond to the world, or heavens, outside. Or, alternatively, the glass was deliberately designed to attract our attention, to inspire devotion or admiration and it would require a particularly strong act of imagination to go beyond the coloured images to the world beyond.

Today, of course, things are different. Stained glass is less prevalent and the quality of glass in many windows provides the illusion of direct access to the outside world, an illusion which sometimes proves to be painful or costly. Now it is possible to forget the windows altogether. To forget, that is, until someone throws a stone at them.

The business of discovering men may be understood both in terms of seeing through or going beyond man-made constructions or images and in terms of recognizing the constructions for what they are, in other words as seeing the glass as glass and not simply as a transparent window on the world. The process of ideological critique or demystification is usually presented in terms of exposing, of digging beneath or going beyond. But it may also be understood as a matter of taking the surface seriously, examining how it is constructed and how it functions.

There is, at one level, nothing very hidden or mysterious about men. An average television news broadcast will move from the battlefield, to the floor of the Stock Exchange, to the picket line and on to the football field. There will be interviews with top-level officials, stockbrokers, union bosses, police chiefs and football captains. Women will, indeed, appear and in increasing numbers although very often the covert message would seem to be that they are doing a man's job in a man's world. Despite various waves of feminism, the presence of men in the world would seem to be very much part of the taken-for-granted.

Yet feminism has, over the decades, thrown stones at windows, shattering the reverential images of the past and reminding us of the reality that has remained hidden through being so transparent. The search for men and the recognition of their activities as the activities of gendered individuals rather than of ungendered representatives of 'humanity' has been initiated by women. This challenge has taken a variety of forms: a reminder of the hidden work of women that takes place outside the public gaze; a reminder of the gendered character of so much of the everyday activity that is routinely taken for granted; an exposure of the inequalities, oppressions and exploitations that characterize and structure many relationships between women and men in society; and a critical exposure of the ideological mystifications that obscure these inequalities or present them as natural or immutable.

It is feminism, then, that has put the critical study of men and masculinities on to the agenda. Any attempt, therefore, on the part of men to engage in such studies must be working within, and sometimes against, this context established by women and feminism. It is not a disinterested search for knowledge or insight. Yet, clearly, such an activity on the part of men is full of difficulties of all kinds. If men have been involved in the construction of a world that is simultaneously a world of and for men and a world which allows men to disappear into an undifferentiated humanity, how can these self-same men subject this world to critical enquiry? And if they do engage in this kind of enquiry is there not the danger that this will become another construction, part of the continuous outpouring of men into a man-made world?

This book is an attempt to explore some of these problems. I want to consider some of the theoretical, practical and political difficulties involved in the critical study of men and masculinities, especially where such studies are themselves conducted by men. I shall first contextualize the discussion by considering the various responses of men to the feminist movement. Next, I shall present a general overview of the methodological and conceptual difficulties involved in the studies of men from within the social sciences. Three possible strategies are outlined:

(a) The re-examination of some classical texts within sociology in order to bring out the 'hidden' stories about masculinity that they tell;
(b) The re-examination of some well documented areas within sociology; here I intend to focus on studies of men at work, looking especially at workshop ethnographies;
(c) The examination of situations where masculinity may become, in various ways, problematic. Here I shall focus on the impact of male unemployment; changes in the gender balance at the workplace or the experience of men in hitherto female occupations; and the impact of the movement for female suffrage.

In the penultimate chapter, I shall consider questions of methodology directly, asking whether there is such a thing as a 'feminist methodology' and whether there are dangers in men using or appropriating such assumed methodologies. In particular I shall look at the usages of experience in social research. The conclusion will sum up the main themes of the book, under the general heading of 'studying men in a patriarchal society'.

It will be noted that a large section of this book deals with areas of work and employment or unemployment. This is deliberate. In the first place, work in the sense of paid employment has traditionally been seen as a central life interest and a major source of status and identity, especially (although this is not always spelt out) for men. One consequence of this assumption is that many of the classic studies and important debates within sociology have been around issues to do with work and the workplace; for examples, the Hawthorne studies, the 'Affluent Worker' studies, studies of bureaucracy, the labour process, deskilling and so on. In the second place, sociological conceptualizations of 'work' have come under increasing critical scrutiny in recent years. While there are several reasons for this, including the growth of large-scale unemployment and the development of advanced information technology, one of the most important influences has been the growth of a feminist critique of conventional understandings of the term 'work' and the gender-blindness of many of the existing studies and arguments.

It might be argued that I should have concentrated on other areas, perhaps more obviously to do with men and masculinities. These might include crime and delinquency (especially, football hooliganism) sport and sexual violence. While I recognize the importance of these issues and have, indeed, begun to explore some of them (Morgan 1988; 1990) my feeling is that they are perhaps too obvious. We have, generally speaking, little difficulty in thinking of men and masculinities when we talk about Rambo or football violence. It is somewhat more complex when we come to think about men in the more everyday or routine areas of life.

There are one or two further points to be made. Following current usages, I shall refer to 'masculinities' rather than 'masculinity'. There is much to be gained from such a practice, especially as a protection against reification and essentialism. Yet, I shall argue in the concluding chapter, there may be some dangers in this reconstruction, a blunting of the critical edge developed in feminist analyses. On balance, I think that the advantage lies with the plural term rather than with the singular but the issue needs further discussion.

In the second place, I write as a sociologist. Negatively, this means that I pay scant attention to psychological or philosophical debates and my use of historical material is a sociological use of such material rather than the work of an historian. Positively, this means that I am writing within a discipline or a tradition that I have been associated with for some thirty-odd years and that my points of reference are often literature and debates within this tradition. This tradition continuously addresses itself to some sense of the 'social', however this misleadingly simple term might be understood, and some sense of the interplay between 'individuals' and the social. I see the exploration of the interplays between social actors and structures within history and the explication of the various ways in which these interplays have been conceptualized by ordinary social actors as well as by sociologists as a source of continual fascination and puzzlement. It is in this exploration of puzzles and paradoxes in everyday social living that I find my main motivation for continuing work as a sociologist and my source of an understanding of sociology as a critical discipline. It is critical not in the superficial sense of finding fault with or blaming particular social arrangements, but rather in showing that there is often something rather strange and mysterious about everyday social life. It is not so much a matter of criticizing certain social practices but rather one of showing them to be *social* practices in the first place, social that is rather than natural or idiosyncratically individual.

This clearly has special importance in the consideration of issues of gender. Consider, for example, the critical examination of the way in which gender enters routine conversational practices. West and Zimmerman, for example, considered the extent to which women in fact had limited speaking rights in conversations with or including men. They often entered the conversation with phrases such as 'D'ya know what?', indicating their uncertain status as co-conversationalists. Men were more likely to interrupt and women to accept or to give way to these interruptions (West and Zimmerman 1977). This kind of research was critical in that it drew attention to practices which were often ignored, unobserved or obscured. (For the sake of argument, it does not matter at this point whether West and Zimmerman's conclusions were correct or true for all gendered conversational encounters.) The next level of critical enquiry is to begin to attempt to explain such practices and to seek for such an explanation in social or cultural terms rather than in biology or individual psychology. The very fact that women (through assertiveness training) and men (through some men's groups) may begin to question and to change these practices should be enough to convince us that natural or biological explanations will not take us very far.

Another aspect of my understanding of sociology is the critical recognition of the interplay between observer and observed as well as of the interplay between actors and social structures. In the present context what this means is a recognition that while one of the main motivations in conducting this enquiry is the desire to explore puzzles and paradoxes, another motivation is something to do with my own identity as a man. What this apparently simple formulation actually means will be the subject of discussion later in the book. For the moment, let me remind myself and the reader that I am a man writing about men and masculinities and that this itself constitutes further sources of problems and paradoxes.

CHAPTER 1

Men and feminism

All the studies written by men and about men and masculinities in the recent decade have underlined the importance of feminist research, scholarship and critique in stimulating their own studies. One of the central difficulties in attempting to write about masculinity is that, as a topic, it did not really exist until feminists began to attack the presuppositions of traditional political and social theory (Brittan 1989: 178). Feminism provided the context, the overall set of assumptions within which the current studies of men and masculinities are being conducted. These assumptions would include a recognition of the importance of gender divisions as a major (often *the* major) way of ordering or structuring social relationships, a recognition of the imbalances of power in the relationships between men and women within society, a recognition of the all-pervasiveness of these imbalances in thought, action and representations, and the recognition that these imbalances were open to challenge, criticism and transformation. These themes clearly shaped many of the writings about men and masculinities, emerging most obviously in discussions of sexual and domestic violence, pornography, sexual harassment and divisions of labour within the home and in the labour market. Feminism did not provide the sole influence – the experiences and writing of gay men in particular contributed to the exploration of inequalities and relationships between men and the need to pluralize 'masculinities' – but it was, and remains, the major influence.

Certainly all the recent texts and collections of papers make note of the influence of feminism and gay studies: 'For at least two decades, the women's movement (and also, since 1969, the gay liberation movement) has suggested that the traditional enactments of masculinity were in desperate needs of overhaul' (Kimmel 1987c: 9–10). Similarly, Connell writes: 'But theories don't grow on trees; theorizing is itself a social practice with a politics. Most of the radical theorizing of gender has been done by women or gay men' (Connell 1987: xi). Brod's collection similarly bears constant evidence of the influence of feminism (Brod 1987) as does the collection edited by Kaufman, which also has more detailed discussions of gay masculinities (Kaufman 1987).

What does it mean to say that feminism has provided the major influence in the development of the studies of masculinities? In the first place it would seem that this is not solely an intellectual influence. People do not conventionally write of the influence of feminism in quite the same way that they might write of the influence of phenomenology or of Habermas. Indeed, it may be argued that men run the danger of playing down this kind of influence of feminism through a misrecognition of feminism as being about women and women alone and through a failure to recognize the significant scholarly contributions of feminist women in debates about, for examples, epistemology or the analysis of cultural representations and practices (see Stanley 1990a, 1990b). In the desire to demonstrate the relative paucity of material about men and masculinity in comparison with the volumes of work explicitly about women, there was a danger of forgetting that all the feminist inspired debates about 'partriarchy' (however that term might be understood) were themselves about men and masculinity. Sometimes it seemed that men claimed the influence of feminism while continuing to quote other men and continuing to include the writings of men in their collections of articles (Hanmer 1990).

It is likely that, when recent studies of men and masculinity refer to the influence of feminism it is less likely to be the influence of a particular set of texts or body of scholarship (as might be the case when we speak of the influence of 'phenomenology') and more the influence of a particular social and political movement which had certain consequences for the ways in which some men see their lives. In a variety of ways and for a variety of reasons, men became aware of, or were made aware of their systematic involvement in gender inequalities, of the fact that talk about women's rights and the position of women in society could not be cordoned off from consideration of men and their positions in society. Some men came to call themselves 'feminists' (or hoped that others might call them 'feminists'), others sought to form or to join groups of men responding to the challenge of feminism or seeking to provide a critical and experiential exploration of their own practices and others came to feel a

[7]

diffuse sense of unease or a variety of more or less immediate pressures that caused them to look at the topics on their reading lists or their involvement in the home or in parenthood.

Clearly not all men, not even all men engaged in sociological work, were influenced by feminism and even those men who were aware of the feminist critique were not influenced in the same way. However, it may be argued that all men, potentially at least, were affected by a set of historical and structural changes that had an impact on the gender order as a whole. Most of the texts already referred to also pointed to these structural factors contributing to some men questioning their positions in society. These included the restructuring of the labour market, higher rates of divorce and remarriage, the loss of an Imperial role (in Britain) and so on. Of course some of these changes in work, employment and the family were affected by the growing women's movement or contributed to the growth of that movement. The cumulative effect of all these trends was to challenge the ideology of the male breadwinner or provider (never or rarely true in practice) and the more or less strong and exclusive anchorage of male identity in the occupational or public sphere.

Again, just as there is no automatic response on the part of men to the ideas and practices of feminism, so there need not be any immediate response on the part of men to the kinds of structural changes that have been outlined. Or, if we find responses, we have no reason to suppose that these would be all in the same direction. Nevertheless, there was some talk of a crisis in masculinity and male identity. Hodson, for example, uses the word 'crisis' and suggests that: 'One of the primary reasons for the modern male crisis is the fact that women have been so successful in identifying the female crisis' (Hodson 1984: 3). In some cases certain historical parallels were suggested. Kimmel for example talks in one place of an 'era of transition' (Kimmel 1987c: 9) and elsewhere of a 'crisis of masculinity' (Kimmel 1987c: 13; 1987b: 143–53). In discussing the idea of a 'crisis' he seeks parallels between the present situation and two earlier periods: Restoration England during the period 1688 to 1714 and the United States during the period 1880 to 1914. He sees these as 'two precursors of the contemporary crisis of masculinity' (Kimmel 1987b: 123). In both cases, he argues, major shifts in economic and political relations led to shifts in domestic relations and in relations between the sexes and that these contributed to an overall crisis of

[8]

masculinity. Whether or not Kimmel's analysis is sustained by further research (and it would seem that such research is both necessary and desirable) a variety of important points would seem to be raised by such a discussion. In the first place, it is argued that it is proper or illuminating to write about a crisis in terms of masculinity. In the second place, such a crisis is not unique in human history. Thirdly, an analysis of these crises should seek out wider economic and political changes and discuss the ways in which these changes are mediated through domestic and gender relations.

Kimmel's approach usefully reminds us that it is important to take a broad historical perspective and to explore historical comparisons if only to discover what is especially unique or distinctive about the present situation. Historical parallels can be misleading if they led one to suppose that there might be some semi-automatic relationship between structural change and personal response. A crisis, or perhaps rather widely disseminated talk about crisis, does not conventionally produce a single unified response but a range of responses. This has certainly been recognized in some of the more recent discussions. For example, Kimmel's account of the period 1880–1914 in the United States, discusses three possible sets of responses to the 'crisis': pro-feminist men, anti-feminist men and pro-male men (Kimmel 1987b: 143–53). To some extent, Kimmel is encouraging us to seek parallels in our own times. Certainly it is possible to find striking examples of each position for both periods and probably for other societies. The pro-feminist position is part of the subject of this present discussion and has some more detailed treatment in Chapter 7. All that might be said at this point is a reminder that it is probably wrong to talk about a single 'pro-feminist' position since it is also difficult to talk about a single 'feminist pattern'. Pro-feminist men's positions may be divided between 'liberal' and 'radical' (e.g. Brod 1987) just as similar distinctions have been discussed within 'feminism' itself but this represents only a slight step in the direction of a more sophisticated analysis. It is also doubtful whether distinctions have a great deal of meaning for earlier historical periods.

In the case of 'anti-feminist men' we are dealing with overt opposition to feminist groups, often constructed in part as a kind of male backlash. Again we are not talking about a single position here, just as we are not talking about a single tone. The opposition may be elaborated and articulated (e.g. in terms of biological models, social necessity or cultural tradition) or it may be muttered and implied (jokes about 'bra-burning', for example, or mutters about 'Women's Libbers'). Often the opposition is couched in terms of 'women having gone too far'.

'Anti-feminist' men overlap with but can be distinguished from pro-male men or 'masculinism' (Allen 1987). Here the emphasis may be less on attacking the ideas and practices of feminists or suffragettes and more on asserting or constructing 'traditional' masculinities. There may be a 'rediscovery' of frontier values of rugged masculinity, of sport and the open air and of the strengths and supports that can be gained from fellowship with other men. Much of this may be misogynist and at least latently homosexual (if often also homophobic). The modern pro-male man may be absorbed in martial arts or weaponry, sport and drinking although he may, conceivably, be also interested in fathering and male friendships.

It its likely that the most widespread 'response' on the part of men to feminism has been one of a diffuse if rarely articulated opposition. A popular examination of men in modern Britain argued that the 'average' man was relatively little affected at first, but became more hostile later as the movement achieved greater prominence (Ford 1985: 292–5). The notion of 'going too far' appeared to be a common theme, focusing upon the widely disseminated (if probably mythical) image of 'bra-burning'. In a neat twist on the 'nature/culture' division, women who allegedly burnt their bras were behaving 'unnaturally'. Ford concludes: 'But for the most part I found that men from all classes, ages and backgrounds were willing to fight powerful rearguard actions to defend the traditional male and female roles' (Ford 1985: 297–8). Somewhat similar pessimistic conclusions came from another overview, published at around the same time: 'it was very rare for a man to admit that his own life had been touched by the changes happening to women' (Ingham 1984: 200). Ingham found that few men were opposed to equal pay or employment opportunities. Yet most men felt that men and women were fundamentally different, that it was difficult if not impossible to know women outside marriage or a sexual relationship and that, once more, the women's liberation movement had gone 'too far'. Her general conclusion was: 'But if there was a quiet movement of British men, they were keeping very quiet indeed, especially

[10]

when it came to questioning the daily routines of their lives' (ibid.: 8).

Classifications such as those proposed by Kimmel, although undoubtedly useful as a preliminary sorting out of a complex set of responses, leave me with a certain unease. In the first place, although this may not always be the intention, there is a hint of moral or political evaluation in such typologies, a sorting out of ideological sheep from goats. In everyday discussions about the sexism of male colleagues or family members there are often more than echoes of the cry of the Pharisee – 'God, I thank thee that I am not like other men' – and it is possible that such considerations may have entered more sociological discourse. At a more scholarly level, any typology or classification can have the effect of editing out ambiguities and complexities, a sense of change and process and the interplay between history and experience. Take, for example, the implied contrast in this quotation from Kimmel: 'a terrified retreat to traditional constructions; to others it has inspired a serious re-evaluation of traditional worldwide . . .' (Kimmel 1987a: 10). For a start it is, clearly, not 'us' who are in 'terrified retreat'. In the second place there is the implied contrast between 'traditional' and 'modern' constructions. (We also find this in the quotation from Ford earlier.) Yet as the discussion of 'pro-male men' shows, 'traditions' are invented, amalgams of real and imagined signifiers from the past are put together to give meaning to maleness and being a man in the present. Just as, now, we are required to explore the range of masculinities that might be discovered is it not possible that an equal, if differently accented, range of masculinities might be found in the past?

Perhaps this point about the complexities of men's responses may be made clear with one or two examples. Just as feminists have seen considerable value, politically and possibly theoretically, in exploring the meanings attached to the phrase, 'I'm not a feminist but' so too it might be possible to explore the commonly heard phrase, 'I suppose you would call me a male chauvinist'. These phrases are clearly not equivalent (indeed in some ways they are in opposition to each other) although they do have some features in common. Both recognize that feminism and the feminist critique are on the agenda. There is a recognition of a discourse taking place which, even if it is not fully or even particularly embraced, has some kind of consequence for the speaker's life. In the case of the 'male chauvinist' phrase, there is some kind of recognition of change and relativity, even where the speaker might wish to reject it for himself. The position is seen or presented as one which is chosen rather than as something which is unassailably and existentially rooted in an ontologically secure understanding of the world. In some modest way, it might be seen as a post-modern utterance. We also know, or have reason to suspect, that little can be read off from such an utterance. The speaker may be more or less 'chauvinist' than his interviewer. There are differences between public and private accounts (Cornwell 1984), with this chauvinist statement being very much a public account, and there are differences between values and practices.

Another reminder of the possible complexities of men's responses comes in Walczak's small-scale study: 'Two men have been personally very deeply hurt by some feminists and still have highly egalitarian views in spite of this. Both of them have also been hurt by prejudice, one because of his colour, the other because of being gay' (Walczak 1988: 135). This reminds us that encounters with feminism can be awkward and painful and that masculine responses and identities may be, indeed always are, mediated through other identities.

Seeing the matter in more processual terms we have a good illustration of what might be done in Esseveld's study of American women entering their middle age (Esseveld 1988). This is essentially a life-course approach, allowing women to speak open-endedly through a series of interviews and looking back over their lives as well as making assessments of their present situations. These were children who married and began to have their children before the feminism of the 1970s and who were sometimes looked upon with a certain condescension by later generations. Yet they also came to respond, in different ways, to feminism and to begin to make some kinds of connections between more general understandings of the situation of women in society and their own domestic and employment experiences.

Could Esseveld's study be adapted to the study of men over the life-course or over some section of their life-course? The possibility of doing something of this kind is demonstrated by Kimball looking at men who have come to challenge or reject traditional masculine gender roles, especially within the family (Kimball 1989). A variety of facts are taken into consideration including

[12]

parental influences, experience of living on one's own for a period of time, the experiences and orientations of partners and so on. While these are listed here as a set of background variables that might predispose individual men to challenge gender assumptions, it is likely that they could be arranged or structured into a more sequential, life-course framework.

In another account, Connell considers his own position as a 'heterosexual man, married, middle-aged, with a tenured academic job in an affluent country' (Connell 1987: xi), and asks how it was that he became interested in the current debates around gender and feminism. He notes an early unease with models of conventional masculinity which, coupled with student activism, led him to read works like Firestone's *The Dialectics of Sex* (Firestone 1971) with some sympathy and interest. He responded positively to a socialism that sought to identify theory with practice, both political and personal, and he learns from living with a woman working for a women's health centre and from working with women engaged on various projects of feminist research (ibid.: xi–xii). His experience, and doubtless the experiences of others known to him, leads him to attempt some tentative generalizations of the factors that encourage some men away from the defence of patriarchy. Generally these would include a recognition that there are at least some points of overlap between the experiences of men and women and that these are often reinforced by the relationships that they have with actual women in family or cohabiting relationships. Further, there is a recognition that not all men are the same and that some groups or categories in particular suffer from the oppressiveness of the present gender order, 'effeminate or unassertive heterosexuals' as well as gays for example. There may also be a recognition that change is taking place anyway and some men may respond to this with a picture of pragmatic acceptance or a whole hearted endorsement (Connell 1987: xiii; see also Snodgrass 1977; Seidler 1989).

When I think about my own autobiography (a theme that I shall be taking up more explicitly in Chapter 8) some of the complexities begin to emerge. If asked to account for my interest in gender and the critical study of masculinities I could provide a range of possible responses. In the first place, I might point to doubts about my own adequacy as a male in society. In various ways I felt myself to be an outsider at grammar school in the

1950s. I suffered from asthma, a fact which effectively kept me from regular or effective participation in athletic pursuits, especially football. Sport was important not so much as a source of prestige but as a basis for membership of male groups. I longed to join the games that took place almost instantly once the break bells had rung and to be part of that camaraderie which included not only performance but also intimate knowledge about football teams and players. Eventually, I gravitated to a group of other non-sporty boys where we discussed books and films, made comics and 'flicker films' and formed a kind of secret society. Yet I retained admiration for the boys who seemed to be so much more obviously at ease with their bodies and with each other. This sense of being apart from but wanting to belong to more obviously 'masculine' groups continued through National Service (Morgan 1987) and my early years at university.

Similar problems with masculine identity revolved around my relationship with girls. My school was a coeducational one although in my case, and presumably in contradiction to theory, this did not allow for easy relationships between the sexes. In the early years, there was a kind of secret sexual apartheid where boys and girls coexisted in the same institution but seemed to have very little to do with each other and any apparent crossing of the line was the subject of gossip and ridicule. I think that one of my reasons for opting for science subjects at the end of my second year was the definition of science as a boy's activity, something associated with exciting matters such as explosions and inventing things. (Instead, it turned out to involve long boring periods which consisted of nothing other than weighing substances.) I became intensely interested in girls but, as I saw it, very ill-equipped to approach them in what might be defined as the appropriate manner. The business of chatting-up, flirtation and asking for dates seemed to be beyond me and the formalities of dances at that time (where you were expected to show some proficiency in dance steps and to ask your partner for a dance) increased rather than reduced the sense of distance. I was much happier on those occasions when I could talk to girls naturally, on those occasions where it did not seem necessary or required to define the interaction in more sexual terms.

I could develop this autobiographical stream further and deeper, perhaps engaging in some quasi-Freudian self-analysis. However, two points need to be made here. Clearly, the diffuse anxieties that I felt at school and later were not defined by me at the time as 'problems about masculine identity'. This was a later, much later, construction brought about by my introduction to feminist thought and analysis. If I conceptualized my sense of difference and unease at all it was more likely to be in terms of family background and accent. I came from a lower middle-class (or respectable working-class) Methodist background. My family lived in a North London suburb called Hatch End, and going to my grammar school at Harrow Weald entailed some rather complicated journeys on public transport or a longish walk. Most of the other boys came from Harrow and Wealdstone, were non-church-goers and had fairly identifiable North London accents. Masculinity and its discontents was only part of an over-determined package.

Further, it cannot be said that these experiences 'caused' my interest in gender and gender identity. Wimps, although the term was not current then, may develop into scholars or artists or they may develop a kind of hypermasculinity with an interest in body-building and martial arts. Clearly other factors were at work.

An alternative account might go like this. During the long vacations when I was an undergraduate, I worked as a 'garden labourer' for the local authority. This entailed, for the most part, mowing grass verges with the odd bit of weeding. It also entailed long tea and lunch breaks and even longer breaks when it was raining. I came to know John, an art student who introduced me to Kafka and, more importantly, Simone de Beauvoir. He lent me a copy of *The Second Sex*. Actually, as I discovered later, it was only half of *The Second Sex*, a paperback with a Renoiresque nude on the front and the sentence: 'The Subject is Woman in All Her Aspects!' Thoughtfully, John had provided a brown paper cover. Conventional autobiographies would, at this point, say 'This changed my life'. Did it? I certainly read it with considerable interest and found that it made sense of a lot of things that I had observed and experienced. It was certainly more interesting and intellectually exciting than most of the books (admittedly, not many at that time) to deal with the 'changing roles of women' which were currently on sociology reading lists.

I have continued to refer to Simone de Beauvoir and to reread *The Second Sex* (the complete version this time). But the books that we read, even the most influential ones, do not necessarily enter into our lives in a naturalistic cause–effect fashion. They

[15]

become part of the resources that we may draw upon in the light of subsequent readings and experiences.

One such experience took place in 1978. I had been invited to take part as a tutor in a British Sociological Association Summer School on 'Feminism and Social Research'. This was presumably as a result of my *Social Theory and the Family* (Morgan 1975) which had included fairly extensive references to feminist writings, something that was rare in sociological texts of the time. There was one other male tutor and three men who had enrolled in the school. The rest were women. This itself was in sharp contrast to the conventional academic or research gathering where women still tended to be in the minority. On the first evening, the position of the male tutors was challenged at a plenary session. Jenny Shaw, the director of the school, and the other women tutors bravely supported us but it was a reminder that the times were a-changing. Men, especially men in positions of power, were regarded with suspicion and although I had intellectually appreciated this in my reading of feminist texts such as Firestone and Millett, this was almost the first time that I had directly encountered this opposition. I felt uncomfortable when a women-only study group was announced and slightly hurt when my attempts to present a sociological critique of 'patriarchy' appeared to fall on deaf ears. Just as, in earlier years, I had looked on with envy at the easy camaraderie of male groups, so I felt some kind of longing and exclusion in the face of some of the more obvious manifestations of sisterhood – mutual concern and support, physical ease with each other, and so on. Yet I do not want to present too stark a picture. What was impressive, and what heartened me, was the large amount of support, interest and encouragement that I did get from many of the women, the students as well as the tutors. Later, I came to reflect on the contrast between my situation there and the situation of many women who find themselves in a minority at conference or similar gatherings and are subjected to even more tangible exclusions, perhaps accompanied by sexual harassment and paternalism (Morgan 1981).

This was clearly an important and influential event, almost certainly more important than any one text might have been. But it took on a special, more fixed significance when I was asked by Helen Roberts to contribute to a conference on research methodology, in particular to a session on 'non-sexist methodology'. This was my first piece of writing on masculinity and was included in a collection edited by Helen Roberts (Morgan 1981). In this paper I referred to my experience at the 1978 Summer School. In this paper I also used themes of men and masculinity in order to look back at some of my empirical research in the past. Generally the conclusion that I came to was that in my research I had problematized women (by writing, for example, about 'women at work') but I had ignored men, even where, as in the case of a study of Anglican bishops, I was writing about men. There was a difference between the large number of texts that were implicitly about men and the relatively small number of texts which were overtly and explicitly about men. I also reflected upon some other experiences in academic institutions, most notably departmental seminars, redefining these in terms of gender characteristics. Thus the tendency to describe many such events in terms more appropriate for gladiatorial combat I described as an example of 'academic machismo'.

In this extended autobiographical example, we can begin to see some of the complexities involved in the idea of 'influence' as it applies to feminism and the practices of men. If we reject a straightforward linear account (the traditional and possibly male autobiographical model) with its implied chains of causes and effects we may find a much more complex set of interplays between past and present and between personal biography and historical change. Thus my presentation at a conference on research methods became the occasion for the public recognition of the 1978 Summer School as an important event, as well as the re-interpretation of a whole host of other experiences, previous pieces of research and sociological texts. This sense of constant autobiographical work, the interplay between past events and experiences and occasions upon which one might be called upon to provide accounts, is something that I have tried to develop subsequently (Morgan 1978; 1990a). Fuller, more systematic accounts, would need to include historical events and wider structural changes and the ways in which these were fed into my life and my attempts to construct my autobiographies. These would include the experience of National Service, the expansion of Higher Education and the growth of sociology as a discipline as well as the whole host of events and factors that led to the growth of the feminist movement in Britain.

What I have tried to show in the previous few pages is that when writers, currently writing on men and masculinities, are

[17]

talking about the influence of feminism they are talking about a process of considerable complexity. If, as I believe to be the case, this is not simply a ritual genuflection, the recognition of the influence of feminism includes not only the influence of particular texts (itself not a straightforward process) but also a much more diffuse but often more profound influence on everyday practices and ways of seeing the world. The influence is not simply upon theories – indeed it is possible that men's theories have not been influenced enough by key feminist writers – but also upon sociology as a set of practices. These would include the processes of writing and diffusion, and the social relationships of academic production in research, teaching and administration. It includes not only relationships with colleagues and research staff but also with secretaries and administrative staff and with sexual or domestic partners. These influences may be felt, in some measure, by all male sociologists whether or not they happen to be writing about men and masculinities.

If we talk about the influence of feminism upon studies of men this should not be seen as a once-and-for-all achievement. Feminisms change and the critical studies of masculinities change, both within a changing environment. It is not simply the response of men to feminisms but also the response of women and feminists to these mens' responses. Some feminists have treated these developments with a cautious but welcoming optimism (e.g. Segal 1988; 1989). Others have been much more sceptical and suspicious (e.g. Canaan and Griffin 1990). 'Wimp' can be a term of disapproval amongst feminists as well as amongst groups of men and it is not unknown for some feminists, certainly some women, to be heard saying that they prefer the old men to the new men on the grounds that at least one knew where one was with the old version. Men in their turn are responding to these responses from women and feminists.

The argument up to this point may be restated in terms of a couple of broad propositions. In the first place it may be stated that feminism is not, and never was, simply about women and their problems. Men, their thoughts and practices, are clearly implicated and increasingly they recognize this, even where they do not welcome it, as when they argue that 'women have gone too far', or state 'I suppose you would call me a male chauvinist'. In the second place, even where we are considering the narrow field of sociology and related disciplines, the impact of feminism

[18]

has not been solely in terms of ideas or topics. 'Doing sociology' is located in a set of gendered social relationships – the 'academic mode of production' (Morgan 1981; Stanley 1990a) – and theories and findings cannot be detached from the conditions of their discovery.

However, in talking about the impact of feminism on sociology we are also talking about the impact on research agendas. One way of exploring this is to consider the articles published in the main learned journals. In an article on gender as a 'key variable' (Morgan 1986) I referred to a small survey of the journals *Sociology* and the *American Sociological Review*, journals representing the official publications of the British and the American professional associations. Generally, my conclusions were:

(a) Gender is more often assumed that either stated or used. It is still possible to find articles where one has to guess the gender of the research subjects or where this does not emerge as a result of a cursory inspection (e.g. a sample of 'felons' might reasonably be assumed to be a sample of men; a sample of 'adults' is more difficult).

(b) 'Men only' studies continue to be numerous in both journals (e.g. in studies of social mobility or crime) but in the majority of these cases, gender is not treated as a topic in its own right. The practice of basing social mobility studies on the study of men only has been subjected to criticism within the pages of *Sociology* during the 1980s although nobody has yet seriously suggested looking at studies of social mobility as sources of information about *men*, the lives and experiences of such men and about social constructions of men's careers.

(c) Women are the subject of analysis relatively infrequently (although this appears to be changing) and where they do form the research subjects, they are more likely than men to be problematized. By problematized, I mean that their gender is seen as a key variable; it is put to the centre of the stage. The research is claiming to tell us something specifically about the situation of women, as mothers, employees or in some other capacity.

(d) Studies which are based upon samples of men *and* women are more numerous in the American journal; direct comparisons and the use of gender as a test variable are more likely to appear in the *American Sociological Review*.

[19]

As far as I can see relatively little has changed since I wrote that particular article. In a rather quick survey of five major journals in 1988 (the *American Journal of Sociology*, the *American Sociological Review*, the *British Journal of Sociology*, the *Sociological Review* and *Sociology*) I found that none of them included any treatment of men as a topic in its own right. In 8 cases men were explicitly treated as a resource, i.e. as constituting the basis for a sample. The figures for women were 8 and 5 respectively. Men *and* women were the subjects, with varying degrees of explicitness, of 47 papers. However, the overwhelming number of papers (96) included virtually no reference to gender; for the most part these dealt with theoretical or methodological issues or used collectivities as their units of investigation. Gender, both as a topic or resource as a key variable, would still seem to be relatively marginal to the mainstream of sociological journal publishing. An American survey, looking at ten sociological publications over the period 1974–83 found an increase (14 per cent to 21 per cent) in the proportion of gendered papers, most of which treating 'sex as a variable' rather than constituting a critical analysis of gender as a topic in its own right (Ward and Grant 1985). A tentative linking of these trends with the proportions of women on editorial boards (part of the 'academic mode of production') gave rise to some concern about the future.

It has been noted that a large number of articles in these journals would seem to be irrelevant to this discussion in that they do not include references to gender nor, it would seem, would they be expected to do so. One such set of articles would be mainly theoretical in emphasis. There would seem to be a general assumption that theory, unless explicitly stated, does not deal with gender. The implication (and we have to guess here since it is rarely, if ever, spelt out) would seem to be that the objects of sociological theorizing are at a higher level of generality than issues of gender. The entities that form the substance of routine theoretical argument – classes, societies, nations, systems, roles, individuals, actors and so on – do not appear to be gendered. Whether they should be and what the consequences might be if they were so treated is a matter to be deferred for further discussion. Certainly some feminist writers are not content to leave theorizing to the men or to treat it as an ungendered practice (e.g. Sydie 1987; Smith 1988; Stanley 1990a).

[20]

The second group of papers where questions of gender do not seem to arise are those which have collectivities rather than individuals as units of research. Instead of using surveys of individuals (the most common form of sociological enquiry reflected in the pages of these journals) they use surveys of collectivities – nations, cities, urban areas or whatever. Clearly such entities normally include both men and women, often in more or less equal proportions. Whether, however, this means that gender disappears is a question of some complexity. A comparison between different kinds of organizations, for example, might well be affected by the different sex ratios at different levels of the organizations concerned. In the discussion of interaction between individuals and aggregated characteristics, gender could be a key variable.

Another set of papers where issues of gender fail to appear are those to do with methodology. Here methodology would seem to be understood in relatively technical, numerical and positivistic terms. Issues of gender or epistemology rarely seem to emerge. I provide a fuller discussion of these issues in Chapter 8.

There are other possible indicators of the impact of feminism, other than the topics of articles published. For example, it would be interesting to look at various Examination Boards and the changing syllabuses at school and undergraduate levels. Clearly we need to go beyond the mere counting of references to men and women and make some more qualitative assessment. Here, Stanley, for example, has argued for a more optimistic picture, maintaining that feminism has had a profound impact on sociology in certain key areas of the discipline, namely the studies of the family, of work and of violence. She also recognizes a growing interest in the study of men (Stanley 1990a).

The process by which the influence of feminism has made itself felt upon the practices of sociology, and especially the studies of men and masculinity, have been complex and variable. For one thing, not all studies of men (e.g. some studies of crime and delinquency) show a direct feminist impact. The degree of impact, as we have seen, is also variable and still rather difficult to assess. But it would certainly seem to be the case that there is still a lot of work to be done. This book is intended to map out what some of this work might look like and to indicate what some of the theoretical, epistemological and conceptual issues might be.

To conclude this chapter it might be worth speculating on some of the motives for writing about men and masculinities and how that these might affect the development of this area of study. Assessments of motivations are always tricky and what follows represents little more than a series of guesses based upon reading and experience over the past few years.

One motivation might be based upon a recognition that it is no longer possible, or safe, for a man to write about women. (See, for example, some of the reviews of and debates about David Bouchier's book on feminism (Bouchier 1983; *Network* May 1984).) This is in part a sociology of knowledge question, to be considered later in this book, and a question of sexual politics. Men who wish to make some kind of intervention into debates about gender might feel that it is more prudent to turn their attention to studies of men and masculinities.

This may merge with a second kind of motivation, that is more of a reaction against the feminist critique. There may be a feeling that men have been ignored in the focus of research and debate on women. There may be a feeling that feminist accounts have oversimplified the lives and experiences of men (in debates about pornography, for example) and men may not always recognize themselves in the accounts provided by feminists. There may be, also, a kind of envy of women, especially around their apparent claims to the 'softer' more emotional aspects of life. This may lead to a kind of 'critical cross-dressing' (Showalter 1987), a desire in some respects to become like women, or, rather, like certain dominant constructions of women and their feelings.

Thirdly, there may be a kind of identification with feminist women, as a consequence of one's own experiences being given new meanings by the writings of feminists. These may be gay men or men who fail, in some way or another, to conform to what are seen as the expected standards of masculinity. In some cases this may lead to a generalized critique of the dominance of rigid sex role systems or models of heterosexuality, although this may still coexist with an understanding of the overall unequal power relationships between men and women within society.

Finally, there may be a recognition of the justness of the feminist arguments and their relevance for the theories and lives of men. In some cases this may lead to a kind of guilty recognition of one's own complicity in systems of sexual oppression. In other cases this may conform to an overall, and perhaps slightly abstract, ethical or political orientation to sexual injustices (Thomas 1990).

We should also not discount other motivations, including various forms of opportunism, personal, careerist or sexual. However, excluding these, we can find a variety of overlapping motivations for men responding in more or less direct and positive ways to feminism. Some of these may have the consequence of a new ghettoization of men's studies. Some may be more likely to arouse the suspicion of feminists than others. I can see elements of most of these in my own motivation to study men and masculinity. There is much work to be done and we – that is men and women interested in the study of men and masculinities – should not allow motivational analysis to get in the way of our studies. At the same time we, especially the men, need to stand back from time to time and to think hard and critically about our motivations and their possible consequences for the gender order in which we work.

CHAPTER 2

Problems of studying men

With increasing social conflict, differences in the values, attitudes and modes of thought of groups develop to the point where the orientation which these groups previously had in common is overshadowed by incompatible differences. Not only do there develop distinct universes of discourse, but the existence of any one universe challenges the validity and legitimacy of the others. The co-existence of these conflicting perspectives and interpretations within the same society leads to an active and reciprocal *distrust* between groups.

(Merton 1957: 457, italics in original)

Introduction

Phillip Hodson, the author of a book based upon a BBC television series on *Men* quotes these words of Sheila Rowbotham written in 1973: 'I sensed something very complicated was going on in the heads of men who were about my age. It's for them to write about this. I wish they would very soon' (Quoted in Hodson 1984: 5). Since 1973, of course, Rowbotham's wish would have seemed to have come true. There have been scores of books, articles and indeed journals and periodicals devoted to the subject of men and, for the most part, written by men. These writings have been personal, autobiographical and confessional or they have been more theoretical and analytical. Some have celebrated men and masculinity, some others have denounced the practices of their own gender; many, if not most of all, have seen a need for some kind of change, personal and/or political. Men have demanded (as have some women) that men should 'get in touch with their feelings', or that they should confront the violence that they have perpetrated or of which they are capable, that they

[24]

should take a critical look at all their practices in the home, in interpersonal relationships, in public life and at work. Yet, perhaps, we still have a long way to go. Recently, after a day conference on issues of men and masculinity, one woman stated to me and the other male participants that she 'still did not know what it felt like to be a man'.

This complaint, like the decontextualized quotation from Sheila Rowbotham above, would seem to suggest two things. In the first place, there is the suggestion that there is some kind of existential reality which is in some way locked inside men and to which women have no access. Secondly, and following from this, it is up to men to make these experiences available to each other and to women. A further implication would suggest the necessity for this in order to transcend the fruitless and increasingly dangerous battle of the sexes. Women, it is argued, have already experienced considerable changes often within their own lifetimes; it is now up to men to do the same, and one important step in this direction is for men to talk honestly about their own feelings, experiences and being in the world.

At one level I agree with this line of argument. And yet, at another level, there is something that worries me a little. To what extent can we say that there is something going on 'in the heads' of men, something that is shared by all men but which is not available to women? This is a sociology of knowledge question, a question about the location and limits of human understanding, to which I shall return later in this chapter. Further, haven't men been writing about men, and about women, too, for centuries? This is part of the gender division of labour, an issue addressed by several feminist literary critics and historians (Spender 1982; Russ 1983), whereby men have had the power, the leisure and the resources with which to write and with which, also, to exclude, marginalize or trivialize the writings of women. Surely there must be something about what 'it feels like to be a man' in all those volumes of fiction, of autobiography, confessions, diaries, histories and letters?

For example, I have a reasonably large number of American crime novels. In one of them I read:

Her body looked lean and supple beneath her uniform, which was short and about a size too small. She had a tiny waist, narrow hips, and breasts that were not large, but firm

[25]

and beautifully formed. Her legs, which she was showing me a lot of, were muscular and perfectly proportioned, with well-rounded calves and neat, trim ankles. She caught me looking at them and crossed her legs.

(Lyons 1989: 134)

Lyons is seen, with some justice, as a highly respected crime-writer, writing in the Raymond Chandler tradition. It is possible to argue that although the novel, in conforming to the conventions of this genre, is written in the first person, the author does not identify with the perspective of his protagonist. But does this, all the same, tell us something about maleness and male experience? Does it tell us that men see women in terms of a 'naming of parts' (can you really *see* a real woman in this description?) and that they see the responses of women to men as a mixture of provocation and denial? We may reject such passages as sexist but do they not tell us something about male experience and male perceptions? And if an ordinary crime novel can tell us this, might we gain even more insight from many volumes of memoirs and biographies?

Immediately however, several qualifications come to mind. For one thing, this is clearly part of a male *heterosexual* perspective. There is at least this modification to the idea of a uniformed male experience. Moreover, we have to learn how to read this passage as being a passage about men. We have to recognize it as part of a particular genre of writing in which we read echoes of other similar novels of the same kind and possibly of movies about the same themes or locations. We can, for example, read this passage as being about an *American* male as well as about a heterosexual male.

The point would seem to be, therefore, that it is not so much a question of an absence of texts about men and male experience, but a lack of familiarity on the part of readers, men and women, with reading texts in a particular way coupled with a relative lack of texts about men which are explicitly signalled as such. Unless we are prepared to read it in this way, a book by a male writer about a man or men will not necessarily be seen as being about issues of men and masculinity. Realizing the importance of reading old texts in new ways may help us to understand an apparent paradox. Sheila Rowbotham wrote a book about women called *Hidden From History* (Rowbotham 1974). The title has come to stand for a wide-ranging feminist project of recovering the lives of ordinary and extraordinary women and bringing them out of the shadows into the foreground. Similarly, texts – novels, poems, plays, paintings and so on – by women have been rediscovered and re-evaluated. The extensive list of Virago titles of writings by women in the past and present serve as a tangible sign of this process. Yet, at the time Sheila Rowbotham was writing, you could go into any reasonably well-stocked bookshop or library and find several volumes dealing explicitly with women. The number of books dealing explicitly with men would be much fewer, perhaps non-existent. The same was true at the time when Virginia Woolf was writing *A Room of One's Own* and the same is true today, for if the number of books dealing explicitly with men has grown enormously, the number of volumes explicitly signalled as being about, and by and for, women has grown at least at the same rate.

We should note, in passing, that in earlier decades many of the books that dealt explicitly with women were written by men. Men wrote about women's bodies, their reproductive capacities, their sexuality, their temperament and their 'nature'. Now, of course, it is likely that the majority of titles dealing with women will also be written by women. Nevertheless, this fact points to one feature about the relative distribution of books about men and women. While the number of books that were in fact about men and their activities have always greatly outnumbered similar writings about women, the number of books which explicitly dealt with 'Women' greatly outnumbered those dealing directly with 'Men'. One way of restating this is to say that women were far more likely to be problematized than men, a point also noticed in the previous chapter, when I considered articles in sociological journals.

In order to explore this idea of 'problematization' a little further, consider two pairs: Augustus and Gwen John and Leonard and Virginia Woolf. There are some obvious differences between the two pairs. In the first case we are dealing with a brother and sister, in the second with a husband and wife. In the first case, initially at least, the man was more well-known than the woman, in the second the reverse was true. Yet critical discussions of the two women have tended to certain similarities. There will be a discussion of the difficulties facing women who wish to paint or write, difficulties in terms of finding the time and the space for artistic activity, difficulties in gaining critical recognition and so on. In the case of Virginia Woolf, of course, these discussions will be greatly assisted by her own writings on that very subject. There may also be discussions of the feminine qualities exhibited in the works concerned, links being made not simply to the lives of the individuals who created the works as individuals but to their beings as women. To problematize women, therefore, is to treat individuals as in some ways representative of a gendered category and to find some explanation of their lives and works in terms of their membership of that category.

Contrast, however, the treatments of Augustus and Leonard. In the various writings about or by these individuals, the question of their membership of the category 'man' will be much less accentuated. Other factors may come into play, as they do for Gwen and Virgina, such as class, family or ethnic background but questions of male gender and masculinity will be muted to say the least. (There is, in fact, an illuminating parallel if we contrast the treatment of Leonard's Jewish background with the absence of treatment of Virginia's gentile background.) Put differently, in the ways in which these two men have been represented, they have been much less firmly anchored to a gender identity than the two women with whom they were linked through family or marital ties. Generally speaking, the same may be said for all the lives of tinkers, tailors, soldiers, sailors, rich men and poor men, beggarmen and thieves, that occupy the sections labelled biography or autobiography in our libraries.

There would seem to be two interrelated reasons for this. In the first place as English linguistic usage indicators, the identity 'man' may often be read as standing for 'humanity' as a whole. A well-known example is Jacques' 'All the world's a stage' speech in *As You Like It*. The audience is invited at the beginning to hear this speech as being about the human condition as a whole. '*All* the world's a stage, and all the *men and women* merely players.' Yet the actual stages outlined clearly deal with gendered men, at least once we get past the infant stage and before we reach senility; schoolboys, an active male lover, a soldier, a justice. This practice is so widespread that it is routinely taken for granted unless subject to explicit challenges. Similar debates around the language of the Bible and the Prayer Book point to the same kinds of issues, where the deeply rooted and taken-for-granted nature of these linguistic practices is such that women who challenge them are often taken to be strident or extreme. When Rowbotham talked about women's exclusion from history she meant, of course, from a history that was not simply written by men but which was nearly always about men, whose gender somehow got lost in wider categorizations such as 'The English-Speaking People', 'Mankind', and so on.

This sliding of man into mankind reflects another main reason for the relative absence of the problematization of men. The relationships between men and women and society is not simply one of difference (in which case one might expect two different but parallel histories) but of inequalities in terms of power. For the time being, I use the troublesome word 'patriarchy' to signify this control of men over women. This is not an absolute power differential, certainly, but it is one which has consequences for the problems being discussed in this chapter. It means that, over a large number of areas, men are taken as the norm, from which women are seen to deviate. This is, of course, accentuated when we are dealing with the contrasting experiences of men and women in the public sphere where women are more likely to be problematized.

At this stage, however, it is possible to outline why the business of problematizing 'men' may be a little more difficult than might at first be supposed. Conventionally much academic work consists of finding hitherto undeveloped or underdeveloped areas for study and turning attention to these areas. Thus, for example, it may be argued that little has been written, sociologically or historically, about the topic of food and attempts will be made to rectify this omission. Superficially, this may sound like 'there have been many studies of women up to now but relatively few studies of men'. However, it should be clear that the parallel is not an exact one and that the reason for this is to do with the institutions and practices of patriarchy. It is generally the case that the powerful have little reason to reflect on their position in society, for the most part tending to treat their position as normal, just, or inevitable. This is true whether we are thinking of class, race or ethnicity or gender. A sense of crisis, indeed, may be indicated, when at least some members of a dominant category are forced to consider their positions in society. Further, when members of dominant groups do come to, or are forced to, consider their position in society, these considerations may be more in terms of justifications or legitimations rather than in terms of critical analysis. Hence, men do not simply turn to consider men and masculinity as another interesting and hitherto ignored topic. They are often forced to by circumstances or through pressure from women or marginalized groups of men, and their investigations may always be suspect.

The sociology of knowledge

I doubt whether I am alone in having had the experience of making what I considered to be a carefully thought out argument which was then attacked with some such phrase as 'you only say that because you are a man'. Equally, I doubt whether I was alone in feeling a certain bristle of annoyance at having what I considered to be a rational or factual argument relegated to the second division of opinion or the third division of bias. In some cases (although I cannot honestly remember having made this particular move) the man's rejoinder may be: 'Why do women always have to personalize things?' And thus begins the familiar spiral of accusations and counter-accusations that so often characterize the 'battle of the sexes', sometimes comic and sometimes tragic, the very stuff of situation comedies and modern dramas. Men and women, it seems, are always and inevitably talking past each other.

As has already been suggested, it would be wrong to interpret this as simply another version of the 'problems of communication' in the twentieth century. Such exchanges and misunderstandings must, I have argued, be placed in the context of deep-rooted and continuing inequalities in terms of power between men and women. We may, however, treat such utterances as simplified theories in the sociology of knowledge. Very generally, the sociology of knowledge considers the extent to which and the ways in which knowledge is shaped and limited by the social positions of those who lay claims to the ownership or generation of that knowledge. In other words, knowledge does not simply represent unmediated or disinterested discoveries of insights; knowledge and the ability to determine what counts as knowledge is unevenly distributed within a given society. In the various Marxist versions, these dominant forms of knowledge may be attributed to the ruling class. In other versions, different social groups (whether dominant or not) may generate their own versions and understandings of the world in which they live. Thus schoolteachers are not simply seen as handing on the accumulated knowledge of the society in which they live, but may also be seen as having class interests both indirectly (as supportive of the ruling class) and directly (as employees of the state, as professionals with particular and specific sets of interests, and so on). While the extensive debates around the sociology of knowledge have focused upon divisions in terms of class and status group and sometimes in terms of some other categories such as generation, it is only recently that gender has been taken as a relevant category of analysis. Thus some feminist writers have written about 'malestream' sociology, a neat reminder both of the dominance of men within sociological and academic discourse and the ways in which this has shaped what is to be researched, how it is to be researched and the uses of such research. In short, gender in common with many other categories of analysis in the sociology of knowledge, may be seen as shaping what may and may not be said.

Issues of the sociology of knowledge, the exploration of the ways in which knowledges are socially located, shade into issues of epistemology, the study of how we come to know, the grounds of or warrants for our knowledges. However, more explicit discussion of epistemology is deferred to Chapter 8, where it is linked to discussions of method and methodology. To some extent, the distinction is arbitrary; I see this present section as dealing with the exploration of what it means to see knowledge as gendered and some of the consequences that might flow from this understanding, while in the later chapter I consider more specifically what might be done in response to this recognition.

The American sociologist Robert K. Merton usefully and lucidly set out some of the key issues in the sociology of knowledge and some of the questions that he asked may be usefully adapted to the analysis of gender (Merton 1957: 456–88). In the first place he asks 'Where is the existential basis of mental production located?'. If we see 'knowledge' as something which is not freely produced by and equally available to everyone in society, then that knowledge must be linked in some way to particular social groupings. But, societies and the groupings within them may be described in a variety of ways: genders, classes, age sets, kinship groupings and so on. What are the relevant categories in this case? Here, the answer would appear to be simple: 'men and women'. Immediately, however, we come up against difficulties. What do the terms 'men' and 'women' mean in this context? Unlike the categories of 'class' or 'status group' they sound like biologically based entities. While, as we shall see, some versions of a gendered sociology of knowledge do come close to suggesting that men and women naturally think differently and see the world in different ways, the more sociological versions shift the focus from timeless biological essences to complex sociohistorical constructions that use biologically based differences (or perceptions of biological differences) in various ways. The focus is upon 'gender' rather than 'sex', although that distinction is not entirely satisfactory.

Two further assumptions would seem to be implied from this location of the existential basis of mental production in men and women. In the first place, the complex socio-historical constructions called 'men' and 'women' refer to collectivities rather than to individuals, to social institutions rather than to simple aggregations of persons. Thus 'men' refers more to generalized institutions of patriarchy (from which it may be argued all men benefit to some varying degree) rather than to a simple aggregation of all male individuals. It is not enough, for example, to read the life of any one male individual (however dominant) as being simply a function of his gender identity or of the institution of patriarchy. To paraphrase Sartre, Napoleon was a man but not all men are Napoleons. And we may wish to add that Napoleon was not simply a man. Similarly 'women' refers to the generalized constructions of women under institutions of patriarchy, rather than to aggregations of individuals, Ms, Miss and Mrs, in a particular society. Thus individual women may speak and act 'like men' and individual men may appear 'feminine'.

In the second place, the location of the existential basis of knowledge in 'men' and 'women' suggests that it is these entities, and not some other mode of categorization, that are of prime importance. Clearly men and women are never just men and women; they also have class, status and ethnic identities as well. However, the assumption would seem to be that these other bases or social locations are of secondary importance. This is, however, a matter of some considerable debate within feminist writings, especially around the interplays between class, gender and ethnic identities.

The next set of questions that Merton asks deals with the nature of the mental productions that are being sociologically analysed. What, in short, do we mean by knowledge? Early discussions of the sociology of knowledge tended to focus on the products of 'intellectuals'; philosophy, economics, psychology, history and so on. It might also include the physical sciences and artistic production. Later formulations would extend the discussion to 'everything that passes for knowledge' (Berger and Luckmann 1966) in a particular society. It is the latter which is the more relevant in the discussion of gender and the production of knowledge. We are concerned, certainly, with the writings of sociologists, philosophers and literary critics; but we are also concerned with popular interpretations of these productions, with everyday understandings of how society is organized, routine everyday knowledge and interpretations that enable us, all of us, to go about our daily business of living. We are not simply concerned with written texts but also with verbal utterances and possibly also, non-verbal texts such as the ways in which a city is organized or various body languages.

Two further points may be made. In the first place, it would seem to be important to understand knowledge not in terms of a set of thing-like 'items' – books, theories, medical knowledge, folk beliefs and so on – but rather as a set of processes. 'What counts as knowledge' is not a once-and-for-all accomplishment but a process, one often involving the establishment of hierarchies and distinctions, so that certain forms of knowledge may be defined as more valuable, more solidly based than others, is itself part of what passes for knowledge. I 'know' that astrology is a less useful or insightful guide to myself than psychoanalysis. There are competing claims to knowledge, some of which assume a greater prominence or dominance than others; astrology tends to become an entertainment, psychoanalysis an object of 'serious' study.

Secondly, and more relevant to the present discussion, it is worth stressing that the knowledge that is related to the gender base need not necessarily be specifically signalled as gendered topics. Direct gender knowledge would include such matters as theories of penis envy, women's emotionality, men's aggression, homosexuality as a disease, women's collaboration in the act of rape, women drivers and so on. These, and many others, are topics which are directly signalled as being about gender and it is not too difficult to relate such theories and knowledge to their gendered base. However, a gendered sociology of knowledge is also concerned with models of human nature, approved modes of

[33]

scientific enquiry, military strategy, construction of great literature, ideas of fun and leisure, and so on. The inclusiveness of the
knowledge that might be related to the gendered base is not
simply in terms of the degree of elaboration or sophistication of
the knowledge in question, but in the range of knowledge which
might be described as being gendered.

This argument may be illustrated by reference to an apparently
absurd example. An important part of the everyday knowledge of
a society is knowledge about the weather and, in advanced societies, an important source of such knowledge is the daily weather
forecast. At a first glance, statements such as 'There will be a cold
front moving across the North of England' would seem not to
contain a gendered sub-text. However, until quite recently, most
television forecasters on British television at least were men and
the term 'weathermen' was widely used. Even today there is some
implied contrast between the male expert (backed by charts and
isobars) and the female entertainer. Further, the whole scientific
discourse, of which weather forecasting is a part, may be viewed
as being dominated by male or patriarchal assumptions. In this
case, weather is construed as a set of largely impersonal forces,
with little reference to human projects with the possible exception of leisure. (Thus the weather may be defined in terms of its
likely impact on the Test Match, a quintessentially male project.)
The everyday weather forecast is a presentation of expertise
(regardless of whether the presenter be a man or a woman), one
which reinforces a particular view of science, one dealing with
objectivity, quantification, professionalism and specialization. It is
increasingly argued that such understandings of the world and our
way of knowing it are shot through with patriarchal assumptions.
I shall discuss this argument later in the book (Chapter 8) but I
raise it here simply to indicate the possibility of relating an
apparently ungendered activity, that of weather forecasting, to
wider gender divisions within society. If we move away from the
daily and formal, possibly ritualistic, presentations of weather
forecasts to more popular expressions, then gender may sometimes become more apparent. Thus there may be references to
'brass monkey weather' or to a 'good drying day' for example.

The final set of questions relates to the hypothesized or
assumed relationship between the existential base, gender, and the
knowledge products. In the case of gendered knowledge three,
not necessarily mutually exclusive, models would seem to be

implied. In the first place there is a direct causal link implied between the gender base and the socially recognized knowledge. This was implied in the retort 'you say that because you are a man'. In the second place the relationship may be more one of settling limits to what is known or what can be known. Here the statements may be more in terms of strong probabilities rather than of absolute deterination. Hence it may be argued that it is highly unlikely than a man will ever fully understand the experience of sexual harassment or childbirth although, perhaps, not impossible. Much, of course, hinges upon what is meant by the phrase 'fully understand'. Finally, we may see the relationships between the base and the knowledge as one of interaction. For example, the generation of knowledge by male scientists about female sexuality in the nineteenth and early twentieth century (Edwards 1981) has consequences for the way in which men and women are understood and how they understand themselves, socially constructed consequences which can, and probably did, become real in their effects. It may also be the case, of course, that knowledge generated by women, and sometimes men, may have the effect of modifying socially constructed ideas of sexual difference.

Up to now, the models almost seem to suggest two parallel processes of knowledge generation, one for men and the other for women. This would clearly be a practical impossibility in any society; for all everyday purposes men and women do manage to understand each other, that is to have some shared stock of knowledge. More important, however, is the recognition that the relationship between men and women is, among other things, a power relationship. This has a variety of consequences. In the first place, knowledge and what passes for socially significant or acceptable knowledge is affected by this power dimension such that, to some extent, men's knowledge is dominant and constraining upon women. However, secondly, this domination is never absolute and women do develop or elaborate alternative ways of knowing or understanding. Hence the relationship between men's and women's knowledge is one of both dominance and struggle, covert or overt. One of the reasons why many men expressed considerable hostility to certain manifestations of feminism such as consciousness-raising groups and Women's Caucuses was the fear, doubtless justified, of the generation of new forms of knowledge and understanding which were outside the control of men.

[35]

Moving somewhat beyond Merton's framework of analysis, there is a final set of questions to do with the specific institutions or social arrangements which serve as mediators between the gender base and the systems of knowledge. In other words, there is rarely a direct link between gender (however constructed) and knowledge. It is here that we come to consider some of the specific institutions of patriarchies in different societies: family and kinship systems, religious systems, educational institutions and the mass media for examples. Less obvious, but often of equal importance are institutions to do with work and employment, leisure and sport. In modern societies it is likely that two central institutions in the construction of gender knowledge, knowledge about what men and women are, are sport and military service.

One implicit aspect of the generation of gender knowledge which deserves some attention is the degree of gender exclusivity, the extent to which single-gendered institutions can effectively claim a monopolized control over the routine production of gender knowledge. This is not simply a matter of whether an institution is formally labelled as being for men or women only. It is also a reflection of the extent to which the institution demands, and the success with which it backs up these demands, that its knowledge be kept within the group. Thus we are talking about the way in which fraternities and sororities successfully maintain gendered secrets. The apparently ferocious Freemason oath may be seen as a male example of this. Again it should be noted that such separateness does not necessarily mean equality: the everyday practical knowledge generated in men's clubs, pubs and fraternities may be deployed successfully as a means of controlling women, even where women may have their own apparently parallel organizations. However, as the growth of feminism has demonstrated, separate women's groups and institutions (such as women-only newsletters) may develop forms of knowledge which successfully challenges some male dominance.

It is also important to consider the overall context of knowledge production. If we return to the example of the weather forecast it is not so much the formal content of the forecasts, the warm front and the deep troughs, that is gendered as the overall context of meaning within which it is presented. Or, to take another example, a formally gender-neutral statement about marking sociology examination papers may be delivered in the context of a male-dominated board meeting, with the men dominating the discussion and the language and the delivery reflecting dominant masculine styles of interaction. Hence in some cases at least it may not so much be a question of 'you say that because you are a man' but rather 'you say that in that particular way because you are a man'. And here as elsewhere, the context of knowledge production may affect the knowledge itself and the formally ungendered topic may become more distinctly gendered. To say that a particular examination script is clearly of an Upper Second quality *may* not be a gendered utterance, but it may become so when spoken with masculine authority with implied references to objective standards and timeless rationalities.

This discussion of the sociology of gender knowledge has not been a diversion. I hope to have demonstrated that everything that passes for knowledge in society *can* be seen as being to some degree gendered knowledge (and not just topics dealing specifically with gender of sexuality). I hope also to have demonstrated that this argument does raise a variety of complexities and directs us to a whole new set of questions. One particular example of this, taking a more interactional model of the relationship between base and socially recognized knowledge, is the fact that the developing if uneven recognition that a wide range of knowledge has a gendered component, is itself a form of knowledge, one which may – indeed is intended to – modify the gender order itself.

In terms of the problems of studying men, the following questions would seem to arise:

(a) If knowledge is in some measure limited by its gendered base, then to what extent and in what ways is a critical understanding of men and masculinities possible?
(b) This can be put in stronger terms. Since we are dealing with a context of power inequalities, to what extent is it possible or reasonable to expect men to develop those forms of self-knowledge which will inevitably lead to the erosion of male power and privileges?
(c) How far and in what ways are sharings of gendered knowledge possible between men and women?
(d) Is it possible now, or in the future, to talk about genuinely gender-neutral knowledge?

Aspects of these questions will be tackled at various parts of what is to follow although I shall return to these issues specifically in the concluding chapter.

Difficulties in studying men

In the light of these more general observations to do with the sociology of knowledge and the ways in which debates in this area might be applied to issues of gender, I want now to look more specifically at some of the problems involved in the study of men and masculinity. In particular I shall consider issues of power, issues of reification and essentialism and the more down-to-earth problems of finding one's way through the mass of material that in practice may be found to deal with men. (See also Hearn 1989b.)

Inequalities of power

As has been argued at various points in this chapter, a central difficulty in the study of men and masculinity, especially the study of men and masculinity *by men*, is to do with inequalities of power. If we assume that men continue to occupy positions of power and to derive a whole range of privileges from so doing (I shall not demonstrate this here; for some of the supportive material see Connell 1987: 1–20) then any forms of self-knowledge must at least seem to be suspect. Men's writing about men (and indeed about women) may be understood within this framework of understanding as having a strong ideological content. By ideology here, I simply mean a set of ideas and practices which have the consequence of blurring, obscuring, masking or distorting inequalities of gender and contradictions within the gender order. They also may be seen as having the consequence, if you like the function, of providing legitimations for the existing gender order. While this may not necessarily be so, it is probably wise and safe to assume this ideological presence unless we are convinced of the contrary.

With these considerations in mind we may examine two kinds of responses on the part of men to the women's movement. These are the ones I describe as the penitential and the petitional. The penitential (often adopting a confessional mode) may include a recognition of the wrongs that men have done to women, both in general terms and often in particular terms with reference to the experiences or past practices of the writer. This recognition of direct complicity with the institutions of patriarchy will be linked to a desire to make amends, usually through the participation in men's groups designed to question the institutions of patriarchy and to change men's practices within it. In principle, there is nothing wrong with this strategy. However, there are some difficulties. There would seem to be a superficial parallel with the processes of consciousness-raising on the part of women (see Figure 2.1).

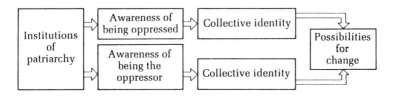

Figure 2.1 Institutions of patriarchy and their possibilities for change

However, while the awareness of being oppressed, where it does not lead to a kind of fatalism, may often be expected to lead to some kind of effective pressure for change, this process is by no means so straightforward for the oppressors, even where their desire for change may be perfectly sincere. The desire for change on the part of men is more likely to take on an ethical dimension rather than an existential or experiential dimension (see Thomas 1990). Or the theories developed on the part of the oppressor to explain or account for their oppression may, indirectly at least, reinforce their ideological power.

In particular, the path to men's gender awareness may divide into two different equally attractive, but ultimately counterproductive, forks. In the first place, leaning too much on the first term of the phrase 'the personal is the political', the emphasis may be too much on personal complicity, possible guilt and the need for personal change. In short, the response may become relatively apolitical. One aspect of this is the 'confession' and it is worth reminding ourselves of the place of confession in Western society (Hepworth and Turner 1982). Individuals conventionally 'feel better' having got previous errors out into the open. Confessions may reinforce notions of the self and the individual. In the religious context they may provide the possibility for absolution, in the criminal context that of punishment, of paying one's debt to society. The confessional context is, indeed, highly structured; just as members of the Catholic Church come to learn what is

[39]

expected in the context of confession, so too do more secular confessions evolve in the context of a fairly stable and limited set of expectations. In our present society, 'True Confessions' are almost inevitably sexual in tone, and the man aware of his complicity in gender oppression may be more willing to write about his masturbatory fantasies than his financial practices. Both, however, may oppress women.

Along the other fork we have the familiar and enticing figure of the 'Over-Socialized Model of Man' (literally, in this case). This removes the questions of individual guilt or blame altogether, by pointing to the power and the pervasiveness of the institutions of patriarchy and the way in which they dominate men and men's practices. Attention may be paid to particular institutions such as socialization practices in the home, in school and sports field and in the media. In some cases references may be made to figures which seem to exemplify the evils of patriarchy: John Wayne, President Lyndon Johnson, Sylvester Stallone and Hugh Hefner are popular examples. This kind of over-socialized or over-structural analysis coupled with the use of exemplars who are doubtless far removed from the actual appearance and demeanour of the writer or speaker may reduce the questions of personal complicity to near zero. Patriarchy is everywhere and nowhere. Of course it is not impossible that men, individually and collectively, may obtain some kind of effective compromise or balance between the personal and the political and that the recognition of the wrongs done to women may become an effective force for change. However, many difficulties would seem to lie in the way.

In considering the alternative mode, the petitional, we are considering the way in which men might come to a realization of the damage done to themselves in the context of a patriarchal society. These may be generalized damages, such as a stifling of the authentic expression of feelings or taboos on tenderness, or particular damages such as those faced by non-conformist men, gays, effeminate or sensitive men, non-athletic men and so on. The dangers of this mode have already been mentioned. They centre on the false parallelism between the sufferings of men in the patriarchal system and the sufferings of women in the same system. Such an approach leads to the downgrading of issues of power and dominance. This approach may also share some strands with the petitional approach, an over-socialized emphasis, focusing upon the distortions brought about by the socialization process or by the school system.

One practical question that emerges in the discussion of men and masculinity, is whether men should talk about 'we' or 'they' (Eardley 1985: 87–8). To talk about 'they' would seem to imply a denial of personal complicity or agency. Writings about masculinity are often replete with images which are far removed, one might suspect, from the worlds and lifestyles of the writers: Charles Atlas flexing his muscles, Rambo stripped to the waist and carrying huge phallic weapons, Ian Botham hitting them for six. Yet 'we' is often a dangerous word also. Who is this 'we'? Is it the particular group or network to which I happen to belong? Is it all 'right-on' men? Or is it all men in my particular society, if not the whole world? Does it imply a dividing-off of them versus us? Or does it imply a kind of pseudo community of interests, linking the person in the full-time academic post, the unemployed steel-worker, and the overemployed stockbroker? Accentuate the 'in group' and you are likely to run the risk of generalizing from the experiences of a few, possibly highly selected individuals and hence laying oneself open to easy rejection. Accentuate the universal, and you run the risk of creating false communities and constructing a generalized masculinity.

Essentialism, reductionism and reification
A second set of problems, already implied in what I have just written, is to do with essentialism, reductionism and reification. By essentialism I mean a tendency or desire to discover some essential gender core associated with men and masculinity. This core may be in biological or psychological terms or it may be less definite than that. A common manifestation of essentialism is the presentation or masculinity in terms of a set of more or less fixed traits; aggressiveness, rationality and so on. All individuals who are identified as 'men' are assumed to have some essential set of characteristics which are in some ways profoundly anchored to that title. One variation may see this as a kind of continuum, with some men conforming more closely to the norm and others falling short of it.

Essentialism overlaps with reductionism. Here we are referring to the reduction of social or cultural practices, in this case gendered practices, to the sum of individual characteristics. These characteristics may be in terms of psychological traits, psycho-

[41]

analytical processes or biological characteristics. Reductionism implies a loss of complexity and diversity, a reduction of the importance of cultural differences in favour of universal basic similarities.

Both these overlap with reification, the practice of treating social and cultural products as if they were things. The idea of 'thing' here conveys a sense of something that is external to the observer, that is unchanged by the intervention of the observer and is not dependent upon the standpoint of different observers. Two or more different observers, for example, will agree that a stone is a stone, that it was a stone yesterday and will continue to be a stone tomorrow. This attribution of 'thinghood' is particularly appropriate in the discussion of issues of gender since certain models of gender to appear to have this kind of reificatory tendency, 'men are men and women are women', a tendency which is reinforced in a capitalist and patriarchal culture. Women may be regarded as 'sex objects' and men may often be defined as surrounded by a kind of character armour which resists change and is threatened by diversity. Reification is easy when confronted by a troop of soldiers marching, a group of workers leaving the factory gates or a room full of men in dinner jackets.

Taking these three overlapping ideas together, essentialism, reductionism and reification we have: 'the popular cultural belief that masculinity is a coherent entity across a number of behavioural and emotional dimensions' (Blumstein and Schwartz 1977: 80). The study of men by men may be particularly prone to this danger for a variety of reasons. Simplified models of patriarchy or male power may be deployed to link one's own experience and understandings to wider social processes. Or, again, as we have seen, men may conclude that they have 'needs' which are not being met in the present-day society. Or, yet again, in the desire to move away from gender stereotypes, to free society from the destructive effects of masculinity, there may be a kind of stereotyping of stereotypes and investigations of masculinity will go where it is conventionally expected to find masculinity, that is on the sports field, in the army or in solidly male work groups.

At this point it might be relevant to mention the opposite problem, that of over-individualizing men. Ingham, in her study based on interviews with a sample of men, found, initially at least, a certain amount of puzzlement on the part of her respondents (Ingham 1984). Men were likely to say 'well, men are all different', that 'you can't generalize', 'we are all individuals'. It may be that this kind of understanding of men as individuals is part of the process of construction of masculinity in a modern society. In a society with an increasingly complex division of labour, which lays stress on a considerable amount of social and geographical mobility and which lays particular emphasis upon individual achievement, this understanding of masculinity and men might be expected to be particularly widespread. While women too are closely affected by these wider social currents, their individualities might be more muted given the social constructions around motherhood and childbirth and the 'naturalness' of the mother–child bond as opposed to the more remote and uncertain father–child bond and given also the continuing greater tendency for men to occupy positions in the public sphere. In popular culture, male heroes tend to come in all shapes and sizes, ages and colours; the women (e.g. the 'Bond girls') tend to be much more stereotyped and interchangeable.

Hence any attempt to study men may come up against the widespread assumption or pattern of resistance that argues that 'all men are different'. If we need to say that 'maleness' or 'masculinity' is something that links the professional footballer, the sociology student and the cabinet minister with the coal-miner and the bread roundsmen we need to be able to say this in a way that avoids the opposite danger of reification, essentialism and reductionism. It would appear to be a tricky juggling act.

Overabundance of material

A third, more practical difficulty, is to do with the sheer volume of material that potentially becomes available. Once you argue that a large number of writings (not to mention other cultural products) are 'in fact' about men even where they are not deliberately or explicitly signalled as such, then you are faced with considerable problems of selection and the handling of a large mass of texts and data. For example, within easy reach of where I am typing I can pick up H.H. Asquith's letters to Venetia Stanley, a novel about an Oxford don, Joanna Cannan's *High Table*, and the first volume of Armistead Maupin's series about life in San Francisco, *Tales from the City*. None of these have 'men' or 'masculinity' in the title (I have plenty of those, now, as well) but I am sure that each of them will tell me something about these themes. A few minutes at any bookshop or library or indeed by

[43]

our own bookshelves will yield dozens more titles. On what basis shall I select? How can I begin to make sense of this profusion of voices?

Studying men: some strategies

I have argued that the business of men studying men is fraught with all kinds of difficulties, some obvious and some less so. However, difficulties are not impossibilities and I want to conclude this chapter with a discussion of some possible strategies. These are not techniques and what follows is not a methodological cook-book. Some of these will be developed later in this present book; others I hope to develop elsewhere. All of them are presented in the spirit of wanting to open up a discussion and of inviting the reader to supply his, or indeed her, own responses.

In the first place, two general orientations. The first is, by now, a commonplace in Men's Studies, to require that we speak and write of a plurality of men, of masculinities rather than of masculinity. What might this mean in practice? In the first place it might mean the multiplication of categories. For example if we take 'masculine' and 'feminine' to signify a range of culturally defined characteristics which can be assigned to *both* men and women and if we take sexual orientation into account, we already begin to appreciate some diversity and complexity: this is shown diagrammatically in Figure 2.2.

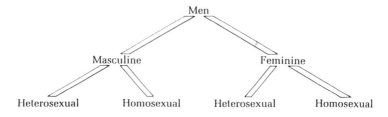

Figure 2.2 Categories of gender and sexual orientation

Similarly we may play around with categories based upon class, ethnicity, age and family or kinship status. While this strategy does serve as a potent reminder of the diversity of experiences with which we are dealing, it does seem to have one potential difficulty, namely that it may lead to the perpetuation of stereo-types rather than their transcendence. We are becoming aware of the potential dangers of the simplistic reference to 'Black men' and 'Black masculinity', just as we are becoming aware of the covert racialism implied in the overuse of the term 'macho'. Working-class masculinities may be discussed in terms of ready-to-hand, conventional and possibly self-serving images: *they* routinely throw their dinners at the back of the fire, drink with their mates every night, beat their wives and so on.

One possible way of handling this is to recognize that there is not simply a diversity of masculinities, rather like a well-stocked supermarket, but that these masculinities are linked to each other, hierarchically, in terms of power. Power, in other words, is a question of relationships between men as well as between men and women. This is implied in Connell's discussion of 'hege-monic masculinities' (Connell 1987). This may not entirely solve the problem of potential stereotyping but does begin to appreciate the dynamic and interconnected characters of masculinities within a particular society. Perhaps another strategy would be to think more in processual and experiential terms and to consider the range of gendered life-courses that take place within society. Here characteristics – age, material status, class, ethnicity and so on – are not simply added to each other but are seen in terms of a dynamic interaction over time and in relation to other life-courses. The practical difficulties of this kind of approach are great but so are the potentialities.

Another tricky problem with the pluralization of masculinities brings us back to questions of essentialism. To talk of a plurality of masculinities seems to imply an array of different statuses each one of which possesses something which we might call a 'mascu-linity' just as champagne, malt whisky, best bitter and sweet sherry are all alcoholic beverages. (This metaphor might be a fruitful one since in all these cases, alcohol is not something which is added to the drinks concerned but is a quality which emerges in the process of their constitution. Moreover, it is possible to speak of different strengths of alcohol as well as of beverages which have marked similarities to the ones listed except that they have the alcohol removed.) Does this not imply a kind of essentialism? There would seem to be two possible responses to this. One is to recognize that 'masculinity' is a term that is used in our society and that, as sociologists, we need to begin to explore the range of

[45]

usages. People do, after all, talk of someone or something as being more or less masculine. The other is to recognize that our use of the term 'masculinities' is a theoretical and political strategy designed to deconstruct conventional stereotypes which may get in the way of understanding the workings of patriarchy. Most people have no difficulty in thinking of Clint Eastwood as 'masculine'. They may have more difficulty in applying the same word to the local bank manager (assuming that manager be a man) and this sense of strangeness or shock may be fruitful in sexual, political or theoretical terms. In the last analysis we should never forget that constructions are just that, constructions, and that there may always be other ways of looking at the same set of phenomena. What may be an aid to our understanding now may serve as a blinker in the future.

One way in which the pluralization of masculinities may be a blinker already is the danger that it may blunt the critical cutting edge of feminism and of some men's responses to it. In the ever-proliferating multiplication of masculinities is there a danger of losing a sense of dominance, of patriarchy and of control? Do we murder to dissect? Might not this pluralization seem, at some stage in the near future, to be yet another male strategy (or at least have the unintended consequences of becoming such a strategy) for the maintenance of male dominance? Again, I want to remain open to this possibility and, where possible, to guard against it. But overall I feel that the only fruitful line of development lies in the recognition of complexity and diversity while also recognizing that these complexities are variations on a deeply entrenched theme.

The other general strategy is indicated in the following quotation: 'It goes without saying that a person's sex is considered an independent variable, not a dependent one, despite the fact that everyone and no one knows what that means' (Sherif 1987: 45). Exactly! The whole language of dependent and independent variables gets in the way of a serious understanding of sex and gender as socio-historical processes. However, as a strategy, consider treating the gender as a dependent variable. In other words, do not consider masculinity as a characteristic that one brings uniformly to each and every encounter. Here the links with biology may become most unhelpful. Men do not routinely remove and replace their sexual organs in everyday encounters. They do, however, sometimes remove their hats or their ties, clench their fists, bare their teeth, smile, weep, relax, straighten up, touch or obviously fail to touch. Gender and masculinities may be understood as part of a Goffmanesque presentation of self, something which is negotiated (implicitly or explicitly) over a whole range of situations. When I was in the Royal Air Force as a National Serviceman, a fairly frequent subject of discussion was the common mistake of using billet talk on leave in the presence of family or girlfriends. 'Fuck my old boots' might be a perfectly acceptable, indeed required, expression in the billet but quite out of place round the Sunday lunch table. In short we should think of doing masculinities rather than of being masculine.

Finally, and more briefly, some more specific strategies, some of which will be explored in subsequent chapters:

(a) Re-reading classics. Take a look at some of the works by the 'founding fathers' of sociology or some of their male heirs. They rarely, if ever, wrote explicitly about men. But their texts can sometimes be reread as being texts about men and masculinities. This is not, of course, an innocent reading, and we should subject the process of rereading such texts to critical scrutiny. The same, of course, may well be true for key texts in history, biographies of famous men, works of literary criticism and so on.

(b) Cases where men and masculinity more or less come explicitly to the fore. Following the point about seeing gender as a dependent variable, we may suggest that some situations are more tightly gendered than others, in the present discussion, more masculinized than others. This is in part a question of all-male establishments but, more than this, where masculinity is more or less explicitly put on the line. Military establishments are a case in point as are single-sex schools, many areas of sport and training for sport, prisons and some places of work such as mining, insurance salesmanship and deep-sea fishing.

(c) Cases where issues of men and masculinity might seem to be called into question, challenged or threatened. Unemployment is a possible case here, as may be retirement. We should also consider explicit challenges through the women's suffrage and feminist movements. We should look at what

[47]

happens when women move into hitherto all-male establishments or institutions (Oxbridge colleges for example) or what
happens when men take up hitherto female occupations.
(d) Make use of autobiography. Keep a dairy. Reflect on the
processes of writing pieces of autobiography or in keeping a
diary.

For a start, then, go to your bookshelf and take down a book.
Any book, don't hesitate for too long. Start reading. What does it
tell you about men and masculinity? What does it tell you about
yourself?

CHAPTER 3
Rereading classics

Introduction

In this chapter I intend to follow up one of the proposals mentioned in the previous one; the idea of rereading certain classic texts within sociology. Before proceeding to this exercise – which is intended to be illustrative rather than definitive – I shall say something about the two terms in the title: 'rereading' and 'classic'.

The sociology of reading is still a relatively underdeveloped area within the discipline and I do not wish to explore all the issues here. The first point is that, contrary to the popular understanding of an individual being absorbed in a book, reading can be understood as a social and a public activity. It is social in that the act of reading, whether formally private or not, is an act embedded in a wider nexus of social relations, just as the production of a text is also a form of social production. It is public in that to read a book, and especially to reread a book, is to enter into the relationships not simply with the text itself but a host of other readers and texts. This is formalized in pedagogic practice within the university or polytechnic. Students are conventionally required to read a chapter or passage and to lead a discussion on that reading with others, including a tutor. In writing essays, students may be encouraged to read what others have had to say about the particular text in question.

What this means is that, secondly, reading is never a purely innocent activity. Even when reading a text for the first time we come to it with certain expectations which are generated through interpersonal interactions or through various prior assumptions, in part generated by previous readings and encounters. The student will, for example, have certain expectations of a text through its location on a particular syllabus, through comments in the lectures, perhaps through previous texts or discussions. The same is true of rereadings. We return to a text with the sounds of other texts echoing in our minds and with the memories of previous texts and discussions interacting with the present re-reading. Yet the reading also has some feature of novelty about it; something has persuaded us, perhaps, to see this text in a slightly different light. It may be said, therefore, that every reading is both a first reading and a rereading.

One particular reading operation deserves particular attention. The notion of 'ideology' has always been a troublesome one within sociology but one of the implications of most of the usages of that term is that we may be required to read, or to reread, certain texts in a particular or novel way. We are being persuaded to 'read between the lines', to seek out themes which may not be explicitly stated, to read absences as well as presences, to 'decode' the text or to discover hidden or suppressed meanings. To give a simple example, feminist writers have reminded readers of the importance of looking at a section of the book which is often passed over, the page of acknowledgements. Here, in male-authored texts, are references to wives and lovers (not usually signalled as such), to secretaries and typists, reminders that much of the work of scholarly production rests upon the almost hidden labour of others, often women (Finch 1983). Other kinds of more complex readings may involve decodings in psychoanalytical terms (e.g. the scatological references in the writings of Luther or Calvin), readings that seek out ethnic or class biases and so on. These 'ideological' readings are more explicit and formalized than other kinds of rereadings but are equally the product of wider social relationships, interactions with feminists, Marxists, other scholars of different persuasions or nationalities and so on.

The second term 'classic' is also very much bound up with the sociology of reading. Conventionally, a 'classic' is a text which has 'stood the test of time', which deserves and requires a multi-plicity of rereadings, which speaks to a wide range of people at different times and so on. Even within the sceptical discipline of sociology some notion of exceptionality is implied on the part of the text and the author even if we may be wary of using the term 'genius'. There is some notion that the work of Weber or text written by Durkheim is inherently better, more worthy of close study, than a host of other texts that we have not heard of, or which we read only with a passing interest or as 'background reading'.

[50]

What we forget is that the establishment of a 'classic' is a social process. Texts have their own histories or careers and the process whereby one text has a flourishing and a long-lived career while another languishing in the equivalent of a 'dead-end job' has been examined in the sociologies of art and literature but has rarely been applied to the products of sociologists themselves. Thus, writing of the careers and reputations of etchers, Lang and Lang write:

> Once an artist dies, his reputation comes to rest irrevocably in other hands. Only a small minority will have achieved the renown and gained a following sufficient to carry them through the ages. The remembrance of most, including some once well-recognised artists with an esoteric circle of admirers, is highly dependent on survivors with an emotional or financial stake in the perpetuation of their reputations.
>
> (Lang and Lang 1988: 92)

In the case of Marx, for example, the situation would seem to be straightforward enough. Survivors had an emotional and political (and perhaps sometimes a financial stake) in the perpetuation of his reputation. Groups, political parties and whole nations came to acknowledge the central importance of Marx's works, in theory and in practice. The processes whereby other central figures or texts in the discipline have come to be seen as central have been less well discussed and certainly deserves attention. The following points would seem to be of relevance. In the first place, a text or author will need to be taken up by some prestigious seat of learning, usually a university. In the case of Weber and Durkheim, this had already begun within their own lifetimes. In the second place, the individuals concerned should have attracted a group of researchers, followers or disciples, to develop or to apply the original theories or insights. In the third place, there is a point where the process becomes cumulative and develops a life of its own so that even severe critics of the original texts perpetuate the reputation through advancing their own careers through perpetuating the memories of earlier texts or scholars. The final stage (associated itself with the growth of higher education and its increasing rationalization) comes where the texts and authors become enshrined in textbooks, the subject of course and examination papers and yet further theses and dissertations.

[51]

The institutions within which texts become established as classics are themselves structured in all kinds of ways. One important consideration is to do with gender. Just as a large number of female etchers with good reputations in their own lifetime (Lang and Lang 1988) may become forgotten after their death, so the writings of women about society and social processes may not become enshrined in the sociological canon. For one thing, women might have been barred, formally or informally, from institutions of higher learning. For another thing, these institutions whether they admitted women or not were, and to a considerable extent still are, highly patriarchal institutions. Hence texts, classics, not only have a history; they have a gendered history. It is not so much that Harriet Martineau or Flora Tristram are necessarily 'better' than a Marx or a Weber; it is that generally students and scholars alike have not had the opportunity to make the comparison. (I am grateful to Liz Stanley for this illustration.)

The notion of a gendered rereading of texts, often assumed to have some classic or near-classic status, is, of course, nothing new in the study of literary works. One of the earliest, one might say 'classic', works in modern feminism invited a critical rereading of such writers as Henry Miller, Hemingway and Lawrence in sexual–political terms (Millett 1977). Since then, feminist rereadings of texts by women and men have developed in volume and theoretical sophistication, bringing to bear insights derived from Marxism, psychoanalysis and various structuralisms and post-structuralisms as well as from various feminist traditions. Men have not been absent from such critical rereadings. Booth, in his fascinating discussion of the 'ethics of fiction', describes his experiences of rereading Ken Kesey's *One Flew Over the Cuckoo's Nest* in the light of feminist critiques (Booth 1988). The conventional and easy identification with its hero or anti-hero (played by Jack Nicholson in the film) becomes more problematic when issues of gender are brought to the fore. Perhaps closer to my current concerns, Schwenger suggests what might be entailed in a rereading of some of the more overtly 'masculine' texts, including those subjected to the earlier critique of Millett (Schwenger 1984). Here, he rediscovers complexity and paradox. Writing of Hemingway he states that 'masculine reserve thus modulates imperceptibly into feminine unknowableness' (ibid.: 50).

Sociology is, of course, not the same as fiction and we would not expect the processes of rereading to be identical in each case.

However, in sociology as in fiction, rereading is a complex, far from innocent social activity and in both cases 'classics' do not automatically take their place in the limelight as a consequence of inherent 'stardom'. Gender is a part of the process of the establishment of 'classics' and gender is, as I shall argue, part of the story, often hidden, that these classics have to tell.

But to turn to the texts themselves. I have selected two here. The first is Weber's *Protestant Ethic and the Spirit of Capitalism*. I first read it in my first year as an undergraduate. I had not heard of it before although I had read Tawney's *Religion and the Rise of Capitalism* before going to university, although with some bewilderment. Shortly into my first year I was asked to read a brief paper based on a couple of chapters and so, in some small measure, I developed some kind of interest (in the full sense of that word) in that text. I found it fascinating, perhaps because of my own background in Methodism and my growing, if inchoate, socialist awareness. It is something that I have read and reread more or less regularly ever since, initially to pass examinations and more recently, of course, in the preparation of lectures and the perpetuation of the text as a classic. I can, I think to my own satisfaction, defend my treatment of it as a 'classic' although it was not until I came to write this particular chapter that I fully realized the social processes involved in the establishment of this central reputation.

The other book is William Foote Whyte's *Street Corner Society*. In an early draft of this section I stated, more or less directly, that this remained after forty-odd years 'one of the few undisputed classics of sociological enquiry'. I argued in terms of the text itself. It was a classic, I argued, partly because of its directness, partly because of its range (students of deviance, political sociology, of ethnic relations and small-group sociology may still read it with profit) and partly because of its detail which makes re-analysis and internal criticism possible. I argued that perhaps one of the main reasons was that it told a simple but dramatic tale; how a man from a 'very consistent upper-class background' (Whyte 1955: 280) went into an Italian slum community and became 'one of the boys' participating in bowling matches, discussing the 'build' of girls passing by on the street corner and illegally repeating votes in an election.

I would still stand by these reasons. These were certainly reasons which attracted me to it in the first place and they

[53]

certainly continue to fascinate new generations of students. But I ignored the processes by which this became established as a text, processes in which I myself as a lecturer and writer in some small measure played a part. For example, I used it as a set text in the first part of an introductory sociology course at the University of Victoria, British Columbia, believing that it was far better to give students a direct sense of what sociology was about rather than to rely upon textbooks. I gave several lectures on this one book, encouraging (with varying degrees of success) students to read it closely and critically. A more significant figure in the perpetuation of this text's reputation was, I suspect, Homans who provided a detailed re-analysis of the bowling group in his book *The Human Group* (Homans 1950). Later I, and doubtless many others, came to direct students to Whyte's Appendix as a model of how to write about participant observation and the research experience.

To some extent this selection is arbitrary. But I hope that the exercise is worthwhile. It will prove to be so, if readers turn to other 'classics' and carry out similar analyses.

The Protestant ethic and the spirit of masculinity

I shall assume here that my readers know something about Weber's *The Protestant Ethic and the Spirit of Capitalism*. In a sense the title says it all. Weber was concerned to investigate the way in which Protestantism, especially those forms of Protestantism stemming from Calvinism, gave some positive sanction to capitalist economic activity. There has always, necessarily, been economic activity and there has always been the pursuit of wealth and gain. What was special about capitalist activity, Weber argued, was its sober rational quality. Profits were not spent in conspicuous consumption but were ploughed back into the enterprise which would then generate more profit and so on. Capitalistic activity was methodical and calculated; labour was rationally controlled and deployed and incomes and expenditures were carefully tallied on a day-to-day basis through rational bookkeeping. The development of, indeed the triumph of, capitalism in the West could in part be explained by the way in which Calvinism, often unintendedly, gave positive approval to or sanction for this kind of activity. Where the Protestant ethic, or something like it, was absent, capitalism failed to develop to the same extent.

Since the various pieces which make up what we now know as *The Protestant Ethic and the Spirit of Capitalism* were gathered together and published, the argument has been subjected to strong and continuous debate on historical, theoretical and methodological grounds. What has been absent in most of these debates, certainly until quite recently, was any discussion of gender. Even Sydie, who provides an interesting gendered rereading of much of Weber's work, does not deal in any detail with this particular work (Sydie 1987). It is clear, firstly, in looking at the book, that while the key terms 'Protestant' and 'capitalism' are non-gender-specific and may formally include both men and women, the book is almost entirely about men. The key figures that Weber discusses – Benjamin Franklin, Baxter, Calvin, Luther and Wesley – are all men. The only reference to women occurs where Weber is providing an example of a traditional orientation to work and resistance on the part of *workers* to systems of payment by results:

> The type of backward traditional form of labour is today very often exemplified by women workers, especially un-married ones. An almost universal complaint of employers of girls, for instance, German girls, is that they are almost entirely unable and unwilling to give up methods of work inherited or once learned in favour of more efficient ones, to adapt themselves to new methods, to learn and to con-centrate their intelligence, or even to use it at all.
>
> (Weber [1904–5] 1930: 62)

At this distance this does seem to be an extraordinarily patronizing passage, made even more extraordinary when we read, in his wife's biography, that Weber was by no means unsympathetic to the feminist cause (Weber 1988). What is more important for the present discussion is that this is the only reference to women in the book.

One of the early themes of the feminist critique of malestream sociology was the drawing attention to such omissions. The point was made, not simply in order to highlight an academic blindspot or injustice, but in order to demonstrate that the inclusion of women into the analysis often affected the analysis as a whole and, at the very least, provided new knowledge and new insights. In the present case, while there have been relatively few attempts to reread Weber for gender themes (but see Sydie 1987) there has been some recognition of the impact of Protestantism on patriarchal ideology. Hamilton (1977), for example, considered the changing nature of patriarchal ideology that came about as a result of the transition from Catholicism to Protestantism, paralleling the transition from feudalism to capitalism. Protestantism, while challenging the doctrines of the evilness of women and the construction of celibacy as the exemplary religious lifestyle, introduced new, and in some ways more restrictive, controls over women within marriage and the family, a 'little church and a little state'. A positive emphasis on conjugal sexuality was combined with a more stringent denunciation of adultery and extramarital sex, especially for women (Hamilton 1977). Oakley, following Hamilton, argued that Protestantism both improved and limited women's status (Oakley 1981: 71).

More recently, there has been some reference to the possibility that Weber's work might be read as a text about men. I referred to this possibility in an earlier article (Morgan 1981) and since then I have found one or two other references. Corrigan and Sayer make some reference to issues of masculinity and its possible relationship to both capitalism and Protestantism (Corrigan and Sayer 1985: 81). Elshtain writes of Luther's masculinization of theology and the privatization of the self, both male and female (Elshtain 1987: 142). Here I want to develop some of these scattered suggestions and references in order to provide for an additional reading of this classic text. Whether or not this will prove to be a fruitful line of enquiry I leave to others to determine.

In the first place consider the characteristics of men as they appear in a variety of psychological tests and investigations. Such characteristics are often based upon the judgement of a team of judges as to whether certain traits are conventionally understood to be either masculine or feminine or both. According to one account, for example, the typical male is:

Someone who is aggressive, independent, unemotional, or hides his emotions; is objective, easily influenced, dominant, likes maths and science; is not excitable in a minor crisis; is

[56]

active, competitive, logical, worldly, skilled in business, direct, knows the ways of the world; is someone whose feelings are not easily hurt; is adventurous, makes decisions easily, never cries, acts as a leader; is self-confident; is not uncomfortable about being aggressive; is ambitious; able to separate feelings from ideas; is not dependent, nor conceited about his appearance; thinks men are superior to women, and talks freely about sex with men.

(Fransella and Frost, cited in Oakley 1981: 64)

This kind of list has been paralleled in many similar studies.

Or, to move to less elevated matters, consider some sentences from a piece of publicity about a sales convention at the Royal Albert Hall in 1983, entitled 'How to Sell Your Way Out of the Recession'. The convention was held between 2 p.m. and 8 p.m.: 'miss the rush hour traffic both ways AND do half a day's work'. Inside, we find that the first session is called: 'How to Develop the Killer Instinct'. We also learn that the leading speaker, John Fenton, 'has been dubbed the Billy Graham of Selling'. Capitalist enterprise is here clearly linked to a kind of secular religion (complete with mass rally in the Albert Hall) and aggressive masculinity.

Generally speaking, it is no difficult task to trace affinities between the list of characteristics drawn up by social psychologists and the ideal type of Protestant–capitalist that emerges from Weber's study. In Weber's work there is the constant reiteration of the word 'rational' and its synonyms: organized, calculated, balanced. In particular, his model of the Calvinist appears very much a man in these terms. Weber writes of his 'systematic self-control', his 'methodologically rationalized ethical conduct' (Weber [1904–5] 1930: 28). It is a dangerous world. There are warnings against putting your trust in your fellow men: 'Only God can be your confidant' (ibid.: 106). The Calvinist should beware of 'loss of time through sociability, idle talk, luxury etc.' (ibid.: 157–8). Similarly, the capitalist, presumably influenced by this ethico-religious orientation, is one of a band who: 'had grown up in the hard school of life, calculating and daring at the same time, above all temperate and reliable, shrewd and completely devoted to their businesses . . .' (ibid.: 69). Such accounts are not confined to Weber's writings. Whatever differences there may have been between the two authors, Tawney provides a very

[57]

similar picture: 'That aim is not personal salvation, but the glorification of God, to be sought, not by prayer only, but by action – the sanctification of the world by strife and labour' (Tawney [1926] 1938: 117). He writes of the 'practical ascetic' (like Weber's 'worldly ascetic'). At one stage military metaphors enter: 'bugle call which summons the elect to the long battle which will end only with their death' (ibid.: 240). Other metaphors are equally masculine in their emphasis: 'hammer out their salvation' . . . 'the service of God, from which all disturbing irrelevancies have been pruned and to which all minor interests are subordinated' (ibid.: 241). A single paragraph contains words like 'discipline', 'rigorous', 'practical discharge of secular duties', 'ethi- cal duties' and so on. With Tawney, as with Weber, there is nothing directly on gender or the family.

A more recent study of Calvin, although more contradictory and complex, certainly provides a range of characteristics that could have come from the social psychologist's list (Bouwsma 1988). Here we find a Calvin that rarely used the first person singular, exercised considerable self-control on the death of his wife, was concerned with order as a central theme, spent much of his time denouncing sins associated with lack of restraint (sexual licence, drunkenness and so on), for whom 'earthly existence is a perpetual warfare' (ibid.: 183). One description of Calvin sounds very familiar: 'Calvin then, was a driven man, driven by external demands but above all by powerful impulses within himself' (ibid.: 29). He might be described today as an overachiever.

One aspect that deserves further attention is the implied attitude to women in some of these accounts and typifications. References to the threats of 'sociability' or 'idle talk' seem to imply a contrast with certain stereotypical notions of women. This is dealt with at greater length by Bouwsma, although the picture is by no means straightforward. One aspect of Calvin showed a near hatred of women and the effeminate: 'It is disgraceful for men to become effeminate and also for women to affect manliness in their dress and gestures' (Quoted in Bouwsma 1988: 35). Calvin presented a justification for Joseph's initial reaction to Mary's pregnancy: '. . . was not of such a soft and effeminate mould as to shelter a crime under his wing on the pretext of compassion' (ibid.: 52). At one stage he described the human foetus as 'living in filth' and women were sometimes associated with disorder and sin. He expressed opposition to feminine weakness and vanities and to practices such as 'gossip'. Within the family, an essential part of the social order, the man was clearly the head while the woman was identified with the body. Yet, as Bouwsma describes him, Calvin was not a straight-forward misogynist of a rather traditional kind. There was also another Calvin, he argues, one which had a positive attitude towards sexuality within marriage and which showed an 'unusual sympathy for female sexuality' (ibid.: 137). The sexes were equal in the eyes of God. Bouwsma argues that Calvin's orientation to what was evil and threatening in the world could be seen in terms of two metaphors. For one, Calvin the central metaphor was 'the abyss'; for the other, the metaphor was 'the labyrinth'. Both these might be seen as feminine symbols, the former threatening to swallow and engulf (see Theweleit 1987), the latter to confuse, entangle and bewitch.

It if is possible to trace these kinds of parallels between concepts of masculinity in contemporary society and the ideal, typical models of the Protestant–capitalist that emerge in the pages of Weber and Tawney, two possible explanations suggest themselves.

In the first case we might imagine a relatively weak con-nection. Weber and Tawney were both men, spending much of their time in the company of other men in single-sex institutions. In the case of Weber at least, matters were a little more com-plicated. He was married to a woman of strong feminist sym-pathies, certainly someone who was far from the model of the supportive housewife. Yet he is also shown to have experienced the classical Oedipal struggle with his classically patriarchal father. He retained strong notions of honour and chivalry throughout his life and saw his work in terms of a kind of heroic struggle. Given the overall unquestioned dominance of men in society and in scholarly production and given his own psychological make-up, there is little to wonder at in finding this gender-blindness in his writings on Protestantism and capitalism. Doubtless some of the same considerations apply to Tawney. Weber and Tawney limited their analysis to the more accessible worlds of men with whom they had some kind of taken-for-granted and unquestioned affinity. All that remains to be done, in a more critical account, is to rewrite the story in such a way as to include the lives and experiences of women.

Alternatively, we may be talking about a stronger kind of connection. The Protestantism discussed by Weber and Tawney not only contributed to the development of capitalism, however one might characterize this relationship, but also to the development of a certain kind of masculinity. If we accept that masculinity is not some kind of universal human essence but is something which is subject to broad historical changes, then it is at least plausible to suggest that the transition from feudalism to capitalism did have some kind of gendered dimension, for men as well as for women. Weber did, indeed, have quite a lot to say about masculinity and patriarchies as they applied in feudal, pre-capitalist societies but had relatively little to say about masculinity in modern societies. Sydie's interesting and useful recovering of Weber's writings about patriarchy (Sydie 1987: 51–88) similarly does not take the story forward into modern society. However, there are some suggestions that Weber might have made that kind of analysis:

> But the modern type of gentleman developed out of the older one only under the influence of Puritanism, which transcended the realm of its strict adherents; the squirarchic, semi-feudal features were gradually assimilated to the ascetic, moralistic and utilitarian ones, but as late as the eighteenth century they were opposed to one another.
> (Weber [1921] 1968: 1063)

It would certainly be fruitful to follow up the suggestions in this passage, which seem to be arguing for a much stronger link between Protestantism and masculinity.

While a complete historical analysis is not possible here, the following points would seem to be of relevance. In the first place there is the question of the separation of home and work. This is given particular emphasis by Weber in his analysis and definition of capitalism in, for example, his stress on the importance of the separation of family from business accounts. But more than that, the capitalist deployment of formally free labour seemed to require such as separation. Since Marx and Weber, many sociologists and historians have pointed to this separation as a crucial feature of the development of an industrial–capitalist society, although more recently the starkness of the implied contrast is being called into question as is the rather limited understanding of the term 'work' in this context (Pahl 1984).

The home/work separation is often treated in parallel with two other distinctions, one between the private and the public and the other between the spheres of women and the spheres of men. Certainly, it is no longer possible to see a complete straight-forward mapping of each of these on to the other two. We are dealing with increasingly complex sets of cross-linkages here, certainly if we are considering the actual social and historical processes of modern society. However, the mapping of these three distinctions on to each other has an ideological significance and it is more likely that it is in the sphere of ideology that we find that Protestantism might have something to contribute to the sharpening definition of these contrasts. The Protestant world, the capitalist world, is a public world and a masculine world, as far removed from the comforts of the home as it was from the traditional controls of the church or the monastery. Yet the home stands as a necessary adjunct to this public world of men. Weber writes of the 'clean and solid comforts of the middle-class home as an ideal' (Weber [1904–5] 1930: 171); it is both a source of renewal and an exemplar of the good life.

In its more modern, more secular forms, the home certainly came to represent comfort, solace and renewal (Davidoff and Hall 1987). But in terms of the original Protestant and Puritan debates, the home was something more than that. The idea of the domestic order as both mirroring and supporting the social order was not a new idea but took on a particular significance with the development of Protestantism. Calvin was clearly no opponent of domestic life and indeed saw the traditional Church's emphasis on celibacy as un-natural. In his stronger version, he saw the family as a major institution of social order. In a more or less straightforwardly Pauline way, he saw the family as entailing the subordination of wives to husbands. All that was excellent came from men and the man was 'head' of the household not only in the modern census sense of the word but in terms of the familiar bodily metaphors (Bouwsma 1988: 88). In his 'softer' version, there was an emphasis on the positive benefits of sexuality within marriage although families continued to be like little churches with the father as the priest (ibid.: 211). More gener-ally, Schochet writes:

The demise of religious chastity and the growing clerical denunciation of virginity as an ideal led, in the writings of

[61]

English Protestants, to a moral elevation of the status of families and to an increasing urging of marriages and the raising of children. Also, the familial head, in the same period began to perform some of the tasks that had previously belonged to the priesthood . . . . As the authority of priests was reduced that of lay household heads was correspondingly elevated.

(Schochet 1975: 57)

We have discussed, briefly, what this meant for women in terms of both gains and losses. What of the impact for men? Perhaps one of the key themes is that of 'responsibility', in the dual sense of having responsibilities for others (a wife and children, possibly employees as well) and being a responsible person. There are strong links, it would seem, to be made between these domestic ideas of responsibility and ideas of self-control, discipline and sober rationality.

Masculinities and their constructions do not exist without femininities and their constructions. One aspect of this might deserve a little further attention. The Calvinist, Weber tells us, aimed to pursue 'rational labour in a calling'. It should be noted that domestic labour (while it might conform to the more traditional Lutheran notions of a calling) has little of these characteristics and, indeed, might be seen as the polar opposite. Domestic labour is subject to processes of continuous destruction – food is consumed, rooms become dirty and untidy as soon as they are cleaned – and it does not have anything of the linear quality of a career, a life systematically and coherently organized around a central project. Thus we are not speaking simply of the separation of the home and the work, symbolically if not always actually, but we are also talking about the elevation of the latter over the former. (Think of the many references to 'filth' in Calvin's writings.)

The second related theme is to do with the familiar one of the control of sexuality. As has been increasingly emphasized and recognized, Puritanism did not entail the downgrading of sexuality. It meant, rather, its ideological location within monogamous marriage where it was both a duty and a legitimate pleasure. The institutional control of sexuality as symbolized by the monastery or the nunnery was replaced by self-control. Yet, as Weber seemed to suggest, sexuality was a constant threat; it was certainly the antithesis of rational labour in a calling and could, therefore, be easily identified with women who remained outside the rational public sphere. Male control over women's sexuality is scarcely new; what does change and what was perhaps novel in the Puritan model were the meanings attached to female sexuality. The traditional circle of sexuality–women–evil was – it might be suggested – gradually replaced by the circle of sexuality–women–irrationality. This was not, certainly, a straightforward transition and early Protestants still saw women as impure and as susceptible to evil forces. They used Catholic witch manuals as an aid to the control of women, for example (Anderson and Gordon 1978). But Puritanism, at least in its English version, did seem to entail some departure from the picture of women as evil and the possible substitution of woman as irrational, thus leading the way for the medicalization of sex, and women, in later centuries (Edwards 1981). Indeed, as Foucault and others might argue, the methodical practice of heterosexual intercourse as outlined in dozens of modern sex manuals may be seen less as an expression of a new hedonism but more as a logical extension of the Puritan work ethic taken back into the home.

One final set of issues seem to be worthy of consideration. Protestantism was not only associated with the rise of capitalism but it was also associated, as Merton and others have argued, with the rise of rational science as we understand the term today (Merton 1957). This was seen statistically in terms of the significant presence of Protestants on bodies such as the Royal Society and, at a deeper level, in the understanding of rational science as the domination of nature. There is clearly a nexus linking capitalism, Protestantism and the development of rational science. What is also possible is to introduce masculinity into this nexus. One example of this is the much-discussed connection between the erosion of witchcraft and magic in the face of a rational science and the medicalization of childbirth and its removal from the hands of women into the hands of men, professionally organized gynaecologists and obstetricians.

Part of the feminist criticism of patriarchy has been the critique of male rationalities which masquerade as universal rationalities and which are concerned with objectivity, detachment and, above all, with the domination of nature. Clearly, as we shall see, this has implications for the very practice of social enquiry. Easlea's *Science and Sexual Oppression* usefully points to the direction of linking

[63]

constructions of science with gender and masculinity although does not look at the religious dimension in any detail (Easlea 1981). Considering the interplay of these elements in history – rationality, gender, capitalism and Protestantism – may provide us with further insights into our own times, and indeed, to those forces which threaten our continued existence.

When I originally thought about this particular exercise, I used the title of this subheading: 'The Protestant ethic and the spirit of masculinity'. There was, of course, something tongue-in-cheek in this exercise, but it did seem to assume what this book has consistently attempted to argue against: namely the idea of a coherent, single model of masculinity. When I had completed an early draft of this section, I realized that when people talked of 'masculinity' they often had in mind something to do with the practice (or the stereotype) of *machismo*, a set of cultural traits and practices especially associated with Latin, Catholic-influenced, societies. These practices were organized around themes of honour and shame and suggested some quite different sets of expectations. Consider some of these sentences from a collection of papers on Mediterranean societies:

> . . . while to lie in order to deceive is quite honourable, to be called a liar in public is a grave affront.
>
> (Pitt-Rivers 1965: 33)
>
> . . . results count for almost everything and intentions for very little.
>
> (Campbell 1965: 145–6)
>
> A true man is one who is prepared to stake everything on one throw of the dice.
>
> (Peristany 1965: 188)

Such an ethic is clearly at right angles to any characterization of the Protestant ethic especially in its outer orientation, its apparent amorality and its lack of rational calculation. The type of masculinity that evolves in these societies is to do with an orientation to externally, communally determined criteria of honour and shame, in turn often revolving around the control, or lack of control, over women. The standards are communally based, the points of reference are the family or the kinship group. Masculinity is something which is constantly being put to the test in claims and counter-claims to pride (Pitt-Rivers 1965: 21) in the complex rules of challenge and riposte in small-scale societies (Bourdieu 1965). All this contrasts with the themes of self-control so much identified with the Protestant model of self.

This would, therefore, reinforce the importance of talking of masculinities rather than a masculinity and would suggest one dimension around which masculinities might be seen to vary, namely that to do with external control and self-control. This is not, of course, simply a matter of Catholic versus Protestant distinction. (For one thing, many of the Mediterranean societies which have been analysed in terms of honour and shame have strong Muslim traditions.) It is, in part, a matter of historical change within Protestant countries (as Elias argued in his many works and as Weber's own life in some measure bears witness). Moreover, it is likely that there is not one single model of Protestant masculinity to be derived from this discussion. The list of traits identified by social psychologists at the beginning of this section could be combined in a variety of permutations to produce a range of masculinities. Similarly, it has already been noted that Calvin's actual writings and life highlighted all kinds of contradictions and variations so that his followers and successors could derive, say, an extreme misogyny or a more or less liberal egalitarianism. What we may conclude at this point is that different complex societies have a range of masculinities which are more or less approved or positively sanctioned and that religion, in this case Protestantism, is one part of the process whereby certain masculinities are accented as well as shaping the limits of acceptable masculinity within a particular society. (For some further discussion see Bologh 1990.)

'Street corner society'

As is often the case, the title says much, in this case perhaps more than was intended. Whyte states that he chose to be deliberately selective in his approach, to eschew the approach of *Middletown*, which attempted to encompass all the traditional institutional areas – family, work, leisure, community and so on – in order to build up a comprehensive picture of a small town. Whyte recognizes that, in his own case, there is little discussion of family or kinship. Instead he seeks to let the part speak for the whole, seeing the group he calls the Nortons and the Italian Community Club as 'representative of a larger part of Cornerville society' (Whyte 1955: 94). He focuses on one or two key processes, inter- and intra-group activities, politics and racketeering to build up a picture of 'street corner society'.

Inevitably, perhaps, such a world is a masculine society. It is a world of corner boys and college boys, little guys and big-shots. When I first read *Street Corner Society* I brought to it remembered and half-remembered bits of American films and musicals: *Guys and Dolls*, *Marty*, the chorus singing 'There is nothing like a dame' in *South Pacific* and possibly the Sergeant Bilko television series. Women feature only through the eyes of the men and boys: as girls to be dated, to be watched, to be fought over and sometimes to marry. The Aphrodite Club girls are seen, for example, through the eyes of the Nortons as a potential source of trouble and division. We learn how the 'feminine' atmosphere of the settlement house (run largely by female social workers) antagonized the corner boys. In terms of his own experience, Whyte found the Martini household where he resided a source of relaxation from the tensions of research as well as a physical base in Cornerville. For 'household' here we should perhaps read women, women who cook for and otherwise service men. But generally the 'street corner society' we read about is a society of men, the masculine worlds of bowling and bars, of clubs and rackets and politics. Women are hidden. The part stands for the whole, the man is society.

In what ways, then, is *Street Corner Society* a study of masculinity? To put the question another way, how far can a study which 'happens' to be about men also be *about* men in a much stronger sense? In the first place, it is a study of domination, of the way in which men struggle for, gain and maintain power in a variety of formal and informal settings. In particular it is a study of domination in areas where the presence of women would appear to be an abnormality. Women may, as happens here, speak at a rally on behalf of a political leader, but they are not expected to compete for office themselves. The aspiring college boys may require women for dances or to play the appropriate parts in a dramatic production, just as the corner boys 'need' girls. While there is little that is explicitly stated in the text, the book does show fairly clearly how the normal taken-for-granted public world is masculine, if only by the very naturalistic way in which this is described. The way in which I read this book, initially, as 'telling it like it is' with relatively few obvious theoretical interventions by the author says much about the congruence, the silent complicity, between the reader, the author of the text and the way in which that particular world was organized.

In the second place, the study is a study of men's homosociability. Masculinity is not, to repeat, the possession or non-possession of certain traits. It is to do with the maintenance of certain kinds of relationships, between men and women and between men. Homosociability is a collective name for an important set of such relationships, referring not simply to the preference of men for each others' company, but for the location of these relationships in public or semi-public regions – the street corner here – and for the particular sets of exchanges and interdependencies that grow up between men. Certainly, the Nortons display a lot of characteristics conventionally defined as 'masculine'. They drink, swear, gamble, stand on street corners and watch the girls and fight. But it is a reflection of Whyte's skill as an observer that he goes beneath the stereotype, although he does not express it in these terms. Within the group there is a lot of tenderness, at least mutual concern. Doc did not reach his position as leader simply in terms of his prowess as a fighter; he is shown by Whyte, for example, to have a sensitive concern for the others in the group, such as Long John and his nightmares. After the book came out, Danny said to Doc: 'Jesus you're really a hell of a guy. If I was a dame I'd marry you' (Whyte 1955: 345).

Street Corner Society also shows us some sources of variation within masculine culture, in this case between the corner boys and the college boys. It reminds us that masculine culture – if there be such a thing – has both centrifugal and centripetal aspects. The college boys manifest striving, ambition, aggressiveness and sometimes manipulative qualities. These are all conventionally defined as masculine 'traits', yet ones which threaten other values such as group loyalties and mutual obligations. Doc and his group, the Nortons, manifest these latter qualities, features of male homosociability, features which may have indeed inhibited Doc's chances for 'getting on', politically and economically. Indeed, we are reminded that in our cultures there are at least two central images of masculinity: the 'lads', the 'gang', the 'boys' at football matches, at street corners, in pubs, bars or secret societies;

and there are the loners, the strivers, the heroes. Here these images are partially manifested in the corner boys and the college boys. They are not confined to Cornerville.

Clearly, there were strong forces working to produce a text allegedly about a 'society' but in practice only dealing with part of that society. Here, as elsewhere the acknowledgements are significant. Only two women feature in Whyte's list, as against 14 men, some of them distinguished social scientists. Of these two, one became Whyte's wife (and helped with the family study although there is little evidence of this in this particular volume) and the other was Kathleen Whyte who 'also did the charts and criticized the manuscript in every stage' (ibid.: viii). Whyte's celebrated Appendix shows in admirable detail his struggles to be accepted and the necessity for his conformity to group norms once he had been accepted. It is likely that a study of women in the community would have been impossible under such circumstances, although there is little evidence to suggest that Whyte ever really regretted this limitation. However, the consequence, albeit unintended, of these pressures and choices was a book that can tell us much about masculinities in all their complexities and diversities.

Some years later, Gans went to another part of the same city to do the research which eventually became *The Urban Villagers* (Gans 1962). He outlined four behaviour types in the area he called 'West End': 'routine seekers', 'action seekers', the 'maladjusted' and the 'middle-class mobiles'. Issues of gender and indeed of masculinity are much more upfront in this book, especially in relation to the 'action seekers'. 'The search for action is a male prerogative' (Gans 1962: 30). This is a peer-group society, and mostly single sex. Children who do well in schools are called sissies. Interestingly, Gans shows how sex segregation takes place *within* the home, thus bringing about a modification of conventional distinctions between the private and the public. Men feel uncomfortable in the presence of women; they fear the greater verbal fluency of the women and they fear that they may become unduly attracted to a woman, thereby 'losing control'. Men feel that they have to control themselves in the presence of 'good girls'. There appears to be a deep-seated fear of 'sissiness' and perhaps of latent homosexuality. Men lack respect for members of the priesthood although they are more ready to accord such respect to nuns.

[68]

One interesting section of Gans's study is his account of responses to the mass media. There is clearly a kind of affinity between the lifestyles and orientation of the male 'action seekers' and many of the heroes of popular crime series. There is also a particular widespread identification with Frank Sinatra, somebody who was presented as being very much his own man, who could face up to opposition from wherever it came and yet who also manifested a kind of self-control and poise. In Gans's study some of the themes that were latent in Whyte's study come to the fore, although we have to bear in mind the changing times.

There would appear to be some differences between the masculinities in the two studies although it is difficult to discern how much of that is due to local cultural differences, to historical differences or to the orientations of the authors. Certainly there seems to be a shift towards a more privatized masculinity in the Gans study. Gans went into bars but did not find that he could gain acceptance there but also suspected that much of the 'action' took place elsewhere. What is perhaps interesting is the way in which Gans's discussion of masculinity focuses almost entirely, as far as one can tell, on the 'action seekers'. One might assume that the other ideal types also have their gendered connotations (especially the 'middle-class mobiles') although this is not systematically discussed. Issues of men and masculinity come to the fore where they might conventionally be expected to be found – in relation to action and action seekers. Perhaps, indeed, there are links between the 'action seekers' in Cornerville and the search for an 'action frame of reference' in sociological history.

Conclusion

This last sentence, of course, raises the principal methodological issue involved in the rereading of texts. In carrying out these rereadings am I not bringing my own understandings of masculinity, perhaps more conventional than I might like to acknowledge, to this reading? Am I not simply finding what I want to find? Further, to continue the re-analysis in terms of a pluralized set of masculinities does not really solve the problem either, since I am assuming some kind of family resemblance between men in a range of different circumstances through my continuing use of that particular word.

[69]

The answer is partly to acknowledge the criticism and to reiterate that I am not providing an innocent reading of these texts. It is a reading which has been shaped by a particular understanding of gender relations, one which has derived largely from the feminist critique of patriarchal institutions and practices. It is based on the belief that in order to understand the workings of these institutions you need to study groups of men and individual men in some detail. It is also shaped by my own participation in a patriarchal society as a man and my faltering attempts at self-understanding that have been brought about by my encounters with feminism and feminists. I acknowledge that it is a partial reading, and that other readings are not only possible but inevitable. I recognize that it is as much a self-reading as an objective detached analysis; much more so, in fact.

When I look at or read about a group of men or individual men can I always expect to find evidence of masculinities? The answer depends on how I understand masculinities. If I see masculinities as a series of traits, about which there is some wide measure of agreement within a particular society and which individuals possess in greater or lesser amounts, then it is theoretically possible that a group of men will fail to manifest those traits. (Groups of men in certain political or therapeutic contexts, possibly.) If, however, I tend to understand masculinities in terms of sets of practices which in varying degrees contribute to the maintenance and reproduction of patriarchal systems then it does perhaps make sense to find masculinities in, sometimes, even the superficially least masculine practices. This may be the case, for example, when men show mutual care and concern for each other under fire in wartime or when they cry openly after having committed some act of violence such as suppressing a riot or a demonstration. Tenderness, crying, mutual concern: in our society (although clearly not in all societies) these are not conventionally defined as masculine characteristics. Yet they can be seen as masculine practices, practices of men, which may be socially legitimated and which, directly or indirectly, support wider systems of control and dominance of men over women and men over men.

It is always possible to have a rereading of a text which is insensitive, which does violence to the evidence presented within a text (no text is completely open) or which shows an ideological blinkering on the part of the reader. It is up to the reader of *this* text to determine whether I am guilty or not of these practices.

What I would hope to do, and what I would hope others would do, is to remain open to the possibilities of surprise and puzzlement. I did not expect to find *so few* references to women in the Weber text. I did not expect to find evidence of mutual concern and tenderness in Whyte's book. I also hope that rereading of such texts will lead, in some measure to a reading of oneself. I am not simply a man, but I am a heterosexual man, a man with a Nonconformist background, a man who has (willingly or unwillingly) participated in all-male groups of one kind or another, and man who has longed for, and sometimes obtained, support and recognition from other men. Rather than simply to see texts as a source of information or ideas or theories about the world, information, ideas and theories which I more or less passively absorb or reject, I attempt to see the text as something that is in a living relationship with myself and that the process of reading deserves as much attention as the actual words on the page.

CHAPTER 4

Danger, men at work

Introduction

Tommy is a big man and his white coat makes him look even bigger. He stands in his boots, his white coat billowing open, hands in trouser pockets, helmet on the back of his head and all shift long – 'he's *murder* on Nights' – he shouts abuse or laughs. He tells many drinking tales, of drinking seven pints in twenty minutes after the 'two till ten' afternoon shift, of how 'no weekend passes without a piss-up in our house', of how his little lad likes a Guinness with his Sunday dinner. Everyone rates him 'a character'. 'Have you seen Tommy yet?' managers would ask us. 'The salt of the earth, Tommy'.

(Nichols and Beynon 1977: 94, italics in original)

The terms 'work' or 'working' and 'men' are often and routinely linked and out of such linkages commonly emerges images like Nichols and Beynon's 'Tommy Robson'. Robson is a foreman, from a coal-mining background and with experience on the shop floor at 'ChemCo' before moving south for the firm. He retains his identification with the North, which continues to be a major point of reference and there is no doubt that Northernness has particular connotations of masculinity in his discourse as well as in the discourse of others. While using the North and the past as points of reference to celebrate working-class strength, he is also critical of the 'soft', 'stupid' or 'bloody-minded' workers of today in the South. Nichols and Beynon do not romanticize this pen-portrait, they do not attempt to disguise his racism and sexism, and they see many contradictions in his position and his attitudes; nevertheless this picture comes across easily as a picture of a working *man*.

One danger, then, in talking about men and their work is of letting figures like Tommy Robson occupy too much of the foreground. We see links between men, class, certain kinds of manual or manufacturing industry and perpetuate a particular stereotypical model of hegemonic masculinity: tough, hard-drinking, little time for softness in men or women but always good for a laugh, one of the lads. What of men who work in offices or professions, who do not conventionally work in all-male groups, or who work with and sometimes for women?

There is a danger that male researchers, possibly from more comfortable backgrounds than the workers that they are studying, will inadvertently perpetuate this model through a process of over-identification. In Gouldner's classic study of *Patterns of Industrial Bureaucracy* (a study that could well have been included in the previous chapter) we find the methodological appendix describing how a largely male research team developed a strong affinity with the masculine world of the miners, possibly identifying with them as opposed to the surface workers. There was an almost self-conscious rejection of the conventional middle-class campus lifestyle and the building up of team solidarity paralleled the solidarity work groups of the miners. They were delighted to prove to the miners that they could 'take it', thereby possibly winning some measure of admiration (Gouldner 1955: 250). Gouldner acknowledges his debt to the 'men at the plant' in these words: 'We were truly sorry when the study was completed, for we had come to like and respect them as "men"' (ibid.: 10, quotation marks in original).

As some of Gouldner's other writings show, he is clearly not unaware of issues to do with gender and, indeed with men as well as women. Yet, apart from one or two fleeting references, the world of Oscar Center (his name for the gypsum mining community) is as masculine as Whyte's street corner society. A stronger emphasis on issues of gender and masculinity might have enhanced this study. In the case of the mineworkers we have a familiar view of the development of patterns of male homo-sociability, the interplay between danger, solidarity working groups, leisure activities and a male egalitarian ethos. The mine versus surface distinction is, in this analysis, a major division within the community. Presumably, the miners feel more masculine, closer to the heart of things, than the surface workers although it is unlikely that the surface workers would themselves feel any less manly. If we look at the level of management, further ambiguities arise. Peele, the new man, is seen as the agent of bureaucratic changes. Perhaps he is seen as less 'manly' than 'Old Doug' as a consequence of his tendency to stand behind the Head Office. Yet he represents another kind of masculine hardness, not the hardness of manual work below the surface in dangerous conditions, but the hardness of bureaucratic and commercial rationality. From Peele's perspective and the perspective of Head Office, the workers are soft with their adherence to traditional values and indulgency patterns. We would rewrite the story of Oscar Center in terms of a classic Western, with Peele as the troubleshooter riding into town to clear up corruption. Inevitably, however, the researcher's identification with the workers inhibits the possibility of such an interpretation of Peele as hero.

Some of the more general issues involved in the study of gender and the workplace have been outlined by Feldberg and Glenn (Feldberg and Glenn 1979). They note that, at the time of writing, women are rarely included in research into work. Further, where women are studied they are the subject of sex-biased interpretations. They distinguish between two frameworks of analysis and interpretation, the job model and the gender model. The job model tends to apply to men and assumes that work is primary and behaviour at work can be explained largely in terms of work-based factors. The gender model tends to apply to women, which assumes that family, not work, is primary and that any forms of behaviour which require analysis are explained largely in terms of extra-work gendered factors.

Feldberg and Glenn make a powerful case for the adoption of similar standards in the interpretation and understanding of men and women in the workplace. Yet the tendency is more in the direction of wanting to see both men and women's behaviours as being made intelligible in terms of intra-work factors rather than considering each, separately and in relation to each other, as gendered subjects. They leave open the question of *how* we go about analysing gender, especially in relation to men and masculinity, in the workplace.

Here, as elsewhere, I argue for the importance of 'bringing *men* back in' although at the same time recognizing the complexities and difficulties in so doing. Consider the 'men' in two titles of well-known books in this area. There is little that is explicitly about *men* in Hughes's influential and insightful collection of papers, *Men and Their Work* (Hughes 1958). Yet there are to be found some interesting discussions of gender in his paper, included in that volume, on 'Dilemmas and contradictions of status'. Or again, where are the men in Dalton's detailed and fascinating *Men Who Manage* (Dalton 1959)? Women feature hardly at all in this study apart from a few references to wives, saleswomen and a 'female department head'. Yet there are *no* references to men, specifically, although the study is one of the richest studies that we have in the analysis of masculinity at work, in the two senses of the word 'work'. Similarly we may ask to what extent is Walker and Guest's *The Man on the Assembly Line* really a study about gendered subjects (Walker and Guest 1952)? How can we read or reread these and many other texts as being 'about' men?

I make no apologies for the fact that, in the following pages, many of the references are now over twenty or thirty years old. For one thing, these studies may still be regarded as 'classics' and may still have something to tell us, even if some of the conditions that they have described may have changed, sometimes beyond recognition. To this extent, this chapter may be seen as a continuation of the previous chapter. In the second place, it is by no means certain that, despite many far-reaching changes in technology and working conditions, there have been significant changes in the ways in which gender routinely enters in everyday working situations. For example, a recent collection of papers shows that issues of gender and sexuality are still very much to the fore in a variety of modern working contexts (Hearn *et al.* 1989). Similarly, a recent study of the British Youth Training Schemes (YTS) suggests that future generations of employees are being shaped by sex stereotypes and gendered assumptions, despite some attempts to challenge and to contest these assumptions (Cockburn 1987).

Work and identity

Work, as Ray Pahl reminds us, is identified with 'employment' in most modern discussions although, partly as a consequence of the approach of Pahl and others, newer, more finely nuanced, understandings of work have evolved (Pahl 1984). I want here, however, to confine the discussion to the more conventional understandings referring to the exchange of labour power for wages or salaries, in activities which are specifically marked off (often in temporal and spatial terms) from other kinds of activities. Work is also, overlapping with this, identified with 'occupation', a particular kind of title or label which is a feature of the ever-increasing complex division of labour in modern societies. These two terms, 'employment' and 'occupation', cover the two aspects of work which would appear to be central in considering issues of gender; the general meaning of the fact or work (or non-work) itself and the more specific meanings attached to particular occupations. In practice, both senses often interact.

Sociological analysis and more recent studies of men indicate agreement about the centrality of work in the lives of men. Work, in both the general and the specific sense, is assumed to be a major basis of identity, and of what it means to be a man. Ford, while finding men initially reluctant to talk about many areas of their lives, discovered little reticence on their part in talking about their work and employment (Ford 1985: 206). Ingham similarly found a dominance of work in the lives of the men she studied (Ingham 1984), and there appeared to be little desire or need to complain about this dominance. They did not, for example, welcome the idea of their having more free time in the future. More theoretically, Cockburn emphasized the importance of seeing patriarchy in terms of relationships between men as well as being about relations between women and men. In her particular study she was concerned about the differences and relationships between skilled and unskilled workers and, of more direct relevance to our particular study, the way in which work is seen as being identified with masculinity (Cockburn 1983: 133). Ford, similarly, refers to the male desire to 'prove oneself' and the idea that the most legitimate way in our society to do this is through work (Ford 1985: 220).

Hughes saw work as being strongly bound up with a sense of self. The particulars of a given form of occupation and the general fact of employment contribute to a sense of self and identity which is far from trivial (Hughes 1958; see also Berger 1964: 211). Nichols and Beynon write: 'a strongly utopian notion of *work* and its significance for mankind persists within the working class' (Nichols and Beynon 1977: 184). Sociologists, social psychologists and, indeed, philosophers would seem to agree on the abiding and central importance of work in what is often a very profound sense.

But how far is this a gendered notion? In response to the question 'Who am I?' men were (and probably still are) more likely than women to answer in terms of a particular occupational title. Women were more likely to respond in terms of gendered or familial titles. Certainly, the assumption has been that the close association of work and personal identity was one particularly appropriate to men, although the significance of this has rarely been explicitly explored, except when the issue becomes problematic in the case of unemployment (see next chapter). Most of the occupations that illustrate Hughes's collection of essays deal with male occupations and this is also true of the collection edited by Berger. Workplaces seem to be the crucibles out of which male identities are forged or through which they are given shape and meaning. For example, a central concept among Newmarket 'racing lads' is the concept of 'bottle' (Filby 1987). It is a new term for an old idea, a set of values to do with nerve, control, being able to take it, and so on. It is a term which has developed more generally in relation to men, perhaps more especially to young men, but in this case as in others takes on a special and particular meaning in the context of a particular work situation. It is not the case that work and work situations create masculinities out of nothing but they are often crucial in giving generalized notions and values specific meanings and anchorages.

What then of women? For the most part it has been assumed, as Feldberg and Glenn complain, that the basis of women's identities are other than the workplace, particularly in the domestic sphere. It is likely, however, that this is an ideological assumption and that, particularly when you control in terms of class, income, level of responsibility and so on, the meanings of work for women and men demonstrate considerable areas of overlap. However, it is also clear that the identification of work with a male sense of self is ideologically related to the wider patterns of the sexual division of labour both at home and at work. Notions of 'responsibility' and 'sacrifice' are often presented in terms of women or in contrast to women. Even where men and women work together in the same or very similar kinds of work, they continue to retain more or less conventional understandings of the gender division of labour (Balzer 1976). All-male work groups may develop strong and oppositional notions of women, using female terms as a form of insult (e.g. in the military). The hostility between Gold's janitors and tenants seemed to be, in part at least, a gendered antagonism with male identity being established in contrast to the 'nagging' women/tenants (Gold 1964). Wives may be seen as supporters of men's work and employment in all kinds of ways (Finch 1983), and their presence in the background may be significant even in those studies where they exist very much on the margins. In Dalton's *Men Who Manage*, for example, we read: 'Later at parties, Haupt's wife boasted of the "new contact" her husband had made and what a "swell guy" Tirpitz was' (Dalton 1959: 75).

If male identity is based upon work and employment, men often need women to confirm and reinforce this sense of identity and selfhood. Or, if not, they often need the implied contrast with women and women's situations, in order to underline the meaning of employment and occupation. The consequences of these understandings, which have complex historical and ideological roots, for women's work in the home has been much explored in recent years.

Certainly much of the discussion about the relationships between work, occupation and identity seems to be conducted implicitly around men and masculine identity. While in reality the situation is much more complicated, it is clear that the assumed secondary status of women within work settings does have consequences for everyday practices and understandings. Indeed, despite the considerable advances made by women in many occupational spheres, the changes in the labour market have yet to make significant inroads into the analysis of work and identity. Clearly work and employment is important to women in all kinds of ways, as complex and as varied as those for men, yet these complexities do not yet appear centrally in the literature.

However, even where occupation and employment are seen as major sources of male identity and sense of self, this understanding is not, it would seem, without contradiction. Nichols and Beynon note the contrast between the utopian notion of work that they describes as persisting in many working-class cultures and the actuality of work and employment in a modern company such as 'ChemCo' (Nichols and Beynon 1977). As in Sennett and Cobb's analysis of the 'hidden injuries of class', when things go wrong, especially when they fail to get promoted or are dismissed, working-class men are likely to blame themselves for these apparent failures (Sennett and Cobb 1977). As Hodson writes: 'Men's relationship with work is complex. They need it in order to survive and yet it can destroy them' (Hodson 1984: 93). Hodson refers in particular to the phenomenon of 'burnout' among managerial and professional workers although the destruction can sometimes be literally true in the case of some particularly dangerous industries. Even at a more abstract level, sociologists and psychologists of work have been very much occupied with the apparently growing lack of meaning in work and employment. Hence the work that is supposed to give workers an overall sense of identity may also weaken, trivialize or truncate that sense of identity. Work, Berger argued, faced 'ontological devaluation' in modern society (Berger 1964: 217) and Walker and Guest's relatively early study was only one of a series of studies which took the theme of 'depersonalization' as a central concern (Walker and Guest 1952). In some cases, sociologists saw work situations as being more or less prone to alienation and depersonalization (Berger 1964; Blauner 1964) although some might argue that these are increasingly features of many kinds of work in an advanced industrial society. Whether or not they are features of work in a post-industrial, post-modern or post-Fordist society is a matter of some contention. Nevertheless, the general point would seem to remain clear, namely that the relationship between work and masculine identity is a contradictory one and what may provide the basis of selfhood in one sense may undermine it in another.

Certainly many observers see workers, men for the most part, as developing considerable skill in making the 'best of a bad job' in using their human imagination and ingenuity in turning work into something more than just a job. Apartment building janitors seek all kinds of ways to enlarge their jobs beyond the merely routine or custodial (Gold 1964) and Nichols and Beynon are not alone at being impressed by the extent to which the workers they studied were able to do something with what they had, even if these responses were themselves contradictory, especially in terms of gender relations (Nichols and Beynon 1977: 193–4). These kinds of example might be multiplied, including industrial sabotage (Taylor and Walton 1971) and general and unspecified larking about (Roy 1960). What these discussions tell us is that the conventional idea of work or a job 'giving' identity and a sense of self is probably too passive. The various features of occupational life – the job itself, the occupational setting, the relationships at work – are part of the raw material out of which a sense of identity is created. Such ways of reshaping the work environment, are not, of course, peculiar to men and there are plenty of accounts of similar practices amongst women workers (Pollert 1981; Purcell 1982; Westwood 1984). It is in the interplay between agency and structure, between employee and workplace that themes of gender, and in this case masculine, identity are elaborated.

Work and masculinities

If work is, or has been, despite all these contradictions, a major feature in the shaping of masculine identities and if there be a growing tendency to write of masculinities rather than of masculinity, does this mean that occupation is a major basis of distinguishing between masculinities? At its most absurd, does this mean that there are as many masculinities as there are occupations? I think that, initially, I did imagine something of the sort, seeing certain fairly taken-for-granted contrasts between mental and manual labour, or between degrees and kinds of skill. Perhaps it was not occupation alone that was the major basis of differentiation but at least the ways in which occupation interacted with class and status. Now I am not so sure, and it seems to me to be plausible to think of different masculinities as cutting across a wide range of often contrasting occupations rather than seeing them as being unproblematically related to occupational status.

For a point of departure let us consider some of the polarities to do with work which Game and Pringle (1983: 28–9) see as being related to issues of gender:

> Skilled/unskilled
>
> Heavy/light
>
> Dangerous/less dangerous
>
> Dirty/clean
>
> Interesting/boring
>
> Mobile/immobile

It can be seen that up to a point these differences can be mapped on to, or associated with, the differences Men/Women or Masculine/Feminine. However, these can only be tendencies or probabilities, not absolute points of differentiation. Plenty of men do jobs which are unskilled, light, hardly at all dangerous, clean, boring and providing little opportunities for mobility of any kind. The reverse is also true for women. From the point of view of my present concerns it is possible to see these as points of differentiation within occupations dominated by men. The implied contrast between male and female jobs may affect the way in which certain male jobs are evaluated, with the more 'female' characteristics tending to be of lower status but again this is probably not inevitable or straightforward. Finally, for the present analysis it is important to stress that such contrasts are socially constructed and situationally relevant rather than fixed differentiations which apply in each and every work situation. Terms like 'dangerous', 'heavy' or 'dirty' for example may have metaphorical as well as an actual significance and, in any event, what may be 'dirty' in one situation may be seen as relatively 'clean' in some other context.

In what follows I shall not deal with all of these contrasts in equal detail. I shall focus on issues of dirty work and dangerous work and also consider a theme not covered in these contrasts, the theme of 'sacrifice' and 'responsibility', themes that in part deal with the intersections between the worlds of work and the worlds of home and family. But first I shall deal, more briefly, with some of the other contrasts.

Beginning, however, with the 'skilled/unskilled' contrast, it can be seen that it deals in average terms with distinctions between men and women in that women have a greater statistical probability of finding themselves in the less skilled jobs, while also dealing with distinctions between men. We should also note at the outset that this does not mean that women are without skills or a sense of craft; very often, indeed, it is the case that the skills and crafts of women have, historically speaking, been downgraded or marginalized in favour of the skills of men. In a recent study Walczak found that: 'The notion that women are good at repetitive work was one of the main themes which found supporters among those who emphasized differences' (Walczak 1988: 72). The gap between 'arts' and 'crafts', for example is one that has become increasingly gendered, as arts become part of a public and commercial arena. Between men, ideas of skill and craftmanship have often been a basis of differentiation, important say in the history of the trade union movement. Cockburn's study of printers argues for a close overlap between ideas of craftmanship and ideas of masculinity (Cockburn 1983: 52).

There would seem to be two interrelated aspects of these ideas of skill and craftmanship, as they apply to themes of masculinity. In the first place there are the skills themselves, dealing with a set of interconnected themes to do with 'being good with one's hands', creating something, deriving satisfaction from a job well done and from the wider recognition of that fact, and of having served a long period of training and apprenticeship to arrive at a particular socially recognized status. In the second place, such skills are social constructs and, more importantly, socially controlled and monopolized such that the practice of these skills in an occupation may well exclude not only women but also other men. Hence while many aspects of skill often have male-gendered connotations, masculinity also enters into the social and collective processes that evolve in order to protect or to monopolize such skills.

Before moving from a discussion of skill, it might be noted that the idea of skill in its more traditional sense seems to be bound up with a rather particular construction of masculinity, one which is at some distance from everyday stereotypes. Skill, traditionally at least, has been associated not simply with the manipulation of things and tools but with a sense of care and finesse, an increasing recognition that formal training and books of rules can only take you so far, patience, and taking pains. Such a sense of skill also has a place in the lives of women, especially where such skills are interpersonal or social, although these may often lack the same degree of public or social recognition. Further, these kinds of skills, associated with craftmanship, are those which are often prone to erosion through social and technological change, through processes of deskilling.

The 'interesting/boring' distinction is more obviously a matter of social construction since it is doubtful whether anything can be considered as inherently one or the other. Further, a *job* may be defined as being boring in itself although the *work* may be interesting through the opportunity for sociable relationships or even the opportunity to daydream. The possibility of enjoying rewards *at* work where the rewards *in* work appear to be fairly minimal (holding the rewards *for* work in terms of pay to be more or less constant) would seem to be something that is shared by both men and women workers. There may be differences in the content of the joking or the conversations, and the sociable relationships may provide the occasion for the production of heightened versions of masculinity or femininity, yet the fact of there being the possibility for such enjoyment would seem to be recognized by both sexes. What is perhaps interesting is the difference in the ways in which much women's work, of the routine manual or non-manual variety, is defined by men, often male supervisors or managers. When I was doing field work in a factory employing a high percentage of women, I often heard foremen or managers saying something to the effect that they did not understand how women put up with such repetitive work, day after day. They went on to suggest that women were in some way better adapted to such work, often stressing the ideas of the 'nimbleness of fingers', presumably seeing factory work as a kind of extension of needlework which all women were supposed to be good at. Kate Purcell found similar constructions, often expressed in the phrase 'men wouldn't stand for it' (Purcell 1982; see also Balzer 1976). Hence gender enters in, not so much in terms of work itself but in terms of the constructed meanings attached to that work, meanings themselves constructed in hierarchically structured labour markets and work situations.

The 'mobility/immobility' distinction similarly does not simply refer to distinctions between men and women but also to distinctions between men. 'Mobility' here has a variety of connotations. A common feature of a definition of a 'good job' is the ability to move around at or outside the place of work. It is likely that men and women share this perception – for one thing it enables the maintenance of sociable relationships – although the ability to, or the chance of, enjoying such mobilities is almost certainly gendered. Mobility of course, also means, social mobility, the movement between jobs and statuses, perhaps entailing geographically mobility as well. These forms of mobility, associated with the notion of a career, are clearly highly gendered; 'Tommy Robson' whom I quoted at the beginning of this chapter moved down South to get a foreman's position while noting that his wife wasn't too keen about the idea at first. It is also important to stress that the idea of a career, the steady movement up a series of hierarchically ordered statuses, and its distinction from a 'mere job', is also the basis of distinctions between men. It is possible to

[83]

see distinctions between the relatively mobile and the relatively immobile as reflecting or constituting different models of masculinity. The mobile career orientation relates to themes of striving and competitiveness and individuality; the relatively immobile, lower-class occupational statuses may play a part in the construction of masculinities based on group solidarity, fraternity and loyalty. The stable upper- or middle-class statuses may reflect or construct a further model of masculinity, one based more on the stable assumption of exercise of power and prestige.

Turning to the 'heavy/light' distinction we have what many might consider to be the heart of masculinity. After all, one of the clinching arguments against across-the-board sex equality in the field of employment is the one of 'who is going to do the heavy work', of who is going to mend roads, drive HGVs and so on. Such distinctions, which it should not be necessary to stress are ideological rather than based upon a careful analysis of relative anatomies or job specifications, would seem to differentiate between types of men's work as well and, by implication, between types of men. The image of John Henry, the man who 'dies with a hammer in his hand', remains a potent one, despite a decreasing need for large hammers, and informs many areas of male iconography, in socialist symbolism as well as in popular culture. Moreover, much traditional 'heavy work' often goes (as we see in Gouldner's study) with many other aspects of masculinities; group solidarity, swearing, drinking, fighting and strict sexual segregation.

However, there are some ambiguities in the way in which the 'heavy/light' distinction sorts out the men from the boys. Heavy work may be associated with certain models of hegemonic masculinity but it may also have strong negative connotations. Nichols and Beynon noted in their analysis of a chemical company that, contrary to Blauner's discussion of such firms, there was still a lot of what was described as 'donkey work' (Nichols and Beynon 1977). Already we begin to see negative connotations; traditionally donkeys are strong, reliable beasts but not noted for their imaginative or innovative capacities. Here we find that much of the donkey work is carried out by young men, another reminder that heavy work is associated with youth as well as with gender and that, with ageing, bodies and muscles may easily fail you. Moreover, in the study we also find the distinction between donkey work/scientific work associated with a distinction between the controlled and the controllers (ibid.: 24). Brawn can become 'mere brawn' or simple 'brute strength', necessary perhaps and sometimes admirable but not the stuff of which true leaders are made. It may be associated with 'thickness' as, from my own experience, where members of the RAF Regiment were described, somewhat unflatteringly, as 'rock apes'. Even in areas of sociological academic life, far removed from manual labour, the pejorative term 'number crunching' is used of those whose style of work more nearly approaches the styles associated with manual labour. Thus while images of masculinity may still tend to emphasize strength and power, these images are not without their negative connotations. Masculinity lies not so much in the inevitable associations between strength and gendered power, but in the processes of division and ordering and negotiation whereby distinctions between heavy and light are made and evaluated.

If the gender connotations associated with the differences 'heavy/light' are found to have their ambiguities, these ambiguities increase in terms of the distinction 'dirty/clean'. Dirt and dirty, as Mary Douglas and others have argued, have all kinds of negative and dangerous connotations (Douglas 1966). 'Dirty rats', 'dirty bastard', 'to do the dirty on somebody'; the associations with pollution and moral disrepute seem to be clear, especially in a society with such strong emphasis on hygiene, cleanliness and the banishing of strong odours (Duroche 1990). Calvin's obsessions of 'filth', with all the deep moral connotations, continues to pervade many aspects of modern society, albeit in a more secular form.

Yet, 'dirty' is not always or straightforwardly negative in connection with work, as Hughes's interesting observations on the subject suggest (Hughes 1958). 'To get one's hands dirty' is to be prepared to get down to the heart of things, to put practice before theory. There are some clear gender connotations here; women are often supposed to prefer a 'clean job', one where they can wear their everyday clothes. But again, dirty with all its ambiguities differentiates between the work of men. There are jobs which are literally dirty such as face workers in coal-mining or workers in slaughterhouses, there are jobs which are symbolically dirty such as police work or undertaking and there are jobs which have a mixture of both, such as, one might suppose, the janitors as described by Gold (Gold 1964). The moral evaluations of dirty work have a variety of strands including necessity ('someone has

[85]

to do it') and a sense of real or symbolic danger in so far as dirty work may be associated with the marginal or minimal areas of society. This kind of work may be the material out of which certain masculinities are shaped. The often described 'masculine' world of the police force may not simply be a product of self-selection, of training or of group solidarity. It may be all of these together with a kind of collective defence against the routine confrontation with social and moral disorder or human cruelty and neglect, reflected in the mangled corpses on the motorway, the old person left to die on her own or the products of domestic violence and neglect. Dirty work often pollutes but it may also be negotiated to give its practitioners a kind of heroic status, the kind of heroism attached to those who do jobs that few of us would be prepared to consider or contemplate.

Certainly, at a more mundane level, the constructions 'clean' and 'dirty' are routinely deployed in everyday work situations with all their moral ambiguities. Dalton's study of managers deals with the familiar distinctions between 'line' and 'staff' management, noting that these were not simply differences in functions but also differences in education, age and style of dress, the last having all the connotations of 'dirty' and 'clean'. The relatively clean and smart suits of staff management might seem offensive or provocative to line management, who may wear work clothes and, symbolically or actually, may have their sleeves rolled up (Dalton 1959: 87–8). Masculinities again, therefore, do not simply reside in some fixed linkings of 'dirty/clean' with different images of men, but rather in the ability of men at work to make these kinds of distinctions and to weave them into their everyday understandings of their work environments. This is not to say that 'dirty/clean' does not distinguish certain styles of masculinity; simply that the distinction is itself not without its ambiguities and the relation between work and masculine gender is more dynamic and more open to process of negotiation than might initially be supposed.

The discussion of the moral ambiguities of the terms 'dirty/ clean' as associated with work also throws some light on certain features of women's work. Much of women's work may be described, symbolically or actually, as dirty work and it may be argued that these forms of dirty work are more firmly anchored to their feminine gender identity than some male 'dirty' work. Top of the list, of course, would come much housework and domestic labour (with the added significance that it is mostly unpaid and little recognized). We would also include some aspects of nursing and caring work and probably also prostitution, where a popular legitimation is that it is socially necessary to cater for fixed 'male needs'.

Another theme closely associated with constructions of masculinity, at play as well as at work, is in terms of danger. Once again we find the constructions 'dangerous/less dangerous' associated with the distinction male/female although the distinction is not a fixed or an absolute one. It may, indeed, be the case that women have worked and continue to work in situations that are threatening to life and health (including the home) but these are in some ways defined as being less serious or less dangerous than the more public dangers of some male work situations. Many forms of modern clerical work, for example, may present all kinds of dangers to posture and eyesight but these may be less dramatic or public than the visible injuries suffered by workers in more obviously 'male occupations'. Certainly, the theme of danger combines with themes of hardship and dirty as part of the construction of quintessentially masculine tasks (Cornwell 1984: 138–9). And certainly there would appear to be an association between certain constructions of masculinity and the avoidance of safety precautions at work.

The danger, however, may once again be symbolic or psychological rather than, or as well as, simply physical. Here again, the work of Hughes may be instructive (Hughes 1958). Work may give individuals the licence to do dangerous things, things which might be prohibited or severely controlled outside of recognized work situations. The use of firearms by army or police is one such obvious example, as is the licence to break the speed limit on the part of the police and others engaged in a car chase or rushing to an emergency. No less dramatic, perhaps, are construction workers all over the world; it is a particularly awe-inspiring spectacle to see workers erecting bamboo scaffolding around multistorey hotels in Hong Kong, for example. Also relevant perhaps is the idea of 'guilty knowledge', the fact that on obtaining a particular occupational title, an individual is often privy to all kinds of secrets, insiders' understandings, knowledge with potentially adverse consequences outside the immediate work environment. Perhaps the extreme case here may be the priest in the Roman Catholic Church, significantly an occupation where the gender distinction is absolute. But most occupations have some kind of 'guilty knowledge' and there may be lingering suspicions that men, erroneously thought to be less prone to gossip and allegedly showing more commitment to work and the organization, are better able to take on such responsibilities.

Even occupations and workplaces which do not, on the surface, seem to be full of dangers may be defined or understood as such, and such understandings may be linked to constructions of masculinity. The world of management that Dalton described was a highly dangerous and agonistic one, a world of back-stabbing, constant threats to one's status and position, a world of 'dog eat dog' (Dalton 1959). How far this is a reflection of Dalton's own orientation to his research is difficult to tell. As someone adopting a quasi-anthropological approach to his 'tribe' he may have been more than usually interested in conflict, struggles for dominance, informal rankings, clique formations, relationships between line and staff and between management and union leaders. I did a rough content analysis of the quotations he used in his chapter on 'Managerial career ladders'. Out of 23 quotations, there were nine expressions of hostility to other groups or individuals and at least 15 references to a view of the workplace that stressed conflict, threat and danger. Only four quotations had no reference to conflict or competition. What was particularly impressive was the picture that emerged of 'danger' and the need for constant watchfulness. It was not competitive in the sense of a race, where the rewards go to the swiftest. It was competitive in that the picture was one of constant manoeuvres and counter-manoeuvres, a world where whom you knew often counted, it was maintained, for more than what you knew.

Themes of strength and forcefulness enter into the informal rankings within the organization that sometimes go against the formal statuses. Thus 'in executive meetings, Stevens clearly was less forceful than Hardy' (ibid.: 23). This was despite the fact that Stevens had a higher formal position in the company. Stevens was seen as being particularly inept for bawling out a worker in front of a group of women. Dalton sums up his study by distinguishing between those who can and who cannot cope with the built-in ambiguities of business life: 'Ambiguity them selects those most able to absorb, or resolve and utilize, conflict for personal and organizational ends. As types the more effective can be called "strong"; the other "weak"' (ibid.: 258). These are probably

Dalton's own constructions and terms although they would not seem too much at variance from the way in which his managers understood their world. Certainly gendered or near-gendered terms were deployed in some of the everyday conflicts. Line management sometimes referred to staff as 'college punks', 'slide rules', 'crackpots', 'pretty boys' and 'chair warmers' (ibid.: 87–8). I have spent a little time with Dalton's study largely because it remains one of the best ethnographic studies of management that we have. It does not seem to be too much at variance with subsequent studies (Burns and Stalker 1961, for example) or more anecdotal discussions of business and organizational life. Despite claims of new managerial styles, there are also new elevations of business men as modern heroes and increasing discussion of the application of new realistic, managerial or commercial practices to areas hitherto supposed to be free from such practices, including universities and voluntary organizations. Some professions may also understand their world in these terms and, as in the case of the law profession, make more or less direct links with male gender (Spencer and Podmore 1987). Within the marriage guidance organization, *Relate*, members often employed distinctions, real and symbolic, between male and managerial styles and female counselling skills (Lewis *et al.* 1991).

One further element, loosely associated with risk and danger is to do with illegal, dishonest or otherwise hidden features of everyday work and economic life. We have no reason to suppose that these features are associated exclusively with men and masculinity although most of the studies concentrate on men and have no recognition of a possible gender dimension (Ditton 1977; Henry 1978; Mars 1982). In Mars's categories of 'hawks', 'donkeys', 'wolves' and 'vultures' women only significantly appear under the second heading, in the form of swindling check-out cashiers. Yet clearly the other categories are redolent of popular themes of masculinity to do with group solidarity, individual enterprise and guilty secrets.

There is another theme linking masculinity and work and that is to do with the idea of responsibility. There would seem to be two aspects to this. In the first place there are the responsibilities associated with the job itself. While it may be possible to make more or less universal statements about the linking of occupations and a sense of masculine self and identity, it would also seem to be the case that certain occupations require, expect and get a much greater identification than others. So-called 'greedy organizations', for example, may demand much of their members in terms of hours and personal loyalty and identification. I have already pointed to one aspect of this strong identification when referring to Hughes's idea of 'guilty knowledge', the idea that in becoming a certain kind of employee one takes on responsibilities with a certain measure of awesomeness. The secret, insider knowledge provides strong psychological links between the individual and the organization and it is likely that these links are seen as stronger for men than for women since it is more legitimate for men to allow work obligations to override other, extra-work, obligations. But these responsibilities are not simply in terms of secrets or guilty knowledge. 'Mr Bishop', a business executive discussed by Underwood, described his job not uncharacteristically, as a 'way of life'. He worked an 80-hour week, arguing that 'we are dealing with the savings of millions of people' (Underwood 1964: 203).

It is likely that many employees, and employers, can define their work as entailing some measures of responsibility in terms such as these; responsibility for money, for the employment of others, for lives and safety or for the quality of a product. Yet even where such understandings, making for strong links between an occupation and a sense of gendered self, are not readily available the idea of responsibility may still be strong in terms of a responsibility for other family members. This usually expressed in terms of being able to 'keep' a wife and a family, often seen as an important measure of working-class male respectability (Lewis 1986: 103). This theme, described as a sense of 'sacrifice' is very much part of Nichols and Beynon's analysis of 'Chemco' workers. The workers are denied any little real opportunities for satisfaction or identification at work and yet continue to maintain the ideology of sacrifice for a wife and children: 'His exploitation in the factory justifies her oppression in the home; and notions of masculinity and motherhood reinforce their mutual dependence' (Nichols and Beynon 1977: 194).

This of course has been a major theme in the analysis of the privatized worker, especially in the discussion of the worker on the assembly line or in the automobile industry. Walker and Guest's assembly-line workers, in common with many such workers since, chose work that was often routine or boring because of the prospect of higher earnings or steady employment

(Walker and Guest 1952: 89). Certainly the theme of sacrifice, the exchange of a more interesting job for a more routine but better paying job in order to support a family, was not far below the surface in their responses, just as it was not far from the responses of Luton's 'affluent workers' (Goldthorpe *et al.* 1968). It would seem that this theme of sacrifice, for men as well as for women, is a deeply rooted one in working-class history and not simply in terms of a man being able to support a family: 'Wait till I'm a man! Won't I work for my mother when I'm a man!' (Ross 1986: 87). The apparent erosion of this idea of responsibility and sacrifice, at least in some sections of society, does not necessarily mean clear and unambiguous moves towards gender equality. The 'flight from responsibility' discussed by Ehrenreich (1983) may often be in response to the apparent attractions of a free-floating 'playboy' image rather than to the demands of the feminist movement.

Again, it should not be supposed that the theme of sacrifice is absent from the lives and experiences of women. Certainly, the ideology of women as 'carers' formal and informal, paid and unpaid, contains within it themes to do with sacrifice as in the phrase 'a labour of love' or talk of 'giving' time to the children or to a relationship. 'Caring', however, while having some affinities with the idea of sacrifice, and certainly with the theme of 'responsibilities', perhaps lacks the heroic qualities associated with the idea of sacrifice. Masculine sacrifice is closer to a state of doing; feminine caring to a state of being (Leira 1983; Holter 1984; Dalley 1988).

Thus there are all kinds of ways in which terms associated with masculinity may be linked with work and employment, in both a specific and a general sense. These ways would seem to cut across particular kinds of employment rather than being associated with particular jobs in any straightforward sense. There are also a variety of mediating factors which may contribute to strengthening the links between gender, occupation and employment, and a strong sense of male self. One obvious aspect is the extent to which the work is organized in groups and the extent to which such groups might provide the occasion for sociable interaction between men. Walker and Guest's study was certainly not the last (or the first) to show the importance of informal interactions as being part of the definition of a 'good job'; more recently, for example, Ford found many of her working-class respondents talking of the pleasure of working in a gang or a group (Ford

1985: 226). The patterns of interaction within such groups has often been the subject of ethnographic analysis, sometimes directly or indirectly drawing attention to the extent and ways in which such groups may provide the opportunity for the elaboration of particular masculine themes through horseplay, trading insults, sexual references and mock homosexual attacks (Roy 1960; Collinson and Collinson 1989). In some cases, especially those associated with traditional trades and apprenticeships, the membership of a working group may be accompanied by initiation rites, again often with strong and overt references to sexuality and aggression. While most of the ethnographic examples have come from groups of manual workers, it should not be assumed that men's groups, formed at or based upon work, are confined to these working-class occupations.

We should also consider the extent to which work situation interacts with class situation in order, sometimes, to accentuate certain models of masculinity. Writing of an Australian working community, Williams makes the point that: 'Working-class male politics rely heavily on the surplus time created by women's domestic production' (Williams 1981: 31). This is a point of some importance. Part of the idea of sacrifice and responsibility referred to earlier may be directed not simply to the immediate features of the work but to voluntary involvement in union and working-class politics. The ways in which such organizations have, and continue to be, structured in such ways as to favour continuing male participation and dominance have been well documented in recent years (Cockburn 1983; Cunnison 1983). Male relations at work are reinforced through male relationships in the union or in working-class politics. Such participations reinforce a sense of separation between home and work and between women and men. The theme of masculinity that may be elaborated in the interplay between workplace, union and class identification may not be the same as the themes elaborated by the 'lads' on the shop floor but they will undoubtedly have some gendered connotations; there may be emphasis on struggle, the importance of solidarity, economist views of labour struggle and so on. Such themes may be reinforced in such communities which are either relatively isolated, geographically, or which have strong traditions of working-class action and identification.

This is not to say that other forms of political and class action do not also have gendered connotations. We know less about the workings of Conservative clubs and parties, employers' organizations and groups like the Masons largely because researchers have been denied access to these centres of class power and action. But from what we know (e.g. of the Masons) we have no reason to suppose that themes of male solidarity and masculinity are absent from these routine political practices and gatherings (Rogers 1988).

Up to now the assumption has been that the work situation consists of all-male or nearly all-male groups. While the labour market is highly gender-segregated, and such segregation often persists within plants and organizations as well as between organizations, mixed-sex work situations are common enough to require some analysis. Do men and women, for example, have different orientation to work even where they are working in the same or similar situation? One cross-national survey suggested that men described a good job in terms of friendly management, friendly relationships with fellow workers, high pay, interesting work and convenient hours (Agassi 1979: 65). There was some variation between countries; fewer significant differences were found in the United States than in Germany or Israel, although the sampling procedures of this particular study make it very difficult to generalize about national differences. When asked 'what would be missed?', men responded in terms of money and a sense of 'feeling useful'; women would miss the money and a 'feeling of independence' (ibid.: 66). Balzer's more impressionistic ethnography attempted to tease out some of the differences between men and women at work. Men tended to discuss sport or life in the army and only occasionally family: 'Most of the women, unlike the men, brought their families to work with them' (Balzer 1976: 23). This was certainly something that I discovered in my period of observation among a workshop of mainly women workers, a process which I called the domestication of the workplace (Morgan 1969). Balzer noted, perhaps rather interestingly, that men tended to go to the bathroom (i.e. toilet) on their own, while women went in pairs (Balzer 1976: 34). However, it would be wrong perhaps to overstate differences in men and women at work, certainly if it is to suggest that these differences are deep-rooted and to focus more on the women as a problem in the workplace. Most studies show that men and women at work, as outside work, have more or less traditional views about the roles of women and men. Thus, in Balzer's study,

[93]

this was true even in the context of a firm that was stressing affirmative action in relation to promotion opportunities and so on for women and ethnic minorities.

Balzer's study is one of the few studies that we have describing interactions between men and women, men and women who were sometimes roughly of equal status on the shop floor. He notes, for example, how the women sometimes adopt quasi-maternal roles to the researcher ('Come and tell Mother about it', ibid.: 44) or the students working in the plant during the summer vacation (ibid.: 186). Emmett and myself certainly found it helpful to analyse some action on the shop floor in these terms (Morgan 1969; Emmett and Morgan 1982). Thus an older woman charge-hand sometimes appeared to adopt a quasi-maternal role towards not only the younger women under her, but also to the two young male foremen in the same department, and formally higher than herself in status. We did not see anything inevitable in this; rather that age, gender and marital status were a range of latent social characteristics which could be deployed, legitimately in many cases, in appropriate or favourable contexts.

One thing I did not write about was 'sexual harassment', partly because the term was hardly in use then. I did use the more benign sounding phrase, 'flirtation' or 'mock flirtation' to des-cribe some of the interactions between managers, foreman and female workers. I did not observe or hear talk of any of the more obvious and oppressive manifestations of sexual harassment (although there were tales of another department, where the workers were not only female but also almost uniformly young and unmarried), and pin-ups, on recollection, seemed to be rela-tively rare in the more masculine areas of the workplace. I am sure that sex entered into many of the verbal interactions between men and women although I cannot say, at this distance, how much of that might have been resented by the women.

Balzer, writing in 1976, does provide some more or less clear examples of sexual harassment although, again, the term is not used and their significance is played down. Thus he describes a woman in 'tight sweaters which showed her large breasts to good advantage' who was subjected to a chorus of grunts whenever she walked past the place where the author was working. He notes that this behaviour only managed to elicit one small smile from the woman concerned on one occasion, although there is no analysis as to why she might have been less than willing to see the joke (Balzer 1976: 29). Generally, the men tended to see it all as good fun, necessary to help pass the time. Sometimes women fail to respond to 'off-colour jokes' (ibid.: 32) but generally women are understood to be taking it all in good part and sometimes being more than capable of returning in kind. Purcell also notes patterns of sexual harassment and interaction on the shop floor, again stressing that it was not always one-way and that women do have ways of fighting back (Purcell 1982).

Thus behaviour in mixed-sex workplaces does not necessarily appear to be modified in terms of gender identification. However, Cockburn argues that: 'Some men would really welcome women as colleagues because it would relax the rigorous standards of masculinity demanded by work today' (Cockburn 1983: 207). This is an important point but does not yet, it would seem, appear to have been subjected to any more detailed analysis. Generally speaking it would seem that the mixture of men and women in roughly equal work statuses does appear to mark out the sphere of work as a male sphere, to which women are expected to conform. In engineering, for example, women are more likely to be the more androgynous while male engineers are more likely to be sex typed (Newton 1987). It is women who are expected to take the sexual banter and kidding in good humour. Men are not expected to demonstrate any increased interest in family or domestic matters as a consequence of the participation of women in the workplace.

However, this discussion does remind us that work situations are not static, either in terms of gender composition or, more generally, in terms of the presence or absence of those features of work that allow for more or less direct anchorage to male identities. Indeed, one of the features of the history of employment and occupations is the decline of strong, traditional male points of anchorage. Mechanization may affect a sense of craftsmanship and more generally male gender identities: 'Machines worked by semiskilled and unskilled labour not only undercut wages but also men's status and value in the workplace and their patriarchal role in the home' (Hunt 1986: 71). Many heavy, dirty, or dangerous jobs have declined or disappeared although, as Nichols and Beynon remind us, it is important not to overstate the decline of 'donkey work' even in some of the more advanced sectors of the economy. The development of new technology, especially at its more sophisticated levels, may provide opportunities for the demonstration of other features of masculinity, this time to do with the manipulation of things and, perhaps indirectly, people. Perhaps more important is the erosion of the idea of full employment itself, although this is perhaps better understood as a return to a more 'normal' labour market situation rather than a temporary departure from normality (Pahl 1984).

Conclusion

Following the widespread argument that work is a major source of identity in modern society, I have explored the implications of this argument for themes to do with men and masculinity. I have attempted to argue against too simplistic a model which would see masculinity as a variable which would be positively associated with features of the workplace such as heavy work, danger, dirty work or solitary work groups seeing these separately or, as is often the case, in interaction. While such work situations generate some of the most traditionally central ideological images of men and masculinity, we should not perhaps be misled by these projections.

A modification of this would be to argue that different work situations generate different models of masculinity. In other words, in recognizing the diversities of masculinities we see one of the main sources of this diversity in features of the occupational environment. Thus there is a kind of masculinity associated with manual work, another with skilled manual work, another with professional or managerial work and so on. These distinctions can be more or less finely drawn. Again, I have the feeling that this may be a little too simplistic. For one thing, the same job or work situation may prove an arena for a variety of masculinities.

The model I am tending towards is a somewhat more complex one which sets a range of 'masculinities' which can be deployed in different mixes in different work situations. This needs further explication. In the first place, by masculinities I am not referring so much to psychological traits which individuals may or may not possess, but rather more to sets of culturally available, recognized and legitimated themes, themes which are more or less identified with certain aspects of being a man in a given society. To some extent these are features or orientations that social actors bring to the workplace and which provide an arena for their deployment. However, there is an interaction between the organizational, technological and ideological structuring of the workplace and these cultural themes. Workplaces set limits for the range of masculinities that might be legitimately deployed. Thus, and obviously, many workplaces will have little scope for the exercise of brawn or brute strength although there may be some attempt to search out their moral equivalents. Workplaces may, further, give positive endorsement for certain characteristics with strong masculinity connotations: group loyalty or aggressiveness for example. Finally, workplaces may be more or less tightly 'gendered', that is masculine or feminine gender work may be strongly required in some situations and more optional in others.

Thus gender does not in any straightforward way arise out of the workplace, nor is it a set of characteristics which are brought, like lunch boxes, into the workplace by the employees. Rather there is an interaction between employees and workplace in this and in many other respects and gender becomes one of the ways, very often one of the most important ways through which individuals make sense of or structure their daily environment. To see not just workers but also men and women introduce some degree of fixity and control over what is often a dynamic, changing and sometimes threatening situation. It is also a way in which men exercise some degree of control, formally and informally, over other men and over women.

There are two further points which require emphasis. The first is to stress that one feature of work in modern society is that it takes place, for the most part, in rationally structured organizations. That bureaucratic rationality may be associated with dominant forms of masculinity, was something suggested in the previous chapter and some of its more complex ramifications will be considered in my penultimate chapter. It is a theme that has received attention in some other works on men and masculinity (e.g. Seidler 1989). What this means is that, whatever the gender composition of particular workplaces and however particular workroles may have strong or weak gender markings, the overall context will be shaped by a rationality which derives from and is supportive of hegemonic masculinity. Hence, of course, the attempt on the part of some feminist groups to provide for structures which present a radical challenge to dominant models of bureaucratic rationality.

One final point is that it is clear that in matters of gender as well as in other matters we cannot confine our analysis to the workplace. As the discussion or responsibility and sacrifice suggested we are often dealing with the points of intersection between work and other relationships, particularly domestic and familial ones but also to do with class and community. Gendered identities which are partially shaped in the workplace also have their impact in the home. As with discussions of leisure, there are a variety of possible models. One model may see a more or less direct causal link between the masculinities developed at work and behaviour and relationships at home. Others may see the home as providing compensations or counterbalances to deprivations or alienations at work. A man may feel his masculinity denied in the routine subordinated work in employment and compensate for this through exerting or attempting to exert a strong patriarchal authority at home. This was part of the argument of Adorno and the Frankfurt school, talking about the erosion of the traditional bases of patriarchal authority at work and at home. Or, the home may be defined as a kind of haven (Davidoff and Hall 1987), a release from the strong masculine demands of the workplace. One possible unexplored feature of the much criticized Parsonian model of the family in industrial society, whereby the family is seen as sustaining adult personalities, is the possibility that the home might provide for the exercise of more 'feminine' or caring qualities on the part of men. Certainly a lot of the recent discussion about fatherhood has stressed this, although also pointing out that this playing at parenthood is often just that, and that real parental responsibility continues to reside with the mother (McKee and O'Brien 1982; Lewis and O'Brien 1987). It may be possible to argue that all three models of the relationship between masculinities at work and at home are of relevance today, although it may be that the first two are declining in legitimacy, at least in their strong forms, while the third is increasing. It need hardly be argued that this does not necessarily mean any fundamental weakening of patriarchal power or male dominance.

CHAPTER 5

Challenges to masculinity: (i) Unemployment

Introduction

The previous chapter explored what has been taken to be one of the main anchorages of male identity, that is work in the sense of paid employment. This anchorage, which sometimes seems so firm and unchanging is, of course, a product of particular sets of historical changes which, among other things, brought about and sharpened the ideological distinction between home and work and the concepts of the 'male breadwinner' and the 'family wage'. These notions, never as firm in practice as they appeared to be in ideology, received a variety of challenges in the second half of the twentieth century. In the first place, economic restructuring led to the decline of many forms of employment which had strong linkages with masculine notions of strength and hard physical labour. In the second place, women (including married women with children) entered the labour force in many places and at different levels providing clear, if uneven, challenges to the links between employment and masculine identity. And finally, as noted at the end of the last chapter, unemployment returned after a relatively brief period of full employment to become an apparent permanent feature of the economic landscape.

Earlier, I argued that one strategy for studying men and masculinities would be to study those situations where masculinity is, as it were, put on the line. Given the natural, everyday assumptions about the gender order and the positions of men within this order, issues of men and masculinity are not conventionally viewed as being in any sense of problematic. Yet there are situations where what has been routinely taken for granted does become problematic, and where issues of men and masculinity come to the fore, more or less explicitly. Such a case might be that of male unemployment. In the light of what has been said about the alleged centrality of employment and occupational status in the lives of men, unemployment might almost be seen as a paradigmatic example of masculinity under challenge. This may also be the same for retirement, perhaps also early retirement, where similar issues involving not only loss of earnings but a loss of a sense of significance or importance may often be entailed. However, here I shall focus on unemployment which was certainly seen by researchers in the 1930s as entailing challenges to masculinity and these themes have persisted, with some important variations, into discussions in the 1970s and 1980s.

Before beginning this discussion one preliminary point, one which should be familiar by now, needs to be made. There are clearly widespread assumptions about the particularly devastating effects, psychologically, on men as a consequence of long-term unemployment. These consequences are explicitly bound up with ideas of male worth. These are part of the assumptions by which people order their everyday lives – very much bound up with the idea of the male breadwinner – and it is likely that some of these assumptions have thereby influenced the conduct of research. For example, it is now widely recognized that assumptions about the centrality of the male breadwinner role have led to underestimates and distortions in the recording and evaluation of female unemployment (Hurstfield 1986). Hence, the issues of masculinity which arise in studies of unemployment in the 1930s and 1980s, *may* be a reflection of the values of the researchers, values which are widely shared by women and men within society as a whole, rather than being simply 'real' psychological processes. Further, the tendency to see unemployment, still, in terms of individual problems rather than public issues may reinforce this association between masculine identity and loss of work. Certainly it would seem that widespread assumptions about individual responsibility plus, in more recent years, moral panics against 'scroungers', will encourage individual men to feel that it is their masculinity and their gender identity which is being put on the line. Hence, there is some kind of circle linking ideas about the centrality of the male breadwinner role, ideas of individual responsibility, and the linkings of masculinity with the effect of unemployment. There may be some partial truth in all of these points taken individually but the cumulative effect may be to make the process seem to be more inevitable, more natural that it in fact is. In this process, social researchers may have played an unwitting role in the perpetuation of this particular vicious circle.

The 1930s

As is well known, there was a variety of studies of unemployment carried out in the 1930s and many of these have come to be regarded as classics of social research. I should stress the word 'variety'. Here we are dealing with a whole Austrian community, a sample of workers in a city close to New York and workers located in a variety of urban areas in England and Wales. The methods of study are equally various, ranging from self-reports in the form of essays written by the long-term unemployed to the rather austere schedule adopted in the Pilgrim Trust survey; from the battery of techniques employed in the Marienthal study to the straightforward observations by Bakke in Greenwich. Finally, the aims and wider concerns show the same degree of variety. In addition to more or less straightforward desires to discover the facts and to assess the effects, there also seemed to be a desire to explore some deeper fears, fears that unemployed workers might fall prey to right-wing or left-wing agitators. There might also have been desires to destroy the myth of the 'work-shy' or the 'sponger'. Komarovsky's study was the most overtly sociological, seeking to test a set of hypotheses rather than to make policy recommendations; the Pilgrim Trust study, on the other hand, was among those more concerned with issues of social policy.

As has been noted by feminist writers recently the focus in most of these studies was with the unemployed *man* (Walby 1983; Evans 1984; Hurstfield 1986). This was sometimes reflected in the actual titles: *The Unemployed Man* (Bakke 1933), *The Unemployed Man and His Family* (Komarovsky 1940). Women may be explicitly excluded from the study as was the case in these two examples or they may be treated separately and viewed as a separate and different problem (Pilgrim Trust 1938). (It is worth noting that in Garraty's overall historical study of the idea of unemployment, there is no mention of gender issues whatsoever (Garraty 1978).) Here I am not so much concerned with the exclusion of women from these studies or with the exploration of the nature and significance of female unemployment, although ultimately these issues cannot be ignored, but with the assumptions about men and masculinity that are revealed through these studies. In particular, I want to explore the widely held assumption that long-term unemployment deprives a man of his sense of social worth largely through the removal of this role as the male breadwinner. Unemployment creates a problem of male gender identity, a point that might logically be derived from the discussion about work in the previous chapter. Many readers may be familiar with Engels's formulation of the problem: 'A man berated his two daughters for going to the public-house and they answered that they were tired of being ordered about, saying, "Damn you, we have to keep you"' (Engels [1845] 1969: 175).

Engels is citing an example provided by Lord Ashley. The precise nature of Engels's own position has given rise to some argument since, while he is clearly critical of the existing domestic arrangements and the patriarchal family just as he is critical of the factory and the capitalist system, he also writes of 'true woman-liness' and 'true manliness'. Clearly in the passage quoted, the reader is being invited to reflect on the deeper effects of un-employment in terms of its effects on the gender order and authority within the family. It is not the loss of earnings that is at issue, it is the loss of authority and the loss of dignity, status and honour that is at stake. It is also worth noting that this passage is as much about disturbances to the generation order as it is to the gender order, a matter of some importance when we come to consider the 1930s.

Since then, historians have further explored these issues which were ambiguously formulated by Engels. Behind the assumption of the male breadwinner lay, as Lewis argues, the assumption of the bourgeois nuclear family and the idea that working for depen-dents provided a major incentive for taking up paid employment, and hence a central role in the maintenance of the wider social order (Lewis 1984: 45). Davidoff and Hall's work has been central in exploring the ways in which notions of gender and family evolved and became crystallized in the nineteenth century, no-ting, for example, the quite different resonances attached to the terms 'womanhood' and 'manhood': 'It was on the basis of claims to *manhood* that the independent respectable workingman pet-itioned for both a living wage and the right of entry to full citizenship through the franchise' (Davidoff, in Newton *et al.* 1983: 18; see also Davidoff and Hall 1987).

Clearly the male breadwinner role is a construction that has a long and complex history, although it is important, as Rathbone was at pains to point out, that it is an idea with a history and not some eternal fact of human existence. The whole point about social constructions however is that they are real in their effects and need to be taken seriously. We might reasonably assume, therefore, that the loss, especially the loss over a long period of time, of the male breadwinner role would have profound effects on the man *as a man*, just as many commentators perceived the effects as coming back into the family unit. Thus, M. Robb M.D. writing on unemployment from 'a medical point of view' in an Appendix to Beales and Lambert's *Memoirs of the Unemployed* notes, among the psychic injuries, economic dependency, social isolation and sexual reactions. 'Sex may serve to express compensatory fantasies', perhaps involving themes of hate or power (Beales and Lambert 1934: 277). More straightforwardly, the Pilgrim Trust researchers noted that 'among many of the families visited, tension between man and wife was apparent' (Pilgrim Trust 1938: 146). Even if we ignore, as we could not ignore now, the use of the phrase 'man and wife' these quotations and several like them are rich with assumptions about the nature of men and masculinity: the assumption of the centrality of the breadwinner role, the profound effects on self and domestic relations that comes with the blow of unemployment, and the possibility that a man will respond to such frustration in ways which are aggressive or violent.

With these and similar assumptions in mind, let us turn to one of the most interesting texts of the 1930s, Beales and Lambert's *Memoirs of the Unemployed* (1934). These were essays written by long-term unemployed men and women who were contacted through evening classes and whose essays were originally published in *The Listener*. In some of these reports we certainly find confirmation of the breadwinner issue: 'I must say that the bitterness, the irritation and gloominess that I experience are merely the result of being unable to give my wife and son the family life which is their right and which they really do deserve . . .' (unemployed collier Banksman, ibid.: 94). This worker also noted with some feeling that his son asked him why he did not work like other fathers did. 'I think my wife looks on me now as a useless piece of goods, and worse than our old table' (unemployed skilled millwright, ibid.: 105). 'It was because I had a family that I made the effort. I believe I should have done nothing at all had I been a single man' (unemployed woodcarver, ibid.: 121). An unemployed London housepainter with six children recalled how his wife had 'not at first realized the difficulty' and had implied that

[103]

he was lazy. This led to quarrels and affected the children in the extent that they went over to her point of view and became, in his view, 'less apt to consider me worthy of their love' (ibid.: 171–2).

It is difficult to read these, and similar accounts, without feeling even at this distance in time a real sense of deep, personal injury. No amount of analysis in terms of 'social construction' or 'patriarchal ideology' should rob these men of that pain. Yet this is not the whole story. In over half of these twenty-five accounts there is no mention of the loss of the breadwinner role at all (or, in the case of the single men, the ability to take on this role); certainly there are few mentions of any notions of masculinity. What does emerge more strongly is something rather different, what the editors call 'the dependence phenomenon': 'the unemployed man's aversion to living on his family, wife or children or brother and to drawing upon his friends . . .' (ibid.: 48). Thus a South Wales miner regrets having to depend on his children, a skilled engineer feels that he is a burden to his wife, an ex-Army officer worries about living with his 'people' at home, a casual labourer does not wish to sponge, and a 'young electrician turned burglar', does not want to be a 'drag' on his parents.

This is something different from a simple loss of a breadwinning role. It is less strongly gender marked, for one thing. In the context of these statements it is possibly as much to do with age, with generation and possibly also with notions of respectability. If we see a sense of reciprocity as something which is very basic to human living, whether we are talking about women or men, then unemployment entails the loss of that ability to engage in reciprocal exchange, and the unwelcome perception of oneself as being more of a receiver than a giver. We may translate that morality (certainly something very deeply rooted even if we reject the idea of a basic human propensity) into gender terms; but at the same time is something that men and women share and can equally understand.

It is, perhaps, worth stressing the point that individuals and authorities were as much concerned with the generational order as with the gender order. Indeed, of course, the full meaning of the term 'patriarchal' would indicate an overlap and interaction between the two. As Crowther points out, the complexities of family obligations entered into the understandings of those who framed and enacted unemployment policy from the 1920s onwards (Crowther 1982: 137). Men did not want to find themselves, as a result of unemployment, dependent upon the earnings of children or wives and young adults did not wish to continue their dependence on parents. In some areas 'dignity money' was paid to provide some alleviation of this sense of dependence (ibid.: 143). There was concern about children leaving home, either in order to avoid obligations to parents or to prevent their unemployed fathers being dependent upon their earnings (see also Deacon and Bradshaw 1983: 17). Here, as in many other cases, gender and generation interact around themes of domestic responsibilities.

Other themes emerge in these self reports. There are suggestions, explored in greater detail in other surveys, that the effect on family and marital relationships is a very complex matter and depends to a large measure on the character of the relationship prior to the onset of unemployment and the expectations that the partners bring to that relationship. Thus, in these accounts, a businessman comes to feel closer to his wife and a South Wales miner feels that, overall, the experience has not changed his family life. Another theme is to do with the loss of skill and the prestige associated with the exercise of that skill, concerns uppermost in the minds of a skilled engineer and a matter of concern to another unemployed engineer. This, as was argued in the previous chapter, may be linked to issues of male gender but is distinguishable from the idea of the breadwinner. Perhaps the strongest sentiment to emerge from these memoirs is a strong scepticism about, indeed rejection of, orthodox politics, a mixture of a kind of fatalism with a strong sense of economic and political realities. Again, we find a merging of genders here, rather than a sharp difference.

The relative lack of reference to the breadwinner role and, more significantly, to questions of masculinity in these memoirs may be a reflection of two different factors.

First, it may be that this sense of a threat to a gender identity is something so deep that few men can bring themselves to recognize it or to give it open expression. This may be another reflection of the alleged reluctance of men to 'disclose' themselves in a variety of interviews or therapeutic situations. A Derbyshire miner's wife suggests something of the sort when she describes her husband as a 'changed man', who 'keeps things to himself' (ibid.: 218). Again, this distaste for disclosure may reflect wider notions of respectability. But if this be the case, this reinforces one of the themes of this book, namely that issues of masculinity do not necessarily leap out of the page or the transcript, and that often a lot of interpretative work is required on the part of the reader or researcher in order to make men speak 'as men'.

Second, it may well be that, in this particular set of writings, we are dealing with a particular group, one which is obviously literate, accustomed to attending evening classes and possibly more critical of everyday assumptions. This is a likely source of bias here. But to recognize this is to remind ourselves, once again, that masculinity is not a unified phenomenon but is something which is shaped by class, educational and other sets of experiences.

Turning to some of the other studies, do we find any further confirmation of the idea of the breadwinner role and the effect of its loss on male gender identity? What often seems to emerge is more a question of assertion and assumption rather than hard evidence. I have already noted the statement by the authors of the Pilgrim Trust report. They also argue for a recognition that things are changing and that widespread long-term unemployment is having a profound effect on traditional breadwinner assumptions (Pilgrim Trust 1938: 199–200). Yet such 'findings' cannot be said to come directly from the evidence collected on the basis of the brief record card which was the main source of their extensive study. Moreover, the more qualitative pieces of evidence here are based upon the interviewers' perceptions rather than actually reported views or opinions. Concern with the loss of the breadwinner role cannot be said to be a central theme in this study although it may be an important background assumption.

Bakke would seem to give an unequivocal endorsement of the 'breadwinner hypothesis': 'Practically every man who had a family showed evidence of the blow his self-confidence had suffered from the fact that the traditional head of the family was not able to perform his natural function' (Bakke 1933: 70). This is an observational study of Greenwich, an area where, as he noted, there was very little evidence of women having worked in paid employment after marriage. Nevertheless, there was an impression amongst the men interviewed that the women were 'taking our jobs' (ibid.: 6–7). But we must be careful. There is a tendency to tell the reader rather than to demonstrate that this is the case. Moreover, when Bakke comes to provide a list of the effects of unemployment, the loss of the breadwinner role is not placed at the head. Towards the end of his study he lists a variety of sources of satisfaction that male workers derive from their work. These include the idea that they are producers who produce wealth (i.e. they are not parasites), the idea of pride in their firm, of wages as a source of relative prestige, home and club or lodge membership. All these have gender connotations although once again we do not find a straightforward reference to the breadwinner/masculinity nexus although the idea of supporting wife and family is clearly important (ibid.: 239–48).

Komarovsky in her study of a sample of 49 families near New York makes the breadwinner hypothesis, or at least one aspect of it, her central topic of enquiry (Komarovsky 1940). Explicitly, she seeks to consider the relationship between a man's role as economic provider with his authority in the family. Men, women and children are interviewed and the results are analysed with considerable methodological sophistication. Whatever the consequences and whatever the ways in which the family members respond to the crisis (which, as we shall see, are various). Komoravosky emphasizes that the breadwinner role is taken for granted by the group that she studied: the unemployed man experiences unemployment as a threat to 'the very touchstone of his manhood' (ibid.: 75). Nevertheless, there is a sense that, here too, this is something which we are being told rather than shown. But even if we are to treat this statement at its face value the important thing, as she emphasizes, are the complex range of responses that might follow from this premise.

The Marienthal study is, explicitly, a study of the effect of large-scale unemployment on a whole community rather than upon individuals, and hence we might be less likely to find reference to the issues under consideration here. Lazarsfeld, introducing this study, deploys a variety of terms, some of which might have a bearing on my theme:

> breakdown of a social structure
>
> reduction of the psychological life space
>
> reduction of a man's effective scope
>
> (Jahoda et al. 1972: x)

As we shall see, gender issues do appear in this study, although not quite in the way in which we find them treated in the other studies. And again, Jahoda *et al.* are as much concerned with the exploration of a variety of responses and their bases.

So far, therefore, this incomplete survey of some of the literature of the 1930s has suggested some limited support for the loss of the breadwinning status thesis, although less than might be supposed and some of this support at least does not seem to emerge directly from the evidence but, rather, appears to constitute part of the general background assumptions of the researchers, assumptions which they often share with their subjects. There are, however, some further themes to be explored. One which has already received some mention is the theme of *respectability* and the extent to which this is in part identified with being able to support a wife and children (see Lewis 1984: 49). The distinctions between the 'rough' and the 'respectable' in working-class communities have a long pedigree in sociological writings and are also to be found in a variety of historical and autobiographical works. This is certainly a theme which is given interesting and sensitive treatment in the Pilgrim Trust report, although here too the picture is far from being straightforward. Interestingly, perhaps, this discussion appears in a chapter called 'Moral problems' and the authors argue that respectability is to do with moral feelings and not simply with social conventions. But this is not just a question of a man being able to support a family. It also involves having enough put by to ensure a 'good' funeral, to avoid the stigma of a pauper's grave. It is associated with privacy and with others outside the immediate network of family relations not knowing your business, a set of beliefs which may be profoundly threatened by long-term unemployment and the accompanying dole and means test. For younger men, the authors argue, the notion of respectability may be associated with the idea of a fair wage, one which reflects one's worth as a hard, reliable or skilled worker (Pilgrim Trust 1938: 180–93).

Respectability, therefore, is more than being simply a question of being able to support a family although, again, this is undoubtedly an important strand. It is a complex set of attitudes and orientations that links and gives meaning to a variety of important everyday situations and serves as an important basis for social status. It is also worth stressing that the meaning of the term certainly varies, at least in emphasis, between genders although this has not been given detailed attention. A lot of the routine everyday 'respectability work', for example, is undoubtedly carried out by women.

It might be interesting to compare the concept of respectability with the concept of maturity. Although the former is solidly a lay framework of understanding, a set of folk-constructions, whereas the latter is partially a 'scientific' construct which has been appropriated in lay contexts, both appear to have an important part to play in underpinning the idea of the male breadwinner role. Ehrenreich, for example, traces the ways in which the psychological usages of the concept of 'maturity' (usually based upon some kind of developmental model) come to give wider support to the importance of the breadwinner role in the 1950s (Ehrenreich 1983: 15–24). This too does not have any direct or overt connections with masculinities although she suggests that one strand that was important in American society was the association with a man's failure as a breadwinner with fear of homosexuality (ibid.: 24). Maturity, like respectability, does have some variations in meaning when applied to men and women. However, it also can have connotations which point to overlaps in the lives and experiences of men and women, with projects and interests that they share rather than pointing to absolute differences.

To turn from this relatively high level of abstraction to more concrete matters, we find that researchers into unemployment in the 1930s were very much concerned with one particular physical manifestation of this condition, one which was described by Bakke as 'loafing' (Bakke 1933: 185–92). Bakke, coming close to the style of mass-observation, did a quantitative study of people loafing around or close to the Labour Exchange and found that approximately 45 per cent were young men and the rest were older women (ibid.: 187–8). This is shown graphically in a photograph that appeared in Hannington's (1937) *The Problem of the Distressed Areas* entitled: 'Dejected – nothing to do' (Illustration no. 5). The Marienthal observers also attempted to quantify standing about and street behaviour in general, finding that men were more likely than women to interrupt their walk; two-thirds of those observed did this at least twice. Women, they argued, 'have considerably less time on their hands' (Jahoda *et al.* 1972: 67).

There are some difficulties with this kind of analysis, especially given the absence of any pre-unemployment observations of the differences between men and women in their public or street behaviours. However, there are also some interesting suggestions. The Marienthal researchers discussed the question of time and the way in which this is affected by unemployment. Taking account of local variations, patterns of shift-work and so on, having a job does not simply mean having a source of income but also in being in a certain place for a fixed period of time. Unemployment, then, threatens a particular nexus linking time, job and gender. Thus unemployed men, as Bakke observed, spent less and not more time in the pub and this may not simply have been a consequence of a lack of finance.

The other dimension inseparable from that of time, is space. No longer finding a location in a 'place' of work, and often feeling 'out of place' or 'in the way' at home, the unemployed men in these studies seem to occupy the area of public space in the street. If the women in the Marienthal study are seen by the observers to be hurrying about their business, this may not simply be a reflection of the fact that there is much for them to do, but that they are moving through territory that had, in some measure, become alien. At the very least we are reminded of the way in which the public versus private distinction refers to a fluid set of changing boundaries rather than to a fixed distinction mapped on to men and women.

All this is highly speculative, but it suggests that the connections between having and losing a job and gender identity are far from being clear-cut and cannot be straightforward encompassed under the all-embracing term of the male breadwinner role. Returning to somewhat more secure ground, we find that all the studies cited are aware that people respond differently to the impact of unemployment and seek to explore some of the bases of these differences. The Marienthal researchers, for example, classified their subjects' responses into those of 'resignation', 'the unbroken', 'the broken or in despair' and 'the apathetic' (Jahoda et al. 1972: 52–4). In looking at the marriages of the villagers, the researchers concluded that there was no simple or single effect of unemployment and that much depended upon the character of the relationship prior to unemployment. Komarovsky makes such variations a central theme and classifies the pre-depression husband–wife relationship in a variety of ways, distinguishing between 'patriarchal', 'matriarchal' and 'balance of power' marriages and also making distinctions according to the grounds upon which the authority of the husband was accepted. What she called 'primary authority' (i.e. that based upon love and respect) was found to lead to greater stability in family relationships during the time of depression than other kinds of authority, perhaps those kinds which were more patriarchal in character (Komarovsky 1940).

Komarovsky's analysis does bring us back to the major theme of this book namely that 'masculinity' is best seen not simply as some kind of quality that is attached to individuals, but a kind of cultural resource, of a set of potentialities which may be realized and shaped in particular contexts. This may be illustrated in the range of factors that she explores: the coercive economic control exercised by the father or husband and the ways in which this may be threatened; the dynamics of prestige and self-esteem of the husband in the eyes of his wife or as he imagines his wife seeing him; the ways in which a loss of money reduces the margins of tolerance within the household; the status-reducing effects of being around the house all the time and so on (ibid.: 23–39). That we are not dealing with a uniform effect or one which is un- ambiguously anchored to notions of masculinity may be illus- trated by this quotation from *Marienthal*: 'We found in our files a number of similar cases, people whose power of resistance, after gradually deteriorating, suffered a sudden collapse. These usually occurred with men whose earlier life had been characterised by ambition and high expectation' (Jahoda *et al.* 1972: 94). The point of this partial re-analysis is not to say that the linkages that have been made between male unemployment, the breadwinner role and issues of masculinity are unimportant. It is certainly not the aim of this chapter to trivialize the issue of unemployment. But it is to argue that the linkages are not inevitable, that they do not involve the deployment of relatively fixed notions of masculinity, and that the mediations between these elements are to do with the ideological construction of the breadwinner role. Here we must follow the path established by Eleanor Rathbone and retraced by Hilary Land and others in problematizing and deconstructing the idea of the breadwinner role (Rathbone 1924/49; Land 1980).

(a) In the first place, Rathbone makes the point that not all men (unemployed or otherwise) have dependents. In a passage that has many echoes in more recent feminist analyses, she ques- tions the stereotypical breadwinner, nuclear-family model: 'it has become customary in sociological writings to treat as the 'normal'

[111]

or standard the five-member family, consisting of husband, wife and three dependent children' (Rathbone 1924/49: 9). She questions the 'Procrustean bed of a uniform wage' and argues that the so-called normal household is very much a minority phenomenon.

(b) The fact that a man may be, formally, a 'breadwinner' does not tell us anything about how the bread will be distributed within the household. Then as now, the question of the allocation of resources within the household was seen to be as important as the question of the allocation of resources between households (ibid.: 41; Brannen and Wilson 1984).

(c) Not all wage-earners are men. In the Pilgrim Trust report there occurs the following sentence: 'What is sometimes the single link they have with their fellow-men has been severed' (Pilgrim Trust 1938: 151). What is interesting, however, is the example that appears close to this particular statement is one dealing with a *woman* worker in Blackburn. In their treatment of women wage-earners, they argue that unemployment among women varies in significance according to region. They cite Blackburn as an example where female unemployment is closer in character to male unemployment (ibid.: 243). The Beales and Lambert collection includes the following statement: 'But I don't welcome the change after nearly nine years of work that I liked and did well. I hate this nothing-to-do. I am strong and I can keep this little house clean in two hours work a day' (unemployed woman, quoted in Beales and Lambert 1934: 87). There is, therefore, not simply the danger of ignoring women at work but also of overstating the differences between male and female employees.

(d) Following on from this, not all persons with dependents are men. Rathbone cites a survey by M. H. Hogg which concluded that 28 per cent of women workers had partial responsibility and 5 per cent had total responsibility for dependents (Rathbone 1924/49: 128).

The assumption about the male breadwinner role was then, as now, an assumption. If we wish to talk about issues of masculinity in connection with unemployment we must therefore consider masculinities as being embedded in particular contexts, relationships and sets of practices. To talk about the quasi-inevitable links between unemployment and male identity is to deflect our attention away on to some apparently universal, timeless or unchallengeable sets of values. The appeal may not be directly to male power or male interests but so some apparently gender-free theme such as 'respectability' or 'maturity'. For the meantime let us leave these issues of the past with another quotation from Rathbone:

> A man likes to feel that he has 'dependents'. He looks in the glass and sees himself as perhaps others seem him – physically negligible, mentally ill-equipped, poor, unimportant, unsuccessful. He looks in the mirror he keeps in his mind and sees his wife clinging to his arm and his children clustering round her skirts, all looking up at him, as the giver of all good gifts, the wage-earner. This picture is very alluring.
>
> (Rathbone, quoted in Lewis 1984: 67)

The 1980s

Up to a point, many of the studies of unemployment in the 1980s reproduced many of the gender themes discovered in the 1930s writings. It is probably not necessary to repeat these arguments at length since they appear very familiar:

> Unemployment carried much greater hardships, materially, during the 1930s depression than it does in the recession today, but comparative studies have shown that the psychological effects are very much the same, that the unemployed go through various stages of reaction to redundancy, ranging from initial shock and disbelief to ultimate fatalism and depression.
>
> (Ingham 1984: 26)

Here she is referring indirectly to the writings of Jahoda who provides a link between studies of unemployment and redundancy in the two periods. In the more recent period there is a tendency to 'neutralize' these processes even more by describing them in terms of a set of stages or quasi-stages through which many, if not all, unemployed men go. This possibly reinforces the links with relatively stable constructions of masculinity. It is certainly worth noting that the more psychologically orientated accounts tend to

[113]

be more likely to refer to issues of masculinity. In a recent discussion, Mattinson (associated with the Tavistock Institute) wrote that: 'For a man obtaining and remaining in paid work was assumed to be a fact of life' (Mattinson 1988: 2). 'A job which overtly defined adult masculinity was clearly important for many men in our sample' (ibid.: 45). However, Mattinson is clearly aware that the distinction between home and work and consequently the identification of the world of work with the world of men, had clearly identifiable historical roots. She also argued, reviving one of the themes of the earlier period, that the different responses to redundancy and unemployment reflected 'old ghosts', particularly individual psychological histories.

Certainly many of the men interviewed in a variety of other surveys express their feelings in familiar terms: 'My wife is right when she says it affects me *as a man*: it isn't the money so much as the feeling men have' (Sinfield 1981: 41). 'I couldn't live off a woman . . . I think I'd leave before I'd live off her. That is the way I am' (man quoted in McKee and Bell 1986: 141). Ford noted how one reaction of unemployed men was that of feeling unable to break the news to their wives (Ford 1985: 233). A recent study includes the following example of a traditional understanding from the North East: 'it takes you out of the manly role. I used to be the breadwinner with my meal on the table. It lowers you. I feel like a lodger in my own house' (man quoted in Wheelock 1990: 63). Interestingly, however, this response was not typical of the men in Wheelock's sample.

An interesting theme which emerges in one account, and one which deserves further study, is that of consumption. It is not entirely new (we remember how Bakke found that the unemployed man stays away from the pub) but it may be of growing significance in a society which is much more clearly identified with consumption rather than production as a basis of identity. Thus Bostyn and Wight argue that 'gender identity pervades almost every area of consumption' (Bostyn and Wight 1987: 143). In the familiar pub situation, where reciprocity and buying rounds are an important feature of masculine drinking culture, the presence of the unemployed may be resented. Masculine self-esteem is expressed through consumption although, it would seem, that they should have earned their right to participate in such patterns.

Again, the point is not to discredit such utterances or to downgrade their importance and reality to those who make them. The pain is real. However, I hope that enough has already been said in this chapter to indicate that we cannot simply take such statements, or the more theoretical elaborations based upon such statements at face value.

Sociological studies of the 1980s have therefore introduced one or two new themes into the discussion. The first is the beginning of a more serious consideration of female unemployment (e.g. Walby 1983; Coyle 1984; Hurstfield 1986; Callender 1987). Much of this recent discussion has focused on the incidence of female unemployment, whether it is higher or lower than male unemployment, and the problems of measuring it. The experiential side has perhaps received less attention, although it is likely that the discussion will include some reference to domestic roles and family-based identities. However, as with some of the quotations from unemployed women in 1930s, there may be a sense that the experiences of women and men in this respect need not necessarily be all that different. Men and women may derive smaller pleasures from similar kinds of work – apart from the money they may mention personal identity, companionship, doing something meaningful and so on. And when unemployed they may refer to frustration, boredom, guilt and loss of self-respect. Some of Coyle's respondents give accounts which can hardly be distinguished from those of men: 'I think we all need to work. I like to work. I'd prefer to go out to work than be at home, even if its only part time' (Coyle 1984: 75–6). 'I don't like being dependent. My husband is very, very good, but it's not my money' (ibid.: 107). One recent study, designed to test some of Jahoda's arguments, found few, if any, differences between groups of full-time employed and unemployed women and men (Henwood and Miles 1987).

It is likely that, male or female, the more identified with work and a particular job is an individual, the greater the shock of unemployment. Women have dependents to support, careers to pursue and a desire for independence and it would not be surprising if reactions of some unemployed men and unemployed women will turn out to be very similar, and that differences within genders might be as great as those between genders. Yet it is still the case that the popular image or presentation of unemployment is in terms of the unemployed man and that most of the discussion about the psychological and personal effects focuses upon the male experience.

Another set of issues that has come to the fore in recent sociological analysis has been in terms of the effect of male unemployment on the sexual division of labour within the home. The growth in the range and amount of female employment (especially for married women), the alleged growth of more companionate or symmetrical marriages in place of more patriarchal ones and the general assumptions about the loosening and variety of personal lifestyles might lead one to suppose a kind of trade-off between work outside the home and work inside the home. In other words, the unemployed man – especially the unemployed man with a partially or wholly employed wife – might be expected to fill up some of his spare time with greater participation in the home.

McKee and Bell claim that they started out with a modified set of assumptions rather similar to the ones outlined in the previous paragraph, but found that they were almost entirely confounded in their study of unemployed men in Kidderminster (McKee and Bell 1986). If anything, unemployment may polarize the experiences of women and men even more and traditional sexual divisions of labour may harden. Women's traditional responsibilities in relation to the management (as opposed to the earning) of money have been even more burdensome when there is less money to go around. Morris's work in Swansea similarly failed to find any evidence of a trade-off between paid employment and domestic activity on the part of the unemployed men and argued that the freedom of manoeuvre in this respect was limited by the workings of the benefits system (which tended to inhibit women seeking paid employment to add to household earnings), the structure of the local labour market and the extent to which men had access to wider networks of information which would enable them to pick up any form of paid employment or money-earning activity that was going (Morris 1987). More simply, the idea of anything approaching a switch in roles between husband and wife would run counter to deeply held cultural expectations. More often than not men found themselves out of place at home, and women tended to agree with this assessment.

The picture is by no means a straightforward one and evidence from different studies and different regions does vary. Certainly one recent study in the North East does provide evidence of a much wider range of responses on the part of couples (Wheelock 1990). This includes exchange-role couples. However, apart from this study it would seem that the optimistic assumptions that men might be more willing to take on domestic responsibilities in the face of unemployment would seem to have, at best, limited support in the evidence. We should perhaps not be surprised about this since similar facts have been found in relation to dual-earner households, namely that increasing female participation in the labour market is not matched by increasing male participation in the home.

The studies of unemployment in the 1980s have also benefited from a wider reformation in the concept of work that has been taking place around the same time. Generally speaking, the equation of 'work' with 'paid employment' has been questioned, partly as a result of the feminist examination of the extent and significance of domestic labour and partly through a recognition of the importance, in many different societies, of the 'informal' sector of the economy. Here too, some initially optimistic expectations were found not to be the case. Unemployed men (or women) did not become more active in the informal economy or in household-based tasks (such as do-it-yourself) as they become involuntarily less involved in the formal economy (Pahl 1984; Wallace and Pahl 1986). Indeed unemployed men were least likely to engage in unpaid informal work outside the household whereas employed women were most likely to engage in these activities, at least in the Isle of Sheppey (Wallace and Pahl 1986). They argue that this difference may reflect the gendered nature of the tasks performed. Informal caring work on the part of women (looking after children, shopping for elderly relatives, etc.) is less likely to be interpreted as 'earning a little bit on the side' than some of the informal activities of unemployed men (mowing a neighbour's lawn, fixing a car). Here again, unemployment may have the consequence of accentuating gender differences and division of labour, although this may be as much to do with wider ideological expectations about the appropriate activities of women and men and less to do with straightforward notions of masculinity being challenged by the fact of unemployment.

Some recent studies, have begun to look at ethnicity as a variable in considering the impact of unemployment (Ullah 1987). In a study of unemployment among Asians, Brah argues that this is an 'experience mediated by gender' (Brah 1986: 67). She too refers to the importance of the ideology of the male breadwinner although stresses this as an ideological construction which takes on slightly different nuances of meaning in some Asian contexts in British society. The obligation to 'provide' may extend beyond the immediate family; hence both married and single men may be affected in rather similar ways by unemployment: 'I can't live off my mother and younger brother. I am supposed to look after them and not the other way around' (quoted in Brah 1986: 68).

Again Brah notes the ways in which male unemployment creates different but equally severe pressures on the women. What is important, however, here, is the reminder of the importance of exploring variations in the impact of unemployment, variations not simply in terms of generalized categories of men and women but also according to class and ethnicity, the latter in the wider context of racialism. Studies of middle-class unemployment (Fineman 1987b) and youth unemployment (Coffield 1987) remind us of the importance of not treating gender as an unmediated category.

Studies of unemployment in the 1980s, therefore, show some considerable measure of continuity with the 1930s, especially around notions of the male breadwinner role. However, there is perhaps more willingness to see this as a complex ideological construction rather than a gendered inevitability and there is a greater interest in exploring the wider impact of unemployment of the gendered division of labour around the household. Further, there is a greater willingness to take female unemployment seriously with the consequence that overlaps, as well as differences, between the experiences of men and women begin to emerge.

Conclusion

The impact of prolonged unemployment and redundancy would seem to be a fruitful area for the exploration of masculinities for it is here, one might assume, that there is a major assault on one of the most fundamental pillars of male identity, that of employment and occupation. It is a time when masculinity, reflected in the ability to provide, comes to be called into question.

[118]

Up to a point these expectations are realized in studies that came from the 1930s and more recently, from the 1980s. However, problems also begin to emerge. It was found necessary to ask questions about the extent to which researchers into male unemployment imported more general assumptions about masculinity and the male role, such that these expectations became part of the reality that was being studied. Further, since the findings of social scientists do have some kind of mediated impact on the way in which people come to see their social world, it is possible that these 'findings' reinforced and solidified widely held gender assumptions.

Hence a deeper examination of some of these studies, together with the development of studies more prone to problematize issues of gender pointed to certain complexities in the analysis. In the first place, while issues of masculinity might be raised by respondents to research questions, they did not inevitably arise, at least not straightforwardly in these terms. The impact of unemployment on male gender identity in the home might, for example, might be mediated by the kind of marital relationship that existed prior to the onset of unemployment. Or other issues might arise, issues to do with respectability or maturity, issues which certainly have gender connotations but which are not straightforwardly anchored to ideas of masculinity or the male breadwinner role. Further, since in practice the male breadwinner role is found to be as much an ideological construction as a reality, the alleged anchorage of male identity to this must itself take on some ideological features.

Perhaps the most interesting point to emerge from this re-analysis is the recognition that, under certain circumstances at least, the experiences of women and men in the face of unemployment need not be all that different. If they do differ this may be as much to do with the hierarchical way in which labour markets are organized, the widespread and deep-rooted character of patriarchal assumptions about men and work and women and the home and wider structures of gender inequalities. Men *are* discovered in the analysis of unemployment but men as different from each other, in some cases, as they are different from women. To explore the impact of unemployment upon men should be to begin to explore one's own assumptions about men in society.

CHAPTER 6

Challenges to masculinity: (ii) Upsets at the workplace

Introduction

We have seen how work and employment have been seen as major anchorages for masculine identity both in the general sense of having employment or regular work and in specific senses of establishing affinities with particular kinds of occupation and particular themes associated with masculinity. We have seen how, in the general sense, that masculine identity may be challenged by unemployment or redundancy. We shall now explore how, under certain circumstances, masculine identities in the more specific sense may be challenged by changes in the labour market.

That the labour market is gendered is one of the taken-for-granted features of social research and, indeed, there has been considerable discussion as to the nature and causes of sexual divisions within work and employment (Walby 1986, 1988). Walby summarizes much of the evidence in these words:

> Women both do jobs which are simply different from those that men do (horizontal segregation) and also work at lower levels in the occupational hierarchy (vertical segregation) . . . . A survey of jobs sampled at the level of the establishment showed that 45 per cent contained no women at all, while 21 per cent employed no men . . . . The Department of Employment/Office of Population Censuses and Surveys survey of 6,000 women showed that 63 per cent of women worked with other women, while among the husbands of these women 81 per cent worked only with other men.
>
> (Walby 1988: 3)

Thus, although women are increasingly found in occupations and at levels where they had previously been absent, their distribution throughout the labour market as a whole is still far from random. Further, as Cockburn vividly points out,

> men are more segregated than women. If we think of occupations as being separate cells, each with its own cell wall, men reach out and penetrate into more of them. We could say that women do not 'defend' their cell walls so effectively against men as men defend their's against incursions of women.
>
> (Cockburn 1988: 30)

Such segregations are not, of course, confined to Britain.

In terms of the present discussion, it may be argued that certain occupational statuses (in both the horizontal and the vertical senses) are more or less strongly identified with dominant models of masculinity. Thus, most forms of manual labour, police work, senior management and insurance selling may all, in their different ways, be identified with particular and more or less approved models of masculinity. Other occupational statuses may be more weakly identified with dominant masculinities or, indeed, with stigmatized models of masculinity: acting, hairdressing, clerical work and so on. It is worth noting that these identifications do vary, to some extent, between cultures. Thus, some Muslim countries may see it as shameful for women to be employed as airline stewards while the reverse is probably true in Britain and most Western societies. One interesting example is that of domestic service in Zambia during the colonial period (Hansen 1986). Up to the early 1960s, domestic service was seen as a male preserve. With this change in gender composition, came changes in the way in which domestic service was perceived such that the status of the work became downgraded and deskilled, and the domestic servant came to be seen as more of a general servant with few specific skills.

This example also underlines the main theme of this chapter, namely that the gender division of labour in work and employment does not remain static. The transitions in domestic service that took place in Zambia were not unusual; they merely took place later than in most other parts of Africa and the world. It might be assumed, therefore, that such transitions have consequences for wider definitions and understandings of the gender order and of masculinities in particular. While accounts of changes in the gendered character of labour markets over time are common enough, information about how such changes are perceived and experienced is still relatively hard to come by except in one or two prominent cases. Nevertheless, such shifts and transitions must remain, potentially, a major source of insight into constructions of masculinities.

Such an analysis is perhaps more complex than might at first appear. In part there is a problem of levels of analysis. At the more macro level we have overall changes in the gender structure of the labour market, the processes by which certain occupations or levels, once the almost exclusive preserve of one gender, cease to be so and may even change completely. At the more micro level we have the experience of men and women as they enter occupations once or still dominated by the opposite gender, or while they remain in occupations that are undergoing marked changes in gender composition. Clearly, there are links between the level of analysis. The extent to which an individual man or woman experiences a particular occupational involvement as presenting problems for gender identities will in part depend upon the extent to which the occupation as a whole is strongly defined in gender terms.

In this analysis it is possible to distinguish between 'invasion', whereby an occupation or a particular status within an occupation becomes dominated (in reality or in perception) by members of a gender previously excluded, and 'tokenism', whereby members of previously excluded genders are admitted but remain in a clear and visible minority. Kanter used an operational definition of less than 15 per cent to define tokenism (Kanter 1977). There may also be processes of parallel developments whereby gender divisions remain marked, although opposite gender occupations may develop in parallel to existing ones: male strippers may be a case in point. Certainly, however, the possibilities may look like the diagram (see Figure 6.1).

There are a variety of points which may be made about this representation. In the first place, the amount of change in occupational composition should not obscure the continuing wider context of inequality whereby men continue to hold the more powerful and prestigious positions. Related to this is the fact that occupations are not themselves homogeneous entities and entry of, say, women at lower levels may not influence the overall pattern of control at the top. Thus women, throughout the world, may be entering the armed services although these bodies still

	Entry of	
	Women	Men
'Invasion'	Clerical work	Personnel management
'Tokenism'	Police, Senior Management	Nurses Health visitors

Figure 6.1 Invasion and tokenism

remain firmly in the control of men. In the second place, the terms 'tokenism' and 'invasion' are somewhat problematic. Much depends upon individual perceptions and what may be 'tokenism' in statistical terms may be perceived as 'invasion' by those already in the occupational status concerned. Further, we should not assume a mechanical parallelism in terms of the experiences of women and men. There are, as we shall see, differences between women as tokens among surgeons and physicians and men as 'tokens' among the nursing staff (Floge and Merrill 1986).

The emphasis in this chapter will be on men in predominantly female occupations or positions, for it is likely that it is there that the sharpest issues of masculinity and masculine identity will arise. However, this is not to say that other situations may not provoke other kinds of issues of masculinity. Certainly the responses on the part of men to the introduction of women often provide vivid illustrations of some of the dominant themes around masculine identity in the wider society. These represent strategic cases for the examination of gender and sexual politics and there is clearly a need for much historical and qualitative research to explore these processes further.

While attention in this chapter is being focused largely on the work situation and paid employment, it is clear that there are other social contexts where similar issues arise. We might, for example, consider marriages where the social status of the man (in terms of occupation, education, or social background) is clearly lower than that of his wife (McRae 1986). We might also consider various other spheres of public life, including areas of education, leisure and politics. Rogers's general survey of men's clubs (treating the term very generally) is concerned largely with the

[123]

ways in which such clubs perpetuate inequalities, in terms of class as well as of gender, although she does have some brief accounts of what happens when all-men institutions become open to women (Rogers 1988). Finally, transvestitism and cross-dressing may tell us a lot about some masculine perceptions of the gender order and of women within it (Woodhouse 1989).

Women in male occupations

'Invasions'

The term 'invasion' is used deliberately here, referring to an argument made by Stouffer: 'As women invade an occupation to the point of becoming a large minority within it, it becomes increasingly unrespectable for a man to be in that occupation' (Stouffer, quoted in Segal 1962: 32). The term also occurs in an account of the introduction of women into factory work in Norway: 'For many men the women were *invaders*. They entered a domain which had previously belonged exclusively to men, except for the occasional women trainee or engineer' (Aga 1983: 102). Clearly the image of the 'monstrous regiment' is not far behind. What is significant is that women do not have to constitute a statistical majority to constitute an 'invasion'. In terms of masculine perceptions, 'tokens' may signify an 'invasion'.

Perhaps the classical case in the sociological literature is that of clerical work. Initially defined as a respectable occupation for men with respectable working-class or lower middle-class backgrounds, clerical work became, in the course of the twentieth century, transformed into a female-dominated sector of the workforce. In Lockwood's terms, the 'black-coated' worker became the 'white-bloused' worker (Lockwood 1966: 122). A similar transformation has occurred in the case of bank-tellers (Prather 1971). It is likely that there might always have been some contrast between conventional constructions of masculinity and the work situation of the average male clerk (Lockwood 1958: 123). The work was, and is, largely sedentary, devoid of much physical risk (although these may have increased with modern technology and the widespread use of women), clean and 'safe'. This clearly contrasted with the more traditional masculine occupations and it is likely that some of the traditional hostility against 'pen-pushers' reflected struggles between different models of masculinity. However, clerical work did have some associations with other features of masculinity, namely a link with bureaucratic rationality, the establishment of order and, sometimes, the manipulation of figures and quantities. More to the point it was of relatively high status, compared with most of the occupations open to women from similar social backgrounds. However, as public and private organizations became larger and more bureaucratically organized, as much of the clerical work became mechanized, routinized and deskilled, as women came to enjoy education roughly equal to that of their male peers and as the apparent financial advantage of clerical work over manual work disappeared or was reversed, so clerical work became more and more feminized. In banks, young men in sober suits (often perhaps seeing their position behind the counter as the lowest stage of a career ladder within banking) came to be replaced by young women dressed equally respectably but more colourfully, while the managerial and professional posts remained dominated by men. This shift took place, in part, as banks ceased, in the eyes of the public at least, to be simply custodians of money or adjuncts to the middle and upper classes (with all the connotations of responsibility discussed in Chapter 4) and became more competitive and more consumer oriented.

There seems to be little doubt that the feminization of clerical work and the lower levels of banking did provoke some kind of crisis of masculinity for some men (Zimmeck 1986). An occupation which was already suspect in terms of some dominant current understandings of masculinity became further undermined. The men who remained were possibly (although there is room for some more research here) seen as effeminate or lacking in drive, or were clearly seen to be working their way up from the shop floor. We know something of the benefits that women gained from this new source of respectable employment (Zimmeck 1986) as well as of the limited nature of these gains over the long term (Crompton and Jones 1984). We still need to know more about the responses of men to these 'invasions' and the feelings and responses of those men who are 'left behind' or who were now entering this occupation as a minority. In this case as we shall see, men become 'tokens'.

One of the factors contributing to the change in sex composition of clerical work was, as we have seen, technical change, and this has been a factor in other areas of employment as well.

[125]

Hunt, writing about opposition on the part of men to mechanization in printing, notes: 'Machines worked by semi-skilled and unskilled labour not only undercut wages but also men's status and value to the workplace and their patriarchal role in the home' (Hunt 1986: 71). This is echoed in Cockburn's well-known study of the printing industry where she argues that technical change made compositors feel that they were doing 'women's work' (Cockburn 1983: 103–4). She quotes one worker as saying: 'If girls can do it, you know, then you are sort of deskilled you know, really' (ibid.: 118). The potentially contaminating effect of being seen to or being thought to be doing 'women's work' is also discussed by Lewis, where it is argued that men might feel their masculinity to be threatened if they were thought to be doing the same work as women in the hosiery trade (Lewis 1984: 103).

Constructions of 'women's work' and 'men's work' although subject to considerable historical and cultural variations may at times be so well drawn that the invasion of the latter by the former may have all the deep connotations associated with ritual pollution. Initially women may be defined, strongly, as being out of place; in the long run it may be the men who feel out of place although they often have many means at their disposal (access to greater career opportunities, sexual harassment) to rectify these particular anomalies.

'Tokens'

A relatively common episode in popular adventure stories of the more traditional kind tells how a 'Dr X' or a 'Professor Y', about to join a team of explorers or the members of a space crew, turns out to be a woman. After the initial expressions of shock, disgust and hostility, a variety of things may happen. In some cases, the woman may prove herself to be as good as any man, although without losing any of her womanly qualities. Perhaps more frequently she may show some signs of female weakness at a crucial moment of danger or crisis, needing to be rescued by one of the men or allowing personal emotions to get in the way of what really needs to be done. Yet again, she may be the source of sexual rivalry and disorder between the men.

This, roughly, is the idea of the analysis of women as 'tokens', a theme developed more systematically by Kanter in her study of men and women in corporations (Kanter 1977). Deriving her theoretical insights from Simmel, she speculated as to the effect of numbers on social interaction at the workplace and how the numerically dominant men respond to and construct the numerically and, often organizationally, subordinate women.

As Aga's study of women in Norwegian factories demonstrates, such processes are not confined to the higher levels of organizational life (Aga 1983). For example, she shows how men either made a point of ignoring the women or, alternatively, acted in an oversolicitous way towards the 'invaders'. The issues raised in this kind of analysis include: the ways in which women are often highly visible in organizational settings and the consequences of this greater visibility; the extent to and the ways in which the dominant men defined or related to the women in terms of available gender stereotypes; and the extent to which gender segregation took place and the likely consequences of this for the careers of women. Thus, women may be defined as 'sexually available', as 'mothers', as 'frigid', as 'frustrated' or as 'lesbians'. In the Norwegian case some of the women were defined as 'left-wing feminists' (Aga 1983). Women's day-to-day behaviour in the office or the boardroom might be readily attributed to some gender-specific characteristic: her periods, her menopause, her domestic responsibilities and so on. Women in such settings may feel excluded from vital sources of exchange of gossip or information that may take place between men in the washrooms, the pub or the bar.

One key aspect associated with the introduction of women into hitherto male-dominated work settings is, of course, sexual harassment. While this can take place in all kinds of situations where women and men meet, and indeed within these gender categories as well, it is likely that it may take on a particular significance in these kinds of 'token' situations. Men may seek to deflect a possible threat to their everyday informal working practices or to their career prospects by attempting to redefine the co-presence of women in overtly sexual terms. Sexual harassment in these kinds of contexts may be, indirectly at least, a mechanism of social control by the dominant men over the subordinate or minority status of women.

Most of the discussion about female tokens has focused on the experiences of, and the effects upon, the women concerned, as minorities in a male environment. There has been less discussion of the men's responses to these changes, and the accounts that we do have seem to suggest, at least implicitly, a more or less uniform response on the part of the men. This is seen as being one of initial and probably continuing hostility, together with attempts on the part of men to control the situation by placing women in more marginal positions, through sexual harassment or through the deployment of gender stereotypes. I suspect that the responses of men may be a little more complex than this, ranging from (as Cockburn suggests) sometimes welcoming the introduction of women as a source of partial release from the demands of an all-encompassing masculine environment, through attempts at accommodation in varying degrees of appropriateness, to the kinds of oppositions and control strategies that have already been mentioned. If it be recognized that masculinities are plural then we should expect such a range of responses. In Aga's Norwegian study, for example, we find that some of the more overt forms of masculine sexual behaviour (the display of pin-ups for example) was modified in the case of those men who belonged to strict religious communities (Aga 1983). What we need to consider in more detail are the ways in which the introduction of tokens may reinforce or bring about some modification in the construction of work-based masculinities. In some other cases it may lead to an accentuation of a kind of masculine protectiveness or chivalry. In yet others, it may heighten the theme of man as a sexual predator.

For example, a common complaint about the introduction of women into the workplace is that it will force men to 'modify their language'. They may feel that they have to edit their routine expletives, or restrict their telling of dirty stories. (That this does not inevitably happen is shown in Balzer's account of factory life: Balzer 1976.) This clearly tells us something about common-sensical constructions of masculine interests, temperaments and groups. Yet some men, at least, may welcome the loss of a compulsion to laugh at jokes which they may actually find offensive. It should be noted in passing, of course, that this fear of having to 'soften one's language' also reinforces certain stereotypes of women as well: women as prudish, easily shockable and in need of protection.

In the case of sexual harassment, it is of course the case that the very term is relatively recent and has come about as a joint consequence of the increasing participation of women in a wider range of work situations and the growth of the feminist movement. The putting of questions to do with sexual harassment on to the union or managerial agenda is an almost classic case of a process whereby the everyday and the seemingly natural is called into question. What might previously be seen as a 'harmless bit of fun', as 'nothing serious, really' or 'what men do naturally', comes to be redefined as a form of sexual exploitation and a limitation of women's freedom especially, although not exclusively, where it occurs between a dominant and a subordinate woman. The boss chasing the secretary around the office was once seen as comic, as a subject for cartoonists; it is now seen as ugly and threatening and a subject for serious critical analysis (Pringle 1988). We need to have more information about the range of responses on the part of men employers and employees to the problematization of sexual harassment and its codification and control. Anecdotal evidence suggests, again, a range of responses. The best known are those responses which seek to deny that there really is a problem, or which seek to trivialize or marginalize it, or which define it in terms of individual weaknesses. Thus, some men might be understood as being particularly 'oversexed' or as experiencing particular difficulties in keeping their feelings, and their hands, to themselves. We know less about those men who have attempted to take the problem seriously and who have sought to modify their own behaviour or the behaviour of their colleagues.

Men in female occupations

'Invasions'

There is one general point to be made about the cases under this heading. This is that the takeover by men of women's occupations and statuses has rarely aroused the same degree of public debate and concern as has alleged invasions of women into occupations dominated by men. This may, perhaps, be seen as a further illustration of the ways in which the activities and positions of men are taken for granted or seen as being natural or inevitable.

One area which has received some attention within the feminist literature relates to childbirth in particular and to medical care in general. In an influential essay, Oakley argued that both these have, over the centuries, witnessed a takeover by men (Oakley 1976). In the case of the management of childbirth, the shift from the informal control and expertise based on communities or networks of women to the control of men was part of a general

[129]

process of the professionalization and medicalization of childbirth. Indeed, it may be seen as part of the process of rationalization discussed in Chapter 3, where the gender connotations of this term were explored. While women did exist, and continue to exist, within the overall framework of the management of childbirth in the form of female doctors and professional midwives, these women have been incorporated into an overall system which is dominated by men. Oakley argues that these shifts were part of a larger shift from a system where healing in general was in the hands of women, wisewomen–witches, to one much more heavily dominated, numerically and organizationally, by men.

A somewhat less heralded illustration of men moving into an occupation hitherto defined as female is provided by the case of personnel management (Legge 1987). In its origins, at the beginning of this century, it was very much a woman's occupation:

> When at the 1913 conference the precursor of the Institute of Personnel Management (IPM) was formed, all but five of its thirty-four founder members were women, including the first president, Mary Wood. By 1927 membership was 420, but fewer than twenty members were men. Between 1918 and 1931, of the eleven institute presidents, six were women.
>
> (Legge 1987: 34)

However, the job was one which was very clearly gender-defined, emphasizing issues of welfare and morals and the supposed nurturing skills of women. As in the early days of social work it tended to have the somewhat pejorative 'Lady Bountiful' image. By 1950, however, the situation had changed and less than half the membership of the IPM were women. This dropped to 20 per cent by 1970 (ibid.: 42). A variety of factors had contributed to this shift but perhaps chief among them was a redefinition of the work and significance of personnel management. It became more identified with issues of industrial relations rather than welfare, in the older sense, and in the climate of the 1950s and 60s industrial relations was being seen as a key to Britain's poor industrial performance. One might almost characterize this shift as being one from the more private sphere to the more public sphere. However, here there was little public debate of 'invasion'.

[130]

Clearly there is more, much more, that could be said about the ways in which men have taken over positions and statuses once seen as the sphere of women and, through this process, have contributed to changing the nature of these positions. However, in terms of conventional understandings, these accounts while important and interesting, do not in themselves problematize issues of men and masculinity. To do this we must explore the situations where men are themselves 'tokens' although it is more than possible that the 'tokens' of one decade may be the 'invasion' of the next.

'Tokens'

In the discussions of men in predominantly or traditionally women's occupations, considerable attention has been given to the position of men in different branches and at different levels of nursing. There are probably several reasons for this but perhaps the foremost is the seeming contrast between the markedly feminine constructions of nursing, to do with care and nurturing, and some dominant constructions of masculinity. Images of the nurse as either a mother figure or a sex object are well known in popular culture. These popular images, of course, only refer to one kind of nursing, the one most visible in a hospital context. As Dingwall points out (Dingwall 1979) the term actually covers a range of different occupational clusters and I shall follow his example and include health visiting under this general heading.

Brown and Stones provide a straightforward account of men in nursing in the British context. They note that in 1972 some 89 per cent of NHS nursing staff were women. However, the minority of men did have some characteristics which tended to differentiate them in terms of other than simply gender. They were less likely to be part-time employees and they were more likely to be qualified. They were more likely to come from social class backgrounds IV and V. Nursing was more likely to be a late choice for men (Brown and Stones 1973).

Brown and Stones's treatment is relatively untheoretical and their approach is organized within a broad 'equality of opportunities' framework. Thus they write of a period of 'male emancipation' during the period 1900–50 (ibid.: 15–17) and argue that the Second World War may have contributed to a weakening of a prejudice against men. Their approach, therefore, tends to see

[131]

the growing participation of men in nursing as a kind of mirror image of the participation of women in areas hitherto occupied by men. As we shall see, this is a somewhat limited perspective.

One American study adopted a more theoretical approach, one derived from Hughes's influential essay on the contradictions and dilemmas of status (included in Hughes 1958). The main concern with this kind of approach is to see status as being compounded of different strands or elements (gender, ethnicity, occupation, age and so on) which are not necessarily congruent with each other. Where incongruities or inconsistencies exist, there are questions as to whether these are felt and perceived as dilemmas and whether any consequences follow from these perceptions. In this particular project (Segal 1962) 22 out of the 101 nurses interviewed were men. This was a somewhat higher percentage than might have been expected, a consequence of the coeducational nature of the school of nursing attached to the particular hospital. Another study of male nurses is clearly influenced by feminist scholarship and focuses more or less directly on issues of male identity (Etzkowitz 1971). A further American study directly addressed itself to the theme of 'tokens' and sought to contrast the careers and experiences of male nurses and female physicians (Floge and Merrill 1986). This discussed, for example, questions of their higher visibility in both cases and the extent to which gender and token status enhanced or hindered career opportunities. Dingwall's sample of health visitors did appear to include slightly higher proportions of men than was the case nationally, although they were still very much in the minority, ranging from 10 per cent for married men under 30 to 3.2 per cent for single men under 30 (Dingwall 1977; 1979).

Even within this handful of studies some themes do begin to emerge. One is to do with different career orientations of men and women. The men in Dingwall's study were more likely to see their undertaking a course in health-visitor training as being a career move, one reflecting 'conventional notions about the life-plans of a male' (Dingwall 1977: 35). The men in Segal's study tended to have clear if limited career objectives (Segal 1962). In most of these studies there are indications of wider social mobility aims, considering the relatively low-status backgrounds of the men who took up nursing or health visiting.

There are signs that men may achieve greater status within the context of the hospital. The men in Segal's study tended to have higher official positions than the women, although this did not necessarily lead to greater job satisfaction: 'in our society, the male winner of a competition with women has but a shallow victory' (Segal 1962: 37).

Floge and Merrill found that their male nurses were more likely to be given leadership roles, whether or not such roles were officially recognized (Floge and Merrill 1986). Members of the public on entering the hospital were sometimes more likely to approach a male nurse for information or help, even passing one or two female nurses of equal status in order to do so. Etzkowitz's impression was that men in nursing often got preferential treatment within the hospital hierarchy (Etzkowitz 1971).

A common theme in these studies, at least the American studies, was the tendency for male nurses to adopt male physicians as a kind of role model. There were some indications of a more informal mode of interaction between male nurse and male physician although this did not appear to lead to wider social interaction outside the work situation. The male nurses, at the same time, wanted to differentiate themselves from other men working within the hospital, notably the lower-status aides. Floge and Merrill's study found more direct interaction between male nurses and physicians than Segal's study. They tended to interact on a basis of near equality, certainly with less of the traditional model of doctor–nurse interaction about it. Female physicians on the other hand, tended to interact on a more informal basis with female nurses and there is some suggestion in their account that what might have been of benefit in career terms for male nurses was not to the benefit of female physicians (Floge and Merrill 1986).

In these studies there are suggestions of a gender division of labour within similar categories or levels of nursing. Segal's nurses were more likely to be found working in male wards with senile patients. Brown and Stones found that there was some feeling that men might be more suited to psychiatric hospitals (Brown and Stones 1973: 94). There was also some expectation that male nurses might be employed in lifting patients, even where this might be formally the job of the aides. Floge and Merrill also found, on the basis of both observations and interviews, that men were more likely to be used in lifting work of this kind although it was often formally denied (Floge and Merrill 1986).

Of particular relevance to our interests are questions of sexual identities, a theme raised in most if not all of these studies. Here

I am using the term to refer to both gender identity and sexual orientation, and in particular to the perception, real or otherwise, that a male nurse was something less than a proper man and was probably also homosexual in orientation. These perceptions of others' perceptions may have some measure of truth about them. Segal notes that around a quarter of the female nurses interviewed suspected the male nurses of effeminate or homosexual tendencies and this contributed to some of the elements of hostility that the women felt towards the men. This theme also emerges in the Floge and Merrill study and in Etzkowitz's account. This latter study also suggests one possible strategy for handling these ambiguities, namely to engage in obvious dating practices or in chatting up the female nurses (Etzkowitz 1971). Other strategies for handling these incongruities might be to seek closer identification with the male physicians (perhaps accepting the erroneous title of doctor when delivered by a patient), emphasizing career objectives, emphasizing themes of technical expertise or not identifying oneself as a nurse outside the work situation (Dingwall 1979).

All these factors do suggest that male nurses as a minority were highly visible and in some measure social isolates, and that issues of masculinity were part of this isolation. However, Floge and Merrill suggest that this isolation was only partial. Their male nurses were not totally excluded from the female networks and their positions within the hospital did have some positive status features that were denied their female colleagues. This is certainly a theme that emerges in other studies.

What is perhaps missing from these studies, with the exception of the article by Dingwall (1979), is anything more than a passing mention of the wider structure of gender inequality within which nursing and similar occupations exist. The medical profession as a whole is, and continues to be, very clearly male dominated both in terms of management and in terms of professional control and definition. While these facts may not directly affect the day-to-day experiences of male nurses they must be seen as a constituting factor in these experiences. It is possible that discussions in terms of 'dilemmas of status' or 'tokenism' tend to modify the effects of gender in favour of more universalistic categories of analysis just as talk of equality of opportunities in this respect bypasses questions of power and control. Certainly, as Dingwall argues, discussions of 'tokenism' may obscure the possibility of a male invasion and nursing becoming a male-dominated profession in more senses than one (Dingwall 1979).

Nursing is not the only occupation to receive this kind of attention. The position of secretary, for example, raises several very similar issues. Cockburn quotes a young man on a Youth Training Scheme: 'If you say "secretary" and say "bloke" it would be a really funny bloke' (Cockburn 1987: 100). Secretaries, like nurses, are strongly identified with stereotypical feminine characteristics: 'If secretaries are represented as women they are also represented almost exclusively in familial or sexual terms: as wives, mothers, spinsters, aunts, mistresses and femmes fatales' (Pringle 1988: 3). As with male nurses, male secretaries when they are found are often assumed to have some kind of problem with their masculinity (ibid.: 168). One of the ways of handling these, by now, familiar ambiguities is to reject the term 'secretary'; this is one of the reasons why male secretaries may be sometimes difficult to find. A preferred term tends to be something like 'administrative assistant'. There is some evidence that, once in, the male secretary moves quickly up the office hierarchy, again a theme familiar from the nursing studies (ibid.: 170–1).

We have seen that one of the issues in considering nursing, was the theme of caring which has strong identifications with constructions of femininity. Another area which has strong connotations of caring is to do with looking after small children. Cockburn has some accounts of young men working with children, often going against traditional gender stereotypes. She notes how one project changed its name from 'Community Health and Care' to 'Community Work' in order to appeal, with only limited success, to men. Unlike nursing and secretarial work, such work has few prospects and low pay, and some of the men she interviewed, regrettably, had to give up child-care for some other better-paid employment (Cockburn 1988).

Cockburn very much supports the idea of the introduction of men into paid child-care work as a way of combating gender stereotypes and of appealing to less aggressive more gentle themes in men's lives. It is a persuasive argument, one which parallels the arguments for encouraging men to play a more central role in parenting. The argument here again is not simply in greater formal equality within the household but also in terms of breaking through the vicious circle, outlined by Chodorow and others, whereby the near exclusive role of women in mothering and child-care reproduces not only mothers but also the harder, more aggressive features of masculinity. The growing boy has, at some stage, to reject the mother, with all her softer caring qualities, in favour of a harder version of masculinity (Chodorow 1978; Dinnerstein 1978).

The argument seems persuasive and attractive although, in Britain at least, this has come under some critical scrutiny in recent years as a consequence of the growing concern about child abuse. These are difficult issues, and it may well be argued that the men who abuse children sexually (and probably physically as well) are those least likely to have made any serious attempt to develop their repertoire of roles to include caring. Nevertheless, in the context of paid child-care, concerns about child abuse may well arouse the fears and suspicions of some mothers and possibly other women child-care workers as well. These concerns, together with perceptions that day nurseries or day-care centres may be seen as women's territory, may certainly inhibit the participation of men in these traditionally female areas of employment.

It is clear that, whatever the particular debates and controversies, all the occupations mentioned so far are understood as presenting some kind of problem for masculine identity. The same may also be said for a major area of unpaid work, that of housework. That this might provoke dilemmas of masculine identity is comically expressed by one of Sue Sharpe's informants who said that she found her husband hoovering on his hands and knees to avoid being seen by the neighbours (Sharpe 1984: 181–2). This is not the place to rehearse the extensive literature on the sexual division of labour within the home and how most of the evidence points to very slow changes in the direction of men's participation even in the face of male unemployment or redundancy (see Chapter 5 for some of this evidence). Most of the findings are, therefore, relatively pessimistic although perhaps we should begin to look more closely at those men who are attempting to take on greater responsibilities within the home. After all, Sharpe's informant was seen as making some kind of effort and her study is not uniformally one of men's avoidance of domestic labour.

One relatively optimistic study is a recent one by Wheelock on *Husbands at Home*. The title is perhaps a little misleading and the study is better understood as an account of the range of responses on the part of men in the North East to unemployment. Her sample is small, 30 families, although the very smallness of the sample may be seen as underlining the wide range of responses that she found. She distinguished between traditional rigid gender divisions of labour, traditionally flexible households, sharing households and exchange-role households. Her sample fell almost exactly into a quarter for each category. She found some breaking down of stereotypes – one wife argued that domestic responsibilities made her husband 'more of a man', although these were perhaps limited in their long-term effect (Wheelock 1990: 113). She argued that the responses on the part of the men and women were more often pragmatic than ideological. For this reason, she used the term 'exchange role' rather than 'reverse role': it was a particular strategy to cope with a particular crisis, one which was compatible with norms of self-respect. We do find husbands willing to take on responsibilities (as opposed to simply helping out) while for the most part retaining the idea that they would rather be in paid employment. There is material for both the optimists and the pessimists here as, I suspect, there is in many similar studies. What does seem to be important for our present discussion is that ideological constructions of masculinity do not seem to be perceived as being put on the line even among exchange-role households.

Parallel lines

There are some jobs or occupations which remain gender specific while, at the same time a kind of parallel, mirror image or shadow occupation develops alongside it, associated with the opposite gender. Thus, 'cricketer' almost inevitably signifies a male cricket player; terms such as 'women cricketers' or even 'lady cricketers' come to be deployed to signify the later development of women's cricket teams. In this section I want to consider, briefly, the example of the male stripper.

Dressel and Petersen's study of the recruitment and socialization of male strippers notes that, for men, this is a non-traditional and deviant occupation. Indeed, some men may seek to disguise their occupation, at least initially (Dressel and Petersen 1982). They point out, perhaps rather unnecessarily, that becoming a male stripper is rarely 'a carefully and deliberately planned occupational move' (ibid.: 390) and that recruitment is usually through informal means. Unlike female strippers, most of the men had not had the experience of 'body work' prior to taking up stripping. However, even in this relatively new and deviant occupation there were signs of the development of an occupational culture. Men were expected to provide their own costumes and 'gimmicks' and not to appropriate material from the acts of other strippers. There were some occupational ethics: they were not supposed to allow members of the audience to fondle their genitals and they were not supposed obviously to date members of the audience. In common with many other 'deviant' occupations, a set of legitimations were being elaborated. A major framework of justification was in terms of 'equal rights for women'. If men could watch strip-tease, women ought to be accorded the same right; it gave women the opportunity for a night out and for 'something different', it gave women sexual outlets where these had been denied for a long time and it was good entertainment. It should be noted, however, that this study was carried out in a 'Bible belt' community and that the strippers here always kept their G-strings on, never exposing their genitals to the audience.

It might seem, superficially, that stripping might be an example of men adopting a traditional feminine occupation with inevitable consequences for their gender identities. As we see, Dressel and Petersen's strippers used the language of sex equality to legitimate their work. However, Barham, seeing male strip-tease from the audience perspective (and from a woman's perspective) raises some different issues (Barham 1985). It would seem that the Australian show that she is describing was altogether raunchier than the one described by Dressel and Petersen. She sees strip-tease as a performance, 'not an imitation of everyday gender relations but rather possible interpretations of them' (ibid.: 51). The show, which seems to contain a lot of aggressiveness, reveals the dangers of independence on the part of women who venture out to the show and symbolically reinstates these women 'under male protection' at the end. At first there is comedy, playfulness and sexual ambiguity but the whole show asserts masculinity in a particular way: 'What is expressed in male strip performance is man's force upon the world' (ibid.: 65). The realization that male strip-tease does not entail a loss of masculinity but a reinstatement of certain facets of masculinity is not absent from Dressel and

Petersen's account, although they have little actual analysis of the performance itself. One of the main perks, possibly motivations, is the opportunity of meeting women: one respondent referred to 'more lays than I can handle' (Dressel and Petersen 1982: 393). Others enjoyed the applause and the overall ego-trip of appearing in front of a group of women determined to have a good time. And, to extrapolate a little, there is 'danger' and 'action' in strip-tease, symbolized when a woman slips a tip inside the band of a G-string. In Barham's account, this sexually charged and socially dangerous situation is modified so as, symbolically, to put the audience at risk and to reassert an aggressive and threatening masculinity. The parallel between male and female strippers would appear to be superficial. Rather than subverting the gender order, it reasserts it. (See also Westwood 1984: 120–2.)

Conclusion

For some time stories of 'women in a man's world' have provided good copy for newspaper or magazine articles and more recently the same has been true for the reverse. Under the heading 'Labour of Love' the *Guardian* told the story of a male midwife (Darking 1989). This account raises many of the themes touched upon in this chapter. The midwife under discussion is clearly in a minority (12 or so out of around 35,000) yet denies that there is anything special about his involvement. He was attracted to the profession by 'the mix of psychological and physical care' (ibid.). He emphasizes the importance of the right qualities rather than the gender while recognizing that some women, within and outside the profession, have serious reservations about men in midwifery. He is conscious of the fact 'that his sex gives him a voice often denied his female colleagues' (ibid.).

Even this short piece can highlight many of the ambiguities and tensions in 'gender crossovers' in occupations. There are certainly challenges to gender-based stereotypes; men can be caring and midwifery often involves hard physical and exhausting work. The whole article is framed by feminist debates and such debates are around whether the involvement of men in such positions represents a serious challenge to patriarchy and the gender order, or whether it provides yet further opportunities for patriarchy to reassert itself in a modern context. The wider issues are to do with how far men can be seen as capable of or willing for change, and the relationships between changes at the individual level (men entering caring occupations or taking on domestic responsibilities) and the societal level.

I shall return to some of these questions in Chapter 9. For the moment I hope that this chapter has begun to show how such 'anomalies' within the gender division of labour can be treated as mini-dramas through which we can begin to explore the tensions and complexities of gender identities and the gender order. Further, it is important to emphasize that issues of men and masculinities are not only to be explored where men enter into apparently new territory; they are also exposed and demonstrated in their responses to women as they, in their turn, enter occupations hitherto closed to them.

CHAPTER 7

Challenges to masculinity: (iii) The suffrage movement

Introduction

Up to now, I have mainly considered indirect challenges to constructions of masculinity in the form of unemployment or redundancy and shifts in the sexual composition of the labour market. However, challenges to masculine dominance and sometimes also to dominant models of masculinity have sometimes been more direct. For the most part, of course, such challenges have come from women. Indeed, as the earlier chapters of this book indicated, the present study would not have come about without the kinds of challenges represented by various strands of feminist theory and practice.

It is, of course, the case that the feminisms to which recent texts on men and masculinity have been responding have been only the most recent of several waves of feminism or proto-feminism. Of particular importance, historically, was the movement for women's suffrage. Such movements, while clearly of central importance in studying the political emancipation of women, are also of importance in a study of men and masculinity. Most obvious are the forms of resistance offered by men to the women's demands (Harrison 1978). These show the lengths to which men might go in order to protect what was seen as their power and privileges. The legitimations of their opposition show, directly or indirectly, their understandings of masculinity as well as their constructions of femininity. Among the opponents to the British suffrage movement, for example, we find a central belief in the natural separation of spheres and a deep-rooted fear as to what might happen, were the distinctions between the sexes to become blurred. There were fears concerning the break-up of the family and of the loss of one central plank in the construction of masculinity, namely the idea of man as the protector. Harrison argues, interestingly, that these fears had a particular historical context in concerns about the state of the nation and what might happen to Britain in a new, tough, Bismarckian world (ibid.: 34).

Harrison is concerned to emphasize the range of responses on the part of men, even amongst those men opposed in some degree to the women's suffrage movement. He points out, indeed, that opposition to the suffrage movement was not necessarily the same as opposition to feminism. This idea of a range of responses, linked to a range of constructions of masculinities, is surely extended further if we consider those men who were supporters of or in favour of women's suffrage. Men were prominent in the struggle for women's suffrage, on both sides of the Atlantic, just as they were to be found in struggles around other feminist or proto-feminist causes such as opposition to the Contagious Diseases Act, or in support of the Married Women's Property Act. Further, many men were willing to call themselves 'feminists' and many women had no difficulty in endorsing that label or in acknowledging their support. Elizabeth Cady Stanton wrote of Mill's *The Subjection of Women* in these terms:

> I lay the book down with a peace and joy I never felt before, for it is the first response from any man to show that he is capable of seeing and feeling all the nice shades and degrees of women's wrongs and the central point of her weakness and degradation.
>
> (Quoted in Rossi 1970: 62)

This judgement is not affected by the tricky question as to the contributions that Harriet Taylor made to the writings of *The Subjection of Women* or to some of Mill's other writings (Rose 1985; Rossi 1970). What matters is that Mill had no problems about putting his name to the work and Stanton had no difficulty about responding positively to a book authored by a man. She was, however, wrong in singling out Mill. Ray Strachey, in her history of the struggle for women's rights and equalities, refers to F.D. Maurice in these terms: 'one of the few men who, in the thirties and forties really believed that women had an existence in this world and the next' (Strachey 1928: 48). Further, in Volume One of Banks's dictionary of British feminists (covering the period 1800–1930) just under one-fifth of her entries deal with men, not simply because they called themselves 'feminists' but because she, as did many of their contemporaries, considered that they had earned that title through their support for unpopular causes and their extensive practical work on their behalf (Banks 1985). Just over a half of these men were born in the first half of the nineteenth century, with three more before 1800. Sylvia Pankhurst referred to: 'Mrs Pethick Lawrence and her husband, who have given their whole lives, their days and nights, and all their hopes and thoughts to the service of the cause' (Pankhurst 1911: Preface). She also notes here the importance of Brailsford and Lord Lytton, although several other men occur in her account, and the accounts of several other women, of the struggles for the vote.

As an example of the nature of some of this support, I quote part of a speech from one of the lesser known supporters, one not included in the Banks survey, Israel Zangwill:

And so to those myriads of tired women who rise in the raw dawn and troop to their cheerless factories and who, when the twilight falls, return not to rest but to the labours of a squalid household, to these the thought of Women's Suffrage, which comes as a sneer to the man about town, comes as a hope and a prayer. Who dares leave that hope unilluminated, that prayer unanswered?

(Zangwill, quoted in Pankhurst 1911: 137)

The point here is not to celebrate such men or to provide a detailed study of them. One such study already exists (Strauss 1982) although there is scope for more work here. What I want to do is to try to assess the nature and significance of such support and to see whether it is possible to say anything about the sources of such support. This clearly has some significance for our own times. I also want to explore some of the possible limitations of or qualifications to this analysis of men's support for the suffrage movement, again considering the possibility for further reflection upon our own times.

My original intention in writing this chapter was to explore some of the issues to do with men and masculinity that might have been raised by this support. Were they, as the title of Strauss's book suggest, *Traitors To The Masculine Cause*? Were they seen by their opponents as being, in some way, less masculine through their support for such movements? Unfortunately, I have not been able to obtain any clear-cut or detailed answers to these

[143]

questions; again, I think that more research and re-analysis is needed into these issues, although a tentative conclusion might be that the issues of masculinity loomed less large than I had initially supposed. Certainly, they do not leap out of the texts. There are several possible reasons for this. We may well find, for example, that a variety of models of masculinity were being deployed by men, and women, on both sides of the debates around women's suffrage and the Contagious Diseases Acts.

It is worth reminding ourselves, however, of the extent and the range of men's support. One image is that of Keir Hardie (who wrote a pamphlet on 'The Citizenship of Women' in 1906) addressing a demonstration on behalf of women's suffrage in Trafalgar Square. The photograph (which appears in Sylvia Pankhurst's history) shows several other men on the platform as well (Pankhurst 1911: 80). There was organizational support as well. Victor Duval and Henry Nevinson, friends of the Pethick-Lawrences, formed the Men's Political Union in 1909; the Men's League for Women's Suffrage had been formed in 1907. In 1909, the Men's Political Union published a leaflet listing 'Prominent Men in Favour of Women's Suffrage'. These included Lord Robert Cecil, Lord Lytton, Sidney Webb, Gilbert Murray, Sir Oliver Lodge, J. M. Barrie, John Galsworthy, Thomas Hardy, John Masefield, Sir Hubert Parry plus some bishops and minor clergy (Brittain 1963: 54).

Many supporters of women's suffrage had also supported an earlier campaign, the one against the Contagious Diseases Acts. These were passed during the 1860s and were in response to growing fears about the extent and impact of venereal diseases on the nation's men, especially those in military organizations, and sought to control the prostitutes that worked near army barracks or naval ports. The sanctions included the possibility of imprisonment and hard labour should they refuse to undergo a medical examination. In one sense, it could be argued that the men who joined women like Josephine Butler in opposing these Acts were risking more than the supporters of women's suffrage, since they were speaking about dangerous or tabooed matters and were calling into question certain taken-for-granted assumptions about male and female sexualities. In particular, of course, they were calling into question a double standard of sexual morality, one which not only differentiated between men and women but also between respectable and non-respectable women. Stansfield who spoke out for repeal in 1874 was one of the first men to break the silence and was much criticized for this (Walkowitz 1980: 97). Walkowitz argues that the Contagious Diseases Acts were one of a 'series of causes' for some radically-minded men in nineteenth-century England (ibid.: 6) and that there was considerable overlap and continuity between the two campaigns.

It has already been noted that support for women's rights and suffrage on the part of men was also found in North America and, again, there were often links between the struggles in both countries. Kimmel argues that such support was one of a range of possible responses on the part of men to a crisis of masculinity in late nineteenth-century America, occasioned by the growth of political democracy and the development of industry (Kimmel 1987b: 138). On the domestic front there was the perceived threat from the 'New Woman', educated and often employed outside the home and having and claiming a voice of her own. Here, as in Britain, there was support for the education of women from sympathetic men as well as support for suffrage. Leach also notes the involvement of men in American feminism of this time and refers, for example, to Thomas Wentworth Higginson as 'the most important American male feminist of his generation' (Leach 1981: 302). Strauss describes Higginson (1823–1911) as being in the John Stuart Mill mould, referring to the range of his radical sympathies and his philosophical interests (Strauss 1982). In the twentieth century, just to provide another example, Floyd Dell's *Love in the Machine Age*, published in the 1920s, provided, Strauss argues, an assault on 'patriarchal capitalism' (ibid.: 266).

The point to be stressed here is that we are not simply dealing with some isolated individuals but something approaching a movement on the part of men, at least a series of overlapping concerns and interpersonal networks. These struggles were not simply on behalf of women's suffrage, but also for a variety of other feminist causes as well, although the nature of their involvements and their understandings of these issues varied considerably. Clearly, any history of feminism must focus centrally on the activities of women; but any such survey would be incomplete without reference to the support and activities of some men, even if the main story is one of opposition or indifference on the part of men.

Backgrounds of 'male feminists'

It would be an irony if we were to explain the participation of men in causes supportive of women in terms of their individual exceptionality since this would be, in some measure, to reproduce some version of a 'great man theory of history'. Exceptional they may have been, but it is also possible to speculate on some of the sociological factors in their backgrounds which predisposed them to take up with such causes or which sustained them in their positions on these public issues. This is very much a preliminary analysis but one, I hope, which has some relevance for today.

The influence of a woman

Undoubtedly, the most important influence in the lives of the men recorded by Banks and elsewhere was the influence of a woman. In some cases this may have been the initial influence, in others the links with women helped to sustain commitment to the cause. At the very least it can be argued that the links with a woman or women prevented any serious weakening of support. The women concerned could be individual women or a set of women within a social circle. They could be related by kinship or marriage or unrelated. The relationship could be marital or non-marital or, even, extramarital. Perhaps one of the best documented examples is the relationship between John Stuart Mill and Harriet Taylor described by Rossi in these terms: 'a complex and subtle mutuality of intellect and sentiment between a man and a woman' (Rossi 1970: 10). Harriet Taylor was clearly of great personal significance to Mill during the period of their acquaintance and especially during their period of marriage from 1851 to 1858. But this was more than the provision of love which, Mill maintained, had been absent in his childhood. It was clearly an intellectual influence and one which was of crucial importance in Mill's own writings on women and other issues.

Many other accounts of the influence of women occur in the various works on the feminism of this time. In the case of Higginson, Leach notes: 'the daily pervasive presence of women in his life from his early years to the moment of his death' (Leach 1981: 302). Sylvia Pankhurst refers to a Mr Bamford Slack MP who: 'agreed to introduce our Bill, largely because his wife was a

Suffragist and helped us to urge our cause' (Pankhurst 1911: 12). But perhaps, the most outstanding case, certainly one of the most attractive, is that of the Pethick-Lawrences. Pethick-Lawrence was not deeply involved in the suffragist cause at first although became interested in it through the examples of two particular strong women: Phillipa Fawcett and Olive Schreiner. However, he wrote: 'I do not suppose that I should ever have become entangled with the suffragettes if it had not been for my wife' (Pethick-Lawrence 1942: 69). He provided considerable financial support for the movement and helped on the planning side. He was instrumental in founding the publication *Votes for Women*, for which he wrote unsigned pieces. He endured a brief experience of prison as a consequence of his support for the suffragettes. Later, he was to be among those who opposed Christobel and Emmeline Pankhurst over matters of tactics and with his wife was expelled from the Women's Social and Political Union. Vera Brittain also stresses the importance of Emmeline Pethick-Lawrence on her husband's involvement and, indeed, wider political career (Brittain 1963: 20).

The case of Keir Hardie is somewhat more complex. There was clearly some influence from his mother, described by his biographer as a 'devout farm servant of remarkable strength of character' (Morgan, K. 1975: 4). Later he was to have 'a series of usually innocent and brief affairs with young left-wing girls he encountered in the socialist movement' (ibid.: 12). This description, particularly the use of the word 'girls', is not without its problems, especially for present-day feminists and their supporters. However, it does suggest the continuing importance of women in sustaining a firm support for their case, even in the face of opposition from other members of his own party. His deepest attachment was to Sylvia Pankhurst, who named children after him. Clearly there was a constant and complex interplay between public and private as Morgan suggests (ibid.: 163).

The list could be extended. Snowden was influenced by Ethel Annikin (Strauss 1982: 208). Brailsford's wife had strong Pankhurst sympathies. There was Dilke's relationship with Emilia Pattison, the wife of the Rector of Lincoln College, Oxford and feminist. Henry Fawcett proposed to Elizabeth Garrett but married her sister. William Fox included Harriet Martineau and Harriet Taylor among his set of friends and William Thompson, one of the earliest in Banks's collection, had a close relationship with Anna Wheeler, a St Simonist and a feminist. Israel Zangwill had an independent-minded mother. A measure of caution must be introduced here. Clearly, there was some presupposition on my part that such relationships were important and similar assumptions may have influenced the biographers. However, the evidence does seem to be clear enough and is probably not all that surprising. One more difficult point of argument is whether such relationships and influences only went as far as the public support for the women's cause or whether it made any difference to the personal lives of these men. Public commitment to a cause, even a feminist cause, could be consistent with a model of radical male politics, one that included public speaking, organizing behind the scenes, lobbying and publicizing. Further, where there were some indications of private lives being affected, the question of causality raises its head. Did the public involvement bring about changes in private lives behaviour or was it the other way around?

Again, perhaps one of the clearest examples of the interrelations between the public and the private is to be found in the case of Pethick-Lawrence. At his golden wedding he told reporters: 'that he had married his wife because she smoked cigarettes, could get off buses when they were moving, and didn't wear gloves when she went for a walk' (Brittain 1963: 196). Pethick-Lawrence's own account of his courtship points to some more serious issues. His proposal to Emmeline Pethick gave rise to a deep and heart-searching discussion of the nature of marriage and whether it was possible to develop in such a way that did not inhibit the full development of the personalities of both parties. In particular, concern was expressed about the traditional 'helpmeet' role expected of the wife of a Member of Parliament (Pethick-Lawrence 1942: 51–2). From all accounts, Pethick-Lawrence was as seriously committed to working out a marriage based on equality and mutual respect as he was to the more public aspects of the suffragist causes.

Similar observations could be made about the much briefer marital relationship between Harriet Taylor and John Stuart Mill. Rossi writes: 'There is no better example of the manner in which they attempted to put in practice the principles they were so firmly committed to on the proper relations between the sexes, than the remarkable statement Mill wrote two months before his marriage' (Rossi 1970: 45). This was a personal declaration of the nature of marriage which was clearly at odds with institutional ecclesiastical understandings and was closer in spirit to modern ideas of companionate marriage. It rejected any patriarchal claims a husband might have over the 'person, property and freedom of action of the other party' (ibid.). It is difficult to know whether the marriage lived up to these ideals although there is no doubt that the commitment was there on both sides.

Elsewhere, Emmeline Pankhurst wrote that 'Dr Pankhurst did not desire that I should turn myself into a household machine' (Pankhurst 1914: 13). However, in other cases it was clear that public commitments did not spill over into private life. Most striking here was perhaps Keir Hardie who 'accepted that in most cases a woman's place should be in the home' (Morgan, K. 1975: 162). This belief was certainly put into practice in relation to his own wife, a woman of working-class origins who remained very much in the shadows of domesticity. Evidence on the domestic lives of many of the other men supporters of women's suffrage is sometimes difficult to come by but it would be surprising if Keir Hardie were a lone exception.

In talking about the influence of women on these men it is important not to tell this as yet another version of the 'behind every great man' cliché. The interplay between public commitments and private relationships has scarcely been explored in the sociology of marriage, which continues to focus on the dynamics of the relationship itself, even where this has been augmented by a deeper understanding of the economic basis and character of marital ties. The conventional models of wives as supporters or helpmeets to their husband's careers has been well documented (Finch 1983) and this probably remains a dominant model in practice as well as in ideology. The processes, interpersonal and psychological, through which marital or other partners sustain or elaborate an understanding of marriage that is at odds with the prevailing norms and which allows for an interplay between public and private, have yet to be explored. In the lives of a Pethick-Lawrence or a J. S. Mill we perhaps have some clues.

Social networks
The sociological analysis of these processes may be taken a little further if we consider another feature that emerges with some clarity in the brief lives outlined by Banks. The importance of

social networks in the lives of nineteenth- and twentieth-century feminists has already been noted (Stanley 1985b) and something similar may be observed in the cases of many of the men considered here. Rather than conduct a detailed analysis, perhaps the case of J. S. Mill might constitute an apt illustration. In the first instance we have the circle of philosophical radicals where there were, among others, the feminist examples of Harriet Grote and Sarah Austin (Rossi 1970: 16). It is likely that Mill and Harriet Taylor first met at the house of William Fox. Harriet Martineau was also present at these meetings. Among these Unitarian radicals, ideals of sex equality were part of the atmosphere. Other friends of Mill were Richard Pankhurst and F. D. Maurice, a Christian Socialist. Other associates of Mill included Dilke, Charles Drysdale, Henry Fawcett and Henry Sidgwick. Following the Richard Pankhurst connection we can move off into other connections such as those around Keir Hardie.

Such analyses are increasingly essential elements in political science, political sociology and political anthropology and there is perhaps some danger that the analysis of networks might develop into something of a technical exercise detached from wider considerations of meaning or significance. Nevertheless, there is no doubt that such networks both provided the intellectual and moral climate which stimulated the interest and commitment to issues such as women's suffrage and sustained that commitment, perhaps in the face of hostility or indifference. Further such networks remind us that the relationships with women, often strong and independent-minded women, should not be analysed in isolation but should be placed in a wider social context. If that wider social context is not to fall back into mere abstraction then something like a network analysis is essential.

Radical movements
Another factor, clearly linked to this network factor, is to do with some kind of background or involvement in a whole range of radical causes or movements. The networks that I described in the last paragraph were but one facet of a wide set of links between causes and movements, linked by a deep and optimistic commitment to reform. More generally, Strauss talks about intellectual and moral antecedents in the Enlightenment (Strauss 1982) while Leach writes of the transportation of American Protestantism in a humanitarian climate (Leach 1981: 302). Coming down to

specific influences, I have already noted the influences of the Philosophical Radicals and the Unitarians on J. S. Mill and his associates. Walkowitz argues that the people involved in campaigning against the Contagious Diseases Acts had similar social and religious backgrounds, namely the North of England, the radical wing of the Liberals and the Quakers (Walkowitz 1980). Similarly, Banks sees as being the main influences on feminism in the period 1840–70 as being the Evangelicals and a general concern with equal rights with socialism and a concern for moral reform entering the period 1870–1920 (Banks 1985). Clearly the connections with socialism were obvious in the case of Keir Hardie but probably of equal importance were his childhood influences around temperance and Evangelical Christianity. His well-known statement that 'Socialism is much more an affair of the heart than of the intellect' almost certainly reflects these influences (Hardie, quoted in Morgan, K. 1975: 204). This perhaps contrasted with the somewhat more rationalistic approaches to reform associated with, say, Richard Pankhurst or Pethwick-Lawrence and these differences may reflect class and educational backgrounds.

These links, connections and influences could be extended. With Brailsford and Stead, the radical commitment extended abroad to include a wider opposition to all kinds of slavery and oppression. Indeed, the metaphor of the slave became a popular one in considering the position of women, and working men, closer to home. Even some of the more free-thinking radicals, whose causes and beliefs might have seemed more of a threat, could be identified with a broad and serious moral concern. Thus Strauss wrote of Bradlaugh, that his 'feminism was a function of his all-embracing belief in human rights – part of the radical tradition' (Strauss 1982: 96). Similar remarks might have been made of Holyoake.

This is not to say that there was some unified and completely coherent radical or reforming movement around a broad platform of causes to which all could give assent. Clearly, there were differences and divisions, both in terms of backgrounds and ideologies. Nevertheless, there was a broad language of reform and this was reinforced through the extensive social networks that linked, sometimes through several stages, groupings and individuals who might not otherwise have had much to do with each other. For the present discussion this means that men who

[151]

supported feminist or proto-feminist causes did not necessarily find themselves isolated. Even if not all their friends supported such feminist causes to the same degree, the idea of standing up for and campaigning for a cause, perhaps seeing this as a moral duty more than anything else, was by no means alien to their immediate circles. What does seem striking about many of the men who supported the cause of women's suffrage, certainly from the standpoint of the present, is that few of them appeared to have any doubts about the particular stand that they were taking. It seemed as natural to oppose slavery as it was to support votes for women and this sense of naturalness may well have been sustained by the particular moral, intellectual and religious traditions of which they formed a part.

Unhappiness and alienation

In contrast to this last point, which suggests perhaps an over-easy identification with a radical tradition and the friends and family who formed networks within these traditions, there is some evidence which points to some elements of unhappiness and perhaps even alienation in the family backgrounds of the men under consideration here. Mill writes of his childhood and growing up 'in the absence of love and in the presence of fear' (quoted in Rossi 1970: 13). At the other end of the social scale, the struggles of the early Keir Hardie in an environment of poverty and drunkenness are well known. Perhaps, as Strachey suggests, there was something in the fact that F. D. Maurice was brought up as the only boy in a family of many children which contributed to his support for women's rights (Strachey 1928: 59–60). This was not necessarily an unhappy family background, however, and generally the picture that Leach provides for the backgrounds of American feminist men does not seem to be repeated in the British accounts to the same extent: 'Many feminist men replicated Higginson's experiences . . . . Many of their fathers were victims of economic failure, weak, nonexistent, unapproachable, cruel or rigidly authoritarian' (Leach 1981: 305).

The difficulties involved in attempting to assess the nature and significance of the more intimate aspects of family backgrounds may be illustrated in the case of Pethick-Lawrence. He refers to his mother in these terms: 'My mother was a very gentle woman who loved peace and harmony' (Pethick-Lawrence 1942: 17). He refers to her Unitarian faith. Yet also his father died when he was

$3^1/2$ years old and he records that he disliked being a child. At school he liked football but found Latin and Greek dull. And so on. It is not clear whether a coherent picture can be constructed here to be entitled 'the makings of a male feminist'. There are two sets of constructions going on here, one involving Pethick-Lawrence's constructions of his own life and childhood and my own reconstruction of aspects of his autobiography. I shall be discussing these issues at some greater length in the next chapter. For the moment, I should prefer to regard the question of some similarities in background in terms of the psycho-dynamics of the family as an open one, but one certainly deserving further more detailed investigation. For the time being I prefer to remain closer to the more prosaic details of supportive social networks involving strong and independent women.

The concept of chivalry

There is, however, one further factor which might be considered as a footnote, although it may be worthy of further investigation. This is to do with the idea of chivalry, an idea which, as Girouard argues, affected a wide range of people and movements in Victorian England and the early part of the twentieth century, including Tennyson, William Morris and the Pre-Raphaelites and Baden-Powell (Girouard 1981). It served as a loose kind of social cement which linked a variety of otherwise very different individuals. Mill himself had elaborated a kind of theory of chivalry. In the first place, there was the softening influence of women. Denied across to means of fighting and warfare they developed other ways of settling differences. This 'softness' (which is clearly not seen in pejorative terms) on the part of women tended to act as a powerful stimulus to men to act as their protectors. The outcome of this convergence was chivalry: 'The chivalrous ideal is the acme of the influence of women's sentiments on the moral cultivation of mankind . . .' (Mill, quoted in Rossi 1970: 224). But he was also aware of the limitations of chivalry and how it left many evils and wrongs unchecked.

It is worth asking questions about the general influence of these notions of chivalry on the men who supported the feminist case. If the idea were so influential, especially amongst the upper and middle classes, as Girouard suggests, then it would be unusual if that influence did not spread to at least some of the men under consideration here. Clearly, the notion itself is flexible enough to

[153]

encourage not only support for the rights of women but also opposition to female suffrage, an opposition based upon strong notions of female difference and male protection. Indeed, the reworking of the Arthurian legends, which formed a major strand in chivalrous iconography, would seem to be more likely to encourage the anti-suffragists than the pro-suffragists. Nevertheless, the idea of righting wrongs that had been done to women might have formed part of the cultural background which men could draw upon, unconsciously, in expressing their support for feminist causes. It may also, as we shall see, highlight some of the weaknesses in this support.

'Traitors to the Masculine Cause'?

Emily Pankhurst described some of the men who supported the cause of women's suffrage in these terms: 'Unquestionably those pioneer men suffered in popularity for their feminist views. Some of them suffered financially, some politically. Yet they never wavered' (Pankhurst 1914: 12). Kimmel notes that, across the Atlantic, the men who supported the suffrage cause were booed and hissed (Kimmel 1987b). It is likely that Keir Hardie's position within the Labour Party was weakened by his outspoken support for women's rights. Later, he was to describe the reactions in the House of Commons to his speech on force-feeding in these terms: 'Had I not heard it I could not have believed that a body of gentlemen would have found reason for mirth and applause' (Hardie, quoted in Strauss 1982: 207). No doubt such illustrations could be multiplied. However, the last quotation brings out the contrast between the men's deprivations and those faced by women. Men were not subjected to force-feeding on this particular occasion and the attacks and deprivations that most men suffered as a consequence of their support for 'the Cause' were for the most part relatively minor compared with those experienced by the women. After all, men making speeches and campaigning were doing what men were supposed to do. Women who did so were stepping outside their allocated spheres and were subject to stronger sanctions as a consequence. Further, and this is closer to the theme of the book, I can find little evidence that the men who did support 'the Cause' were seen as being in any way defective as men. In most cases, it would seem, their masculinity was not called into question.

This is not to say that some men did not, directly or implicitly, call into question some features of masculinity as it was generally understood. For example, Strauss writes of Israel Zangwill in these words: 'He . . . was convinced that women's involvement in politics would act as a corrective to the "male beast" that was asserting itself through jingoism' (Strauss 1982: 220). Clearly, there is some idea here of a link between masculinity and various forms of oppression in the world, a kind of critique that has become very familiar today. Yet the characterization of the women as a corrective to the beast in man was a reworking of some well-established Victorian themes and, in other guises, served as a justification for keeping women out of politics. In this case, however, the angel in the house became the angel in the House.

Somewhat more complex was the approach of Pethick-Lawrence. He outlined critically some possible motives for men's oppositions to women's suffrage. There was the fear of the uses that women might put their vote to, putting emotion before reason. There was the fear that they might impose stricter standards of morality. They might lose their attractiveness through participating in politics. But finally, a major source of the opposition was an 'innate love of domination' (Pethick-Lawrence 1942: 68). This was clearly a problematic notion, although his critical use of this phrase indicated that he was willing to distance himself from some prevailing features of masculinity. Like Zangwill, he saw the connections between masculinity and power.

From William Thompson who wrote, in 1825, 'be rational human beings, not mere male sexual creatures' (Strauss 1982: 19) to Floyd Dell, there were continuing signs of a wide ranging critique of male practices and institutions. In other words there is some evidence to show that the support for the various feminist causes was prepared to take on board some of these wider critiques of taken-for-granted practices. This was perhaps more marked in the struggles around the Contagious Diseases Acts where, almost inevitably, models of male sexuality were called into question. Nevertheless, these critiques of some patriarchal practices were perfectly consistent with other political themes such as the preference for reason against emotion and, perhaps in some cases, a slight reworking of the theme of chivalry. All in all, these critiques of men and their practices were made from a relatively firm base, one rooted as we have seen in a radical tradition and supported through social networks.

Limitations

I have tried to resist the temptation to turn these men into heroes, a temptation which might be all too easy given the possible chivalric influences that have been suggested. Certainly from the standpoint of today certain limitations of these stances may become apparent. One specific example, already mentioned, is Mill's assumption of the authorship of a text which was certainly heavily influenced, to say the least, by Harriet Taylor. Indeed, other influences such as those of William Thompson, may also have been suppressed (Pateman 1988). This may be seen as a specific instance of a more general trend, that is of the limited extent to which, in some cases, political principles were translated into personal practices. Keir Hardie may have been 'the most sensitive person I have known in my life' (Pethick-Lawrence 1942: 64) but the comparison between his relationship with his own wife and with Sylvia Pankhurst must raise some hard questions.

Another possible limitation which has already been mentioned are the constructions of women which emerged through a consideration of these men's lives and proclamations. There was the tendency, already noted, to see women as being innately more reasonable, certainly more moral than men. As the consideration of the working through the chivalric theme demonstrated, there was a clear understanding of sexual difference. Unlike those who opposed women's entry into political life, however, they saw these differences as providing the very rationale for giving women the vote. Hence it might be argued that the involvement of men in the fight for women's suffrage had something of the idea of man as the protector about it and hence, indirectly, reproduced the very patriarchal beliefs that had kept women out of the public arena in the first place.

Again, Pethick-Lawrence provides the most complex illustration of this general issue. Towards the end of his life he elaborated a near-mystical view which saw all human beings as a 'composite fragment of the Great Life' (Pethick-Lawrence 1942: 204). He saw something of the contradiction in the relationships between men and women: 'The mutual attractiveness of men and women for one another is tinged with fear and even with a degree of hostility' (ibid.: 206). Nevertheless, there was a need to transcend the limitations of sex, class and race. However much we may reduce these differences in the case of sex there will always be a 'residual difference' between men and women in the emotional sphere. Developing an argument which has again become familiar in the light of modern feminisms, men tend to look on life as a kind of adventure in its own right, while women see life as a means to an end, namely the future of the humankind. Women as a result tend to be more 'personal and subjective' but for this very reason their voice should be heard in places hitherto dominated by men (ibid.: 207). Whether or not one regards such a viewpoint as progressive or conservative will very much depend on wider understandings of the nature of sexual difference. Pethick-Lawrence clearly saw such an understanding, which it should be remembered referred to a residual not an all-consuming difference, as basic to his commitment to struggles for equality. Today, we might have some reservations.

Pethick–Lawrence also made one other quite revealing statement: 'The wrongs of a class or sex or race have appealed to me more cogently than the purely personal troubles of a particular John or Mary' (Pethick-Lawrence, quoted in Brittain 1963: 31). To some extent, I think, this should be read as a confession, perhaps of weakness, rather than a central statement of belief. Nevertheless, it does link to recent social psychological discussions which suggest that pro-feminist men are still more prone to support their 'feminism' in terms of abstract principles, rather than in terms of particular experiences (Thomas 1990). It is likely that this general orientation was shared by many, if not all, of the pro-feminist men studied in this chapter. Indeed it was left to the women to supply the emotional input that had, for many of them, been denied to them from childhood, through boarding school and into the public arena. Again, the overall orientation of men in their support of women's rights may have reproduced deeper assumptions about the natures of women and men.

Such a discussion of 'limitations' may well seem out of place. Is this not a classic example of failing to understand the past in its own terms, of imposing present-day concerns on to the conflicts and struggles of the past? While it is clearly important to attempt to understand past situations in the terms by which they were shaped and structured, there are limitations to the extent to which this is possible. Indeed, I cannot help bringing present-day pre-occupations into this analysis. Rather like Wayne Booth's discussion of the racism and sexism that he now finds in books that he once considered to be classics, I want to treat these figures of the past as friends (Booth 1988). In this construction of friendship, I do not wish to be blind to these faults as I see them and feel that friendship demands of me that I should make my awareness of these limitations apparent. This is not in order to diminish them, or to condemn them to some wastebin of the past. In some ways it enhances them, through denying them a mythical heroic status. Moreover, it forces me to think more searchingly about my own practices.

Conclusion: on learning lessons from the past

Clearly, there is much that can be learnt from this brief and incomplete exploration. There are specific issues to be explored such as the influence of marital or other couple relationships on modern men, interested in supporting feminism (Snodgrass 1977 has some examples). Certainly the complexities of the links between public stance and private practices are still highly relevant and perhaps always will be. Similarly, the debates about sexual difference, although now cast in a different mould, still continue to reverberate and to provoke.

I have already noted that it would be a narrow response simply to list the limitations of these, for the most part middle-class or upper-class, supporters of women's rights, and to see them as being of little relevance as a consequence. Another equally unfortunate response, in my opinion, would be to identify with these figures and to yearn nostalgically for a simpler age when women not only accepted the support of men but actively welcomed them. Most men today, especially those men who see themselves as supporters of the feminist cause, have had some experience of rejection by women and have retired, puzzled and hurt. Even where there is some understanding of the reasons for this rejection, intellectually or perhaps even deeper, this does not make the pain of rejection any the less. Why can't men and women stand on the same platform as they did in some of the early meetings in the fight for the vote?

Part of the answer, of course, is that the particular struggle was focused around the franchise. In the judgement of at least some of the women fighting for the vote, the support of men was essential. After all, men were on the inside and by definition were the only ones who could introduce Bills supporting the extension of the franchise. If, however, the issue is to do with, say, pornography or sexual harassment it is less obvious that men are initially necessary in order to bring about change. In some cases, of course, it may be felt that men may actually obstruct the advance of feminist causes, even where that may not actually be intended. Further, there are arguments around the nature of political struggle which emphasize the empowering effect when those most affected by the issue in question mobilize themselves around that issue. In all kinds of ways, therefore, the struggles of today are not the struggles of the past, and a sign of nostalgic regret, although understandable, may not be the best response to these past figures.

If we learn from the past, then, it is not as a result of drawing up a checklist of lessons or through the hagiographic establishment of exemplars or role models. We learn from the past, as we learn from anything, through keeping our critical faculties tuned up and maintaining a sense of flow between our own life and the lives of these men, and women, in the past. We seek to understand them in their context but this construction of that context will be shaped by our own concerns and interests. I came, for example, to like Pethick-Lawrence or at least the Pethick-Lawrence that was available to me through a couple of published sources. I realize, of course, that our positions are not interchangeable and the exploration of why this is so, apart from the more obvious reasons, may help me to understand my own situation towards the end of the twentieth century. I shall have more to say about this in Chapter 8.

Men and methodologies

> More recently, a former professor of mine, having heard of my work on gender and science, asked me to tell him just what it was that I have learned about women. I tried to explain, 'It's not women I am learning about so much as men. Even more, it is science.'
>
> (Keller 1985: 3)

Introduction

In this chapter I want to attempt to do two things. In the first place, I want to explore the extent to which and the ways in which, the whole practice of 'doing sociology' is gendered. This means that I shall be asking questions about the way in which sociology, as it has been historically constituted, has been a masculine discipline. This must recognize that part of this history has included the growth of a feminist critique which is both part of and apart from the sociological discipline. In particular, I am concerned to ask questions about how deep this masculine character of the discipline has gone. It is one thing to say that most of the figures who have populated the textbooks and lists of founding fathers have been men. It is another to say that masculinity has pervaded the actual assumptions, theories and methods deployed by sociologists, today as well as in the past. This is, in part, to return to some of the sociology of knowledge questions raised in Chapter 2. Put somewhat starkly, are the 'two sociologies' like Jessie Bernard's (1973) 'two marriages': 'his' and 'hers'?

In the second part of this chapter, I want to consider the extent to which men in sociology, becoming aware of the feminist critique and of their own involvements in a masculine (in all senses of the word) world can make use of or adopt techniques or approaches which might be regarded as 'feminist' in order to make sense of their own worlds in order, in other words, to 'discover men'. Up to a point, I have been doing this, adopting these approaches, in previous chapters. Hence, this chapter may in part be viewed as a critical examination of some of my own practices revealed in these earlier chapters and the assumptions that lay behind them.

Clearly, there are connections between these two parts. Up to a point, the answers in the second part of the chapter will depend upon the answers given to the first set of questions. Again, to put the matter over-simply, if we were to conclude that there are no significant differences between men's sociology and women's sociology in terms of epistemology or methodology, then we might conclude that there is no particular problem for men sensitive to gender issues working in sociology. They can continue to go about their researches in any way they choose. Alternatively, if there really be two sociologists mapped on to the differences between men and women, then such sociologists might find themselves to be in very real difficulties indeed.

A few moments thought will suggest that life must be more complicated than this stark contrast suggests. Not all work on gender is feminist and not all women working within sociology would be described as, or would describe themselves as feminists. Further, 'feminism' is not a monolithic thing; on the contrary, the term signifies a very wide range of theoretical positions and sociological practices. Very often sociological practices would seem to be as much influenced by national or cultural factors as by gender. Articles, whether written by women or men or both, in say the *American Sociological Review* often have more in common with each other than they might have with articles published in the British journal, *Sociology*. To give another example: in the collection of autobiographical essays, *Sociological Lives* (Riley 1988), there are essays by men and women in the sociological profession. They all adopt an autobiographical format and they all tend, with one or two slight exceptions, to see autobiography in straightforward linear terms, as an account of a career (broken or unbroken) and a movement through various more or less discrete stages. The only difference between the men and the women in this collection is that the latter do tend to take account of gender issues, and how these have or have not affected their own careers, while the men, on the whole, do not.

[161]

Issues of method, methodology and epistemology

Nobody attending one of the annual conferences of the British Sociological Association (or, for that matter, a meeting of one of the study groups attached to the BSA) will be unaware of issues of gender. At least one of the conference 'streams' will deal with issues of gender and gender will be treated as a 'key variable' in many, perhaps, most, of the other sessions. There will be meetings of the Women's Caucus and possibly now, some meetings of a Men's Group. The AGM will include a report on the work of the Equality of the Sexes Committee and all the various committees and subcommittees will be required to bear issues of gender in mind when appointing or nominating members. A large number of books on display at the publishers' exhibition will deal with issues of gender.

It is worth remembering how recent all this is. In Britain the turning point was almost certainly the Annual Conference in 1974 at Aberdeen where the theme was 'Sexual Divisions and Society' (Barker and Allen 1976a, 1976b); for further details see Hearn and Morgan 1990; Maynard 1990). Throughout the 1970s (in particular) there was a far-reaching critique of the intellectual 'sexism' in almost all areas of sociological research and theory. There were accounts of how women had been marginalized or trivialized in a whole range of areas of sociological enquiry. There is still room for improvement, in some areas more than others, but it is worth stressing the importance of the transformations that have taken place.

What came to be realized during this period was that the 'intellectual sexism' (Acker 1973) of many areas of sociological enquiry was not simply a piece of intellectual blindness of a kind that has occurred before and will no doubt occur again. These exclusions and marginalizations had real, concrete, material roots. These are what I called part of the 'social relations' of academic production' (Morgan 1981; Stanley 1990a) and it is worth noting that these have changed less noticeably than the actual content of sociological research. Sociology, with a history and a tradition which is predominantly masculine, exists for the most part within social institutions and organizations – universities, polytechnics, research institutions – which are themselves male dominated and often largely male peopled (Hearn 1987). By the social relations of academic production I mean not simply the gender composition of teaching or research staffs and academic hierarchies, but also differences between lecturers and students, full-time staff and temporary staff, directors of research projects and short-term researchers, staff and secretaries, staff and cleaners and so on. I also refer to even more hidden sets of relationships which are often consequential for academic production: relations with spouses, lovers, children and kin.

I am struck by the extent to which my institution is sexually stratified and the ease with which I forget this fact. I come to work, early this time, since I have an examination to invigilate. Since, for most of the working days during term time, I live alone, I have cooked my own breakfast and perhaps carried out some small domestic tasks before leaving for the university. As I arrive in the Department, I greet the cleaner, a woman. I greet two colleagues, Liz and Pete, I accept a bundle of question papers from the Chief Examiner (male) and go over to the Whitworth Hall. On one half of the room there is a preponderance of men students and I am not too surprised to find that they are sitting a physics paper; on the other side there are mostly women sitting a paper in humanities or possibly even sociology. As I stroll around the examination hall I see the paintings of past Vice-Chancellors (no prizes, here) looking down on the bowed heads of the students. My co-invigilators are three men and one women. After the examination I go to the refectory for an orange juice and tonic water (served by a woman), a hot dish (served by a woman) and a cup of coffee (served by a woman). Men very clearly outnumber women in the Senior Common Room. I go back to the Department to talk to a PhD student and I wonder about her career prospects in sociology. I draft a couple of letters and give them to Joan, the secretary. I talk to some students (men and women, but mostly the latter) about their forthcoming examination and finish this just in time to go over to the Senate meeting. Apart from the Vice-Chancellor's secretary, men sit at the front. (Rather oddly, they sit beneath an oil painting of a woman, exposing a large amount of bosom.) There are one or two women scattered around the assembly but they are easily noticeable, in Kanter's terms clearly 'tokens'. One speaker, indeed, refers to 'sensible people wearing ties' in a speech on the University's response to the Union's boycott of examinations. Various men professors bob up

[163]

towards the end of the meeting to tell us of the appointment of new professors – again all men. Before going home, a quick drink in the staff bar served by a woman.

This is the reality with which I live on a day-to-day basis. Of course, there are contradictions and interesting variations. I will sometimes meet the professor of anthropology, Marilyn Strathern, or catch sight of some other senior members of the university who are women; and I have forgotten to mention that the porters, at a low point in the university hierarchy, are all men. But what is surprising is how readily I forget this or how easily I forget that 30 or more years ago, the picture would have been even more stark.

All I am saying, perhaps, is that the university in which I work is shaped by and is part of the wider patriarchal structure of institutions and culture. This is a reality as much as the changes in sociological practice that I have noted earlier in this section are also realities. It will have its own special or peculiar features, no doubt, but the university cannot escape its location in a wider, sexually stratified (and stratified in other ways as well) society. The question is whether this matters in some deeper sense, other than demanding a struggle for equal opportunities in education and employment and against such matters as sexual harassment or discrimination. Do we need to think more profoundly about the whole business of doing sociology?

Again, the argument would seem to be fairly straightforwardly affirmative. Institutions which have been male dominated and male peopled for generations can hardly be expected to have escaped the influence of this cumulative masculinity. Had the question, say, been one of Catholic or Scottish domination over the centuries, few would have any doubts about the relationship between social composition and intellectual product. That the question is still not only relatively unexplored, but continues to be greeted with scepticism and denial, is a reflection of the extent and the depth to which institutions of scholarly production have been dominated by men, such that their definitions become the overriding reality, the dominant rationality. The whole business of sociology (and all other disciplines as well, no doubt) is, as Dorothy Smith argues: 'based on and built up within the male social universe' (Smith 1987: 86). Further, she argues, there are links between the institutional locations of the practices of sociology and the wider structure of the oppression of women. Sociology does not simply reflect, unconsciously or consciously, these wider practices; it also contributes to their reproduction. It does so through the perpetuation of models of society and of human processes which are in fact based upon the experiences and perceptions of one half of humanity; through the continuing marginalization and trivialization of issues to do with gender and women and through the perpetuation of models of social enquiry which, again, reflect a male version of the world. It is this last point, perhaps, which is the most controversial.

Again, there are some points which are more easy to accept than others. While there may be some scepticism as to whether the distinction between 'hard' and 'soft' models of social enquiry or sciences can be straightforwardly mapped on to distinctions between men and women, it can be readily seen, and one might hope accepted, that the continuing deployment of such terms and contrasts may be part of a male perspective, especially where 'hard' and 'soft' are ordered hierarchically such that the closer to the former, the more scientific the practice (Sherif 1987; see also Gherardi and Turner 1987). A fairly obvious link that Sherif notes is the military support for all kinds of methods of psychological testing. Sociologists have, indeed, every reason to question such distinctions and the assumptions that lie behind them since, very often, the discipline as a whole has been labelled a 'soft' discipline as compared with the more quantitative subjects such as economics or the more tightly professionally organized disciplines such as psychology. Thus, we may question whether it is natural or inevitable for a woman to gravitate towards 'soft', qualitative methodologies while the man adopts 'hard' quantitative methods, while accepting that the evaluative deployment of these labels does emerge in the context of a sexually stratified organization.

Similarly, there is some questioning of the style that I and Jessie Bernard, although separately, referred to as the 'machismo' element in research and routine academic practices (Morgan 1981; Bernard, quoted in Millman and Kanter 1987: 31). I might be a little more hesitant about the use of the term now, partly because I think that it is possible to see some diminution of these practices but partly because the use of the term is probably imprecise and possibly racialist. What I was referring to was a set of practices exemplified by the academic seminar. Here, characteristically, the speaker 'defends' his or her argument or thesis; the listeners are called upon to 'attack' after the presentation. The attacks might be conducted with genuine wit or heavy sarcasm, with sceptical appreciation or withering scorn. Graduate students who might be presenting their field work in such a setting would have had many sleepless nights anticipating the ordeal. Academic gossip might recollect the time when Joe really wiped the floor with Mike, when Ken really got the knife in, tales of past battles, demolitions, academic prize fights. The notion that a seminar or the presentation of a paper might be the occasion for some kind of cooperative intellectual undertaking seemed to be somewhat muted. For many, indeed, there could be no other way; the cut and thrust of debate was all, the institutional embodiment of a Popperian process of questioning and falsification.

These practices and assumptions (which were also reflected in some degree in the conduct of tutorials, in the refereeing of papers for academic journals and the conduct of routine business in committees) are still with us, although there has been a growing realization that there might be other ways of doing things. In part, a large part, this growing realization is a consequence of the impact of women and feminism upon the discipline, and from some determined efforts to transform democratic ideals into daily institutional practices. This is not to argue that women are 'naturally' nicer or more gentle than men or to overstate the amount of change that has taken place. Perhaps more to the point is the argument that feminism was a large element in a process of wider institutional questioning that perhaps began with the student revolts of the late 1960s.

It may, therefore, be accepted in some measure that certain routine practices and assumptions within the discipline were shaped by the male dominance of the subject that these are beginning to be questioned and, at least, modified. It may also be accepted that issues of women for a long time were ignored or marginalized within the subject, that this again was a product of the male domination of the subject, and that the rectification of this particular set of anomalies was a long time coming and is still incomplete. But at least gender is routinely on the agenda in many conferences, syllabuses, publishers' lists and journal articles.

However, it will be argued, we still use textbooks which start with the Holy Trinity of Marx, Weber and Durkheim, with possibly side references to Comte, Spencer and Simmel. And there are still widespread assumptions about the greater reliability and validity of quantitative research or that qualitative research's main function is as a kind of adjunct to the real business of research with figures and calculation. There are also widespread assumptions that theory occupies a privileged position within the discipline and that theory at the most elevated levels is gender blind or gender free. Theory also tends, in this understanding, to be something that is largely carried out by chaps. It is at this point that feminist writers encourage us to look at some of the deeper more abiding assumptions of the discipline. They may recognize the advances made in terms of the appointment of women or the introduction of a course on the sociology of women or gender but feel that some of the deeper assumptions have been left untouched.

The problem may be reformulated in the following terms. The traditional mode of social enquiry (and not simply sociological enquiry) was to seek to make universalistic statements that either just related to men or referred to both women and men but ignored the differences between them. The idea of citizenship and the social contract (Pateman 1988) is an example of the former; understandings of marriage as a 'relationship' is an example of the latter (Lewis *et al.* 1991). One simple response, certainly with sociology, to the recognition of this blindspot is to include women, where they had hitherto been excluded or obscured. To a large extent, such an approach leaves existing structures and methodologies untouched. The more complex approach is to argue that the traditional models in fact represented fundamentally masculine ways of viewing the world and the production of knowledge about that world, and that these masculine approaches to the production of knowledge became deeply institutionalized within Western society and perhaps wider. So deeply institutionalized, in fact, that they became the taken-for-granted model for the generation of knowledge about the world and human understanding. Further, any attempt to challenge these assumptions is to run the risk of excommunication from the scientific community as one lacking the necessary seriousness and commitment.

A major feature of a scientific outlook, it might be supposed, is objectivity. To be objective, is, as far as possible, to attempt to see things as they are not as we wish them to be, not through the distorting spectacles of our own presuppositions or existing and unexamined philosophies. The opposite would seem to be one of subjectivity or, more bluntly, bias. Yet we find Keller writing: 'Along with autonomy the very act of separating subject from object – objectivity itself – comes to be associated with masculinity' (Keller 1982: 119). In one sense, this statement may be less radical than it first appears. It is not arguing that objectivity is necessarily and always masculine. Keller is pointing to a process, which can be seen in terms of the whole history of Western science, whereby objectivity and the idea of autonomy have come to be associated with masculinity. This is something more than an accident but less than an inevitability. Nevertheless, it does seem to be suggesting that the scientific stance, with its claim to universality, is in fact profoundly shaped by gender.

An associated term is detachment. As Kanter writes, 'sociology is the quintessential discipline of detachment' (Kanter 1988: 71). Do not all the methodology textbooks celebrate the value of detachment, whether it be in terms of the participant observer blending into the field, the interviewer abstaining from asking leading questions or responding to personal questions or the careful drawing up of an interview schedule? The frequently used term 'the research instrument' encapsulates this theme of detachment. Yet, again, we find this apparently key element in any form of sociological enquiry, qualitative as well as quantitative, being called into question: 'Here, 'masculine' described not a biological category but a cognitive style, an epistemological stance. Its key term is *detachment*: from the emotional life, from the particularities of time and place, from personal quirks, prejudices, and interests, and most centrally, from the object itself' (Bordo 1986: italics in original). Interestingly, many people could quote the second sentence of this quotation and read or hear it in a tone of approval. The reference to 'masculinity' in the first sentence, however, calls it into question. If detachment is identified with masculinity, it again loses its claims to universality. The desire to eliminate sources of bias may simply be another form of, gender-based, bias.

Yet again, another feature of social scientific enquiry would seem to be abstraction. To be sure the sociology capacity for abstraction has often lent itself to parody; my neighbour's party becomes a 'loosely structured interaction situation'. Nevertheless, such parodies are often taken as illustrations of how poorly the media or lay persons understand sociological enquiry. Without abstraction, it may be argued, there is no generalization, and without generalization there is no social science. What we have may be gossip, journalism, various forms of fiction but not any form of disciplined enquiry. Even an invitation to produce an autobiography, may lead to abstraction: 'to ask a sociologist to talk about herself would inevitably lead her to want, instead, to describe a group or class or a social pattern – but not delve at all into personal matters or purely individual events' (Kanter 1988: 71). This, too, has been the subject of critical scrutiny. Dorothy Smith, for example, finds even the writings of two feminists (Hilary Graham and Ann Oakley) influenced by patriarchal styles of presenting sociological research when they write of conflicts 'between medical and maternal frames of reference' rather than 'directly between doctors and patients' (Smith 1989: 54–5).

There are several other features of patriarchal or masculinist thought which have been identified by feminist writers. A thread running throughout malestream sociology, as it runs through malestream science as a whole, is domination. Concepts, models, systems and theories are elaborated to give order to social life, to introduce an element of predictability. In some cases, predictability and control may be the stated aim of a fully-fledged or mature social science. In other cases, the control and domination is more metaphorical. Explorations of 'false consciousness' or 'latent social functions', for examples, may seek to find the reality beneath the ideological smokescreens and rationalizations established by individuals as they go about their daily lives.

Another theme which has sometimes been identified is the tendency to think and write in terms of dichotomies. These may include subjective/objective, feelings/understandings, involved/detached and so on. Even the dilemma, which is often raised in response to feminist critiques, between relativism and realism might itself be a further example of a masculinist version of seeing the world. The tendency to write or speak in terms of dichotomies may itself be part of a wish to dominate, to give order to a world which is much more untidy and a more critical, including feminist, social science should aim to transcend these dichotomies.

In order to explore this feminist epistemological critique, let me take a particular example. Skocpol, writing of sociologists studying gender argues: 'They are producing excellent scholarship on matters that will not be subsumed by the newly fashionable economistic 'rational choice' theories favoured by many male academics' (Skocpol 1988: 157). It is not just an accident that some, although clearly not all, male sociologists might be attracted to some version of 'rational choice' theory. It is objective, detached and abstract. It seeks to give order to a wide range of social phenomena. Like many other similar models or approaches – games, theories, exchange theories and so on – it suggests a tough-minded and individualistic model of both the human subject and of the process of sociological enquiry itself. The fact that rational choice models may well be open to statistical manipulations of some considerable sophistication is itself an added attraction.

Skocpol is clearly not saying that all men in sociology have been seduced by rational choice models or that women in sociology are incapable of working within this particular paradigm. It is important to stress this because one of the accusations sometimes levelled against writers on feminist epistemology is that of 'essentialism'. In other words, particular ways of thinking or living in the world are firmly anchored to biological men or women. Griffiths, a feminist philosopher who is critical of essentialism discusses a set of beliefs which link gender, emotionality and bodies: 'In short, women are "in touch with", "in harmony with", "close to" or "part of" natural things; men are in control of them' (Griffiths 1988: 132). She is critical of these perspectives just as she is critical of some dominant models of doing philosophy; 'philosophers continue to contribute to the commonly held belief in the value of hard heads in control of tough bodies' (ibid.: 142). She herself is arguing for an interdependence, an interplay, between feeling and understanding in philosophical enquiry and the same, no doubt, could be extended to sociological enquiry.

The notion of two fundamentally different ways of viewing the world, based upon a contrast between an ethic of justice and an ethic of care, has been identified with the writings of Gilligan (1982). It is important to note, however, that she stresses that 'the different voice I describe is characterized not by gender but theme' (ibid.: 17). The association of this different voice (which she elaborated in the context of a critical examination of masculine models of children's moral development) with women is 'an empirical observation' not absolute or inevitable. Since Gilligan's discussion can be related to feminist discussions of methodology and epistemology it is important to have this warning against too essentialist a reading. If a feminist sociology is more ready to allow for an interplay between subject and object, and to transcend dichotomies such as those between feeling and understanding, this is not something which arises inevitably out of being biologically female.

But, if these differences are not biologically anchored, where do they come from? To answer this question is to return to some familiar themes in the sociology of science and, more generally, historical sociology. Bordo, whom I quoted earlier, focuses on the thought of Descartes and what she sees as a prevailing 'gyno-phobia' that was prevalent in seventeenth-century Europe, most manifest of course in the persecution of witches (Bordo 1986). Something similar is argued in Easlea's *Science and Sexual Oppression* (1981). More recently, Seidler has seen the problem in the development of the ideas of reason and rationality. Thus he writes: 'This makes masculinity as power invisible, for the rule of men is simply taken as an expression of reason and "normality"' (Seidler 1989: 4). To some extent, we are returning to some of the themes that I raised in Chapter 3 when re-analysing Weber's work on Protestantism and capitalism. It will be remembered that 'rationality' is a key word in Weber's sociology and that it can be argued than an unspoken feature of this analysis is the identifica-tion of Protestantism, capitalist rationality and scientific enquiry. Thus the masculinity of science, including social science, has a material and cultural base, not a biological one.

It should not be imagined that there is any kind of monolithic consensus amongst feminists around these questions of epis-temology. Grimshaw, for example, accepts that there are impor-tant ways in which it can be said that philosophy is gendered but finds problems with talk of the 'maleness' of philosophy (and presumably social science as well) and the related ideals of mascu-linity and femininity. She argues that although gender is a major basis for identification it is never the only one; a person is never *just* a male or female (Grimshaw 1986). It is clear that these kinds of debates are going to go on for some time and this is not the place to provide an overall assessment of them. (For a useful guide and bibliography see Stanley and Wise 1990.) The purpose of this section was to show that the idea of sociology as a masculine undertaking was not simply a question of the gender of its prac-titioners. It was as much a question of the deep assumptions concerning the very nature of sociological enquiry.

In an earlier attempt at investigating these problems, I made a tentative distinction between two kinds of 'rationality'.

'Sociological rationality' I saw as being to do with, in the most general sense, the conduct of sociological enquiry and without which that very enquiry would be impossible. At its very simplest, sociological rationality is to do with an openness of mind, a capacity to be surprised and everything that is implied in the words 'discipline' or 'critical investigation'. This kind of rationality, I argued, inevitably merged with and was distorted by the particular masculine cultures of universities and other places where sociology is conducted. Here the rationality becomes a kind of rhetoric, a dominant ideology, a means of social control (Morgan 1981). I felt that we should attempt to encourage the former while undermining the latter; indeed the two processes should go hand in hand.

Now, I should be critical of this distinction if only because my treatment of the culture of rationality was too shallow in historical terms. I did not consider the deeper historical roots of the very idea of rationality and my suggestion seemed to be that the first form of rationality was some timeless, universal and ahistorical set of guide lines. This is clearly not the case and I should now accept that values of objectivity and detachment are themselves historically shaped and, to that extent, gendered.

However, I should want to preserve something of the idea of 'sociological rationality', if only to remind myself that any form of disciplined enquiry is, and must be, hard work. I would wish to argue that ideas such as 'detachment', 'objectivity' and 'abstraction' (and certainly 'critical enquiry') are not themselves to be condemned out of hand. I should like to think of the feminist critique as going some way to fulfilling, rather than rejecting, the promise of sociological enquiry. After all, the neglect of, say, women in stratification studies or their marginalization in studies of work and employment is not simply a question of ethics or social justice. Sociology that ignores the question of gender is, simply, bad sociology. And similarly, and more profoundly, a sociology that does not continually examine critically its own processes by which what counts as sociological knowledge is being produced is untrue to the critical strands within the sociological tradition.

I should note, further, that feminists have not been alone in emphasizing these critical features of sociological enquiry. Many of their concerns about the dangers of reification and the artificial distinctions between subject and object are to be found in the

Frankfurt School's debates with positivism, in Sartre's methodological writings and in Gouldner's pleas for a 'reflexive sociology'. What is distinctive about the feminist critique is the
combination of many of the strands from this critical tradition,
with a recognition of the central importance of gender, seeing this
not as a category but as a relationship of power. Gender, then, is
not simply another topic but a central division running through
every feature of sociological enquiry.

Recognizing this, what follows in terms of actual sociological
enquiry? Here, perhaps we need to think about the distinctions
between epistemology, methodology and methods (Harding
1987). Up to now we have been largely concerned with issues of
epistemology, the grounds of knowledge about the social world
and how these are shaped by gender. Methodology concerns the
actual logic of social enquiry within particular paradigms (positivism, interactionism and so on) while methods concerns what
social investigators actually do. Here too, there are many debates
about whether distinctive feminist *methods* can be read off from
feminist epistemologies and whether, in principle, men might
take part in, or use, these methods as well as women. Again, I do
not want to get into the details of this debate but to concentrate
on the latter set of issues, ones which have been largely unexplored.

I think that it is possible to list some of the characteristics of
feminist methods although this is bound to be both incomplete
and contestable. Some of the main features would seem to be:

(a) Negatively, a scepticism about any claims which see the
    survey or the structured questionnaire as the central 'research
    instrument' of sociological enquiry. This is not, I understand,
    to argue that feminists cannot use these methods; simply that
    they cannot be elevated to a yardstick by which all other
    methods are judged and that, where they are used, their use
    should be tempered by some of the following considerations.
(b) A recognition of the interplay between researcher and
    researched and the placing of this recognition at the centre of
    the sociological enquiry rather than its relegation to a
    methodological appendix.
(c) A recognition of the importance of experience, both the
    experiences of the researched and of the researcher, again
    considering the interplay between these two. In many cases

[173]

this implies a recognition of the fluidity of the boundaries of the 'field' both in terms of time and space.

(d) A recognition of the political and ethical implications of social inquiry. For the most part the emphasis will be upon sexual politics but that need not exhaust the possibilities.

(e) A recognition of the diversity, partiality and necessary incompleteness of any single mode of sociological enquiry.

(f) As a consequence of this, a recognition of the centrality of an understanding of sociology as a cooperative enterprise, between researcher and researched and between different researchers.

Doubtless this list could be extended. What I want to focus on is the idea of the recognition of a plurality of research approaches, one which includes a willingness to explore new or possibly even stigmatized methods of social enquiry. It is this recognition of diversity and pluralism which some have seen as providing links between a feminist sociology and a post-modern sociology (Stanley 1990a; Stanley and Wise 1990). Thus Cook and Fonow, after producing a list not all that dissimilar from the one above, point to the importance of innovative techniques, including visual techniques, triangulation, linguistic analysis, textual analysis, refined quantitative approaches, collaborative strategies and the use of the situation at hand (Cook and Fonow 1986). A collection on *Feminist Experience in Feminist Research* includes papers on interview relationships, individual responses to sexual violence, accounts of the experience of reading for a PhD, the use of the 'Q Sort' technique in studying lesbianism and reading as a technique (Butler 1984). Stanley's volume on *Feminist Praxis* (1990d) includes a similar wide and unexpected range of topics: accounts of beginning and ending sociological projects, critical examination of the use of statistics, uses of biography and autobiography and a variety of modes of analysing experience including mastectomy, life in a Chinese restaurant, the use of drama by a school teacher in order to get at gender, and the processes of becoming a feminist social worker. One particular emphasis here and elsewhere is upon one of the most basic modes of social enquiry of all, namely reading. This may be reading texts such as biography, or autobiography, or reading and rereading field notes or in reading a photograph or set of photographs. Clearly this emphasis has been of particular importance in my own thinking and will already have been found at various parts of this present book. Similar things might be said about the use of biography and autobiography.

Methods and masculinities

I have suggested that, while there may still be some considerable dispute as to what might constitute feminist methods or whether the term has any validity at all, one broad way of characterizing feminist methods would be in terms of the three words, experiential, eclectic and reflexive. In other words, feminist methods as understood in at least some quarters would focus on the category of 'experience', deploying a variety of methods, orthodox and less orthodox, to this end and always with some reflection on the process whereby such knowledge and understanding is generated. Here I want to focus on how these orientations might affect men engaged in an exploration of masculinities. I shall do this by working through a range of possible methods. I shall conclude with some general observations about the potentialities and limitations for men seeking to make use of these methods.

My first two illustrations deal with the area of biography and autobiography. In some ways this reflects an interest in these issues that has developed among some of my friends and colleagues at Manchester, especially Liz Stanley (Stanley 1990c; 1990d; Morgan 1990a). At this point it is important to spell out differences between two modes of doing autobiography, differences which could (with all the qualifications already discussed) be mapped on to the differences between men and women or at least on to the difference between non-feminists and feminists. Todd, for example, refers to: 'the more male genre of autobiography which sums up a public life, weighing character and temperament ponderously and balancing attributes to make an admirable composite' (Todd 1989: 57). Hence this is not simply a question of women being more likely to mention gender than men, a tendency which we find in the volume edited by Riley (Riley 1988). It is as much a matter of approach, style and form as it is of content. Tentatively we can begin to draw up an ideal typical picture of this feminist auto/biography. It would include a recognition of the interaction between writer and subject. This might seem obvious in the case of an autobiography, perhaps less so in the case of a biography. However, in the case of the former this will entail considering the writer as writer as well as subject; in the case of the latter it will entail a consideration of the interplays between the lives and feelings of writer and subject. This leads to a dissolution or at least a weakening of the dividing line between biography and autobiography.

Related to this is the deployment of the distinction between topic and resource. Put another way this is to do with a critical examination of the process of writing and the process of (self) discovery involved in doing auto/biography. There should be a recognition of different or particular genres in doing biography, genres which may well, as we have seen, be gendered. Thus, the conventional model of a life, usually a public life, that begins with family background and birth and goes on through school, university, early employment, marriage and so on to death or retirement. This should be seen as a particular and pervasive genre. It is particularly pervasive since it parallels conventional understandings of the socio-biological life-cycle and hence has a naturalist quality to it. But it is not the only way of telling a tale although it may be one which is particularly appropriate for public figures.

Many conventional biographies often resemble other monuments to public figures, such as statues or paintings. Here the audience is conventionally called upon to comment upon the likeness or otherwise between the portrait and the subject, between signifier and signified. The aim in a good biography or autobiography is seen as accuracy and likeness both in terms of external details and inner character. In contrast, the more feminist approach to such practices might begin with the emphasis that there are many versions of a person's life. While some of these may be more truthful or accurate than others, they all have a particular truth and importance and the job of the biographer is to allow for as many voices as possible. At the very least there should be the recognition of the partiality of any one account.

Finally, feminist biography may desire to move away from the conventional linear model as described above. This may mean allowing for the play between past and present as it allows for the play between writer and subject. It may mean the concentration of fragments of a life rather than seeking to encompass a 'whole': a photograph, a letter, or a particular memory.

[176]

I said at the beginning that this was an ideal typification of feminist auto/biography. It may also be an idealization of such practices. As Stanley points out, there are plenty of lives of women (including lives of feminist women written by feminist women) which follow the more or less orthodox model. Moreover, it is possible to find lives written by men which have this more experimental quality, Arthur Miller's aptly named *Timebends* for example (Miller 1987). But this is perhaps the point. The aim is not, it would seem, to set up a new orthodoxy to which all right-on feminists and others should adhere; it is simply to stress that the conventional linear model is not the only way of doing auto/biography.

Example 1: The life of A. J. A. Symons

With these general points in mind, I turn to my first example, a life of A. J. A. Symons, written by Julian Symons his younger brother (Symons [1950] 1986). I picked up this volume at a sale of Oxford paperbacks at Lancaster University bookshop. Why this volume? I was looking for some holiday reading and I had vaguely heard of A. J. A. Symons. I was familiar with the author as someone who had written an interesting study of crime fiction. I now realize (at the time of first writing this) that this is a book by a man about a man. To what extent and in what ways can it tell me anything about men and masculinity?

In reading the book there is much that amuses me – especially the description of the somewhat eccentric weekends at Finchingfield – and sometimes things that appal me. There are also one or two puzzles that need further exploration. I am appalled by passages such as the following:

> He did not, I think, greatly enjoy the company of most women, for he demanded in his companions a kind of intelligence which few women possess, and a seriousness which many women positively dislike. He had a great appreciation of humour, but no liking for the inconsequent frivolity which, for those who enjoy the company of women, is one of their chief charms.
>
> (ibid.: 54)

It is clear that this is not simply a portrait of the subject; nor is it simply a display of male prejudices. It is a kind of interaction

[177]

between subject and author, a collaboration (perhaps closer since we are dealing with siblings) which produces this particular construction. We may note the authoritative tone with which Symons writes: 'few women possess', 'many women positively dislike', 'one of their chief charms'. Not note, 'in my opinion' or 'in my experience'.

It is this context that I consider another sentence in the book: 'For some years their life together had been untouched by any serious infidelity on his part' (ibid.: 214). This sounds a bit like conventional 'chaps' talk'. A little bit of infidelity may be OK, but don't overdo it. Unfair, perhaps, on the author? Well, certainly no more unfair than Symons's treatment of Gladys, his brother's wife. Certainly, he recognizes that A. J. A. must have been a little difficult to live with, given his clear preference for male company, his obsessions with collecting things, his propensity to spend household money and his taking Gladys away from her circle of friends into the Essex village of Finchingfield. But it is very difficult to get any sense of Gladys the person at all. She appears briefly on one page, is married on the next and then more or less disappears until the divorce.

Clearly any feminist or feminist-influenced reading of this biography must be sensitive to issues such as these, not simply because they may be read as examples of sexism and not so much in a spirit of righteous indignation, but more as seeing these illustrations as clues to the interplay between writer and subject and serving as a reminder of other versions and other stories that are suppressed in this particular text but which remain to be told. It may, as it did in my case, heighten my reading of this book as a text about men and masculinity. We read of A. J. A.'s early obsession with war games and his lifelong passion for forming clubs (The First Edition Club, The Wine and Food Society and so on). In his biographical writings he was obviously fascinated by a kind of male heroism, the 'man of action', in his case the explorer Stanley. Yet, at the same time, there was an overwhelming sense of the dandy about Symons: in terms of his style of dress and his close attention to such matters; his interest in style and performance and wit and paradox. (His support of the writings of Poe might be one example.) This is not to say that dandyism is necessarily opposed to masculinity; indeed, it may alert us to one particular way of 'doing masculinity' (Schwenger 1984: 128–9).

Somewhat muted in this biography are themes of homosexuality. Homosociability is there, certainly, but there was also
his interest in Oscar Wilde and Baron Corvo (the subject of his
best-known book) and the inclusion in his circle of men like Tom
Driberg. Again the absence is interesting and revealing and not
necessarily all to the author's discredit. Symons's reticence here
may be a question of family loyalty or personal taste or both but
it serves, possibly, as a reminder, that the desire to find out
whether 'x' was 'really' a homosexual or whether he had latent or
suppressed homosexual tendencies is to fall too easily into a
discourse which elevates certain models of sexuality over others
and which has a model of truth which involves the accurate
pinpointings of a subject's sexual activities.

By a curious coincidence, A. J. A. Symons's best-known work,
The Quest for Corvo, is subtitled 'An Experiment in Biography'.
(Symons [1934] 1966). His brother, writing in a preface states
that: 'It blows the gaff on biography, as it were, by refusing for a
moment to make the customary pretence of detachment' (Julian
Symons in Symons [1934] 1966: 10). Apart from serving as a
reminder that there is nothing inherently or essentially feminist or
feminine about writing experimental biography, this realization
does throw up a bewildering set of complexities, rather like a
corridor of mirrors. (It is worth noting that Julian's life of his
brother does not follow a strict linear pattern either.) Here I am,
a man interested in the process of discovering something about
men and masculinities reading a life of a man who wrote the life
of another man. Just as writing the life of another man is, in some
measure (recognized or not) writing one's own life, so too is the
reading of another life the reconstruction of the life of the reader.
A chance encounter in a bookshop may lead in some unexpected
directions.

Example 2: my own life
For the next illustration, I take a fragment of my own life. During
my early adolescence, I came to dread one part of the Harvest
Festival at my local Methodist Church. Probably, almost certainly
in fact, this only occurred on a couple of occasions, although they
inevitably seem more frequent in retrospect. The moment of
dread occurred during the singing of the Manx fisherman's hymn,
'Hear Us, O Lord, in Heaven Thy Dwelling Place'. The singing

[179]

of this hymn was a recognition of the harvest of the sea alongside the more conventionally understood harvest of fruit and vegetables, perhaps a necessary reminder in Pinner where the nearest most members of the congregation got to fishing was a trip to the local Mac Fisheries.

This hymn includes the following stanza:

> Our wives and children we commend to Thee:
> For them we plough the land and plough the deep
> For them by day the golden corn we reap
> By night the silver harvest of the sea.

Conventionally, the minister would ask the men in the congregation to sing this stanza. The women, on the other hand, were requested to sing the following stanza:

> We thank Thee, Lord, for sunshine, dew and rain,
> Broadcast from Heaven by Thine almighty hand –
> Source of all life, unnumbered as the sand –
> Bird, beast and fish, herb, fruit and golden grain.

A mild sense of panic swelled up in me as these stanzas approached. Was I, with voice barely broken and certainly without wife and children, to join in with the men? Or should I sing with the women? The male voices surged above and around me like the seas that were described in the hymn, strong and confident. I knew I wanted to be part of them.

What then does this brief fragment of autobiography tell me/us about the construction of masculinities? One obvious factor, something perhaps lacking in many recent discussions, is the role of religion. Here, of course, I am not so much talking about any formal doctrines but the totality of religious practices, formal and informal. I am talking about what it means to belong to some kind of religious community. It may be suggested that, in modern British society, religion has a somewhat ambiguous relationship with the masculinities. It is true that our religious, Christian or otherwise, leaders are predominantly male and the symbolism in most of the religious traditions is heavily slanted in a masculine direction. Methodism, indeed, may be more masculine than some traditions, lacking (indeed deliberately eschewing) the imagery of the Virgin Mary or the goddesses of some Hindu traditions. John

Wesley, the founder, is presented as a kind of folk hero, riding enormous distances the length and breadth of the country and preaching to large, sometimes hostile, crowds. Chivalric imagery enters into some of the hymns introduced from the nineteenth century onwards.

Yet, at the same time, there is something feminine in the construction of Methodism in modern society. Women predominate in many congregations. Some of the older traditions of Methodism, stressing teetotalism and turning the other cheek, seem to stand at odds with dominant views of masculinity. I felt something of the tension, going to church or Sunday School while other lads were out playing. Yet even this rejection of certain popular ideas of masculinity could have something of the heroic about them:

> Dare to be a Daniel
> Dare to stand alone
> Dare to pass a public house
> And bring your money home.

The point is, of course, that religion does not have a straightforward relationship with any single or dominant model of masculinity. Modern-day Anglicanism, for example, can be seen as a struggle or tension between a variety of versions of masculinities as they debate whether women should be ordained or whether practising gays can remain ministers in the Church. High Church and Evangelical differences often trade, at least stereotypically, on contrasting models of masculinity. Muscular Christianity is by no means dead, and for many a boy, 'gentle Jesus, meek and mild' must have seemed less attractive by far than Christ driving the money-lenders out of the temple.

In this particular cases, religion per se was probably incidental to a much more important factor. The theme here was of a sense, heightened by the sound of male voices singing in unison, of a community of men (perhaps called 'the elders' in other traditions) and a strong sense of wanting to belong to this body. Here, effortlessly, it would seem, there was an identification between the quasi-group of men singing in church and an imagined collectivity of men with wives and children, men as protectors, willing to make sacrifices. I link this, in my memory, with other senses of exclusion and wanting to belong: the asthmatic child wanting to

[181]

join the football team, the young National Serviceman both attracted and repelled by the camaraderie of the billet (Morgan 1987).

Some readers will no doubt find this piece anecdotal or, worse still, self-indulgent. Clearly, I am not saying that there is anything special or unusual about these experiences. Indeed, one of the central features of feminist approaches to biography is the recognition of the importance of getting away from the lives of exceptional men or women, people on the centre of the public stage. Nor am I saying that my experiences can be used to prove any general point such as 'religion is crucial in the construction of masculinities' or 'masculine identity is established through generating a desire to belong'. These may or may not be 'true' in some general sense; they are certainly worth investigating. What I am saying is that any one life, mine as much as that of anyone else, does alert us to possibilities and potentialities. But more important, is to reflect on how these memories were generated, on the complex interplays between past and present that are signalled by even the most straightforward and 'innocent' of recollections. Stories continue to be the main way in which individuals make sense of their daily lives and in telling this particular tale I am inviting you to respond with your stories, with both of us attending to the circumstances of their production. (See also Jackson 1990.)

Example 3: a photograph of Marilyn Monroe

My third illustration will be more brief. Much of what I have said about auto/biography has been said about photography, by Denise Farran in a paper dealing explicitly with a photograph of Marilyn Monroe:

> Photographs do not simply 'display' facts, but rather readers bringing their social knowledge, their ways of seeing, to 'recognize' these. Further, readers will do this in different ways depending on their particular biography and context of reading.
>
> (Farran 1990: 266–7)

She recognizes that one way of viewing the selected photograph is as a 'sexual' photograph, a picture of someone publicized during her life as a 'sex symbol' and adopting here a 'sexually provocative' pose. Feminist critiques have explored the processes of production and consumption of such images, looking at the processes of sexual objectification whereby a woman is presented by (almost certainly) male photographers for consumption by the 'male gaze'. Farran, while not disagreeing with such a critique, wants to take the argument a little further, recognizing the multiplicities of possible readings of this one photograph and how these might be related to features in the reader's own biographies and what they bring to the photograph in terms of knowledge and understandings about the life of the subject of the picture.

There is, however, the presupposition that some heterosexual men will see this picture in sexual terms. If, as is the case, I do not read the photograph in straightforwardly sexual terms or as sexually provocative, what can I learn from this different reading? In the first place, of course, it reinforces the point that Farran is making. I do not find the picture provocative because of what I know about Marilyn Monroe's unhappy life, because of what I have read about the processes of the production of 'sex objects', because of the influence of feminism and feminists and so on. It may be that this particular picture does not 'work' for me or that it is not particularly well reproduced. For example, I have to take the author's word for it that her dress is unzipped at the back; this is not apparent in the picture as it is reproduced.

It may also be the case that I was never particularly 'turned on' by Marilyn Monroe. I enjoyed many of her films, certainly, especially *Some Like It Hot*. But I never, as far as I can remember, found them the slightest bit sexually arousing. Rather like Sue Wise's account of her relationship with Elvis Presley, I found it easier to imagine her, if I imagined her at all, as a friend than as a lover (Wise 1990). Perhaps part of the reason was the contrast between the way in which she was marketed and the image that, for me at least, actually came across. I knew how I was *supposed* to respond, with all the slightly coy this-is-what-real-men-like references to measurements and wiggles. When *Bus Stop* was shown at the RAF cinema there were lecherous references to 'Bust Stop' before the showing but general expressions of puzzlement and perhaps disappointment afterwards. Similarly, the authors of *Coal Is Our Life* describe, briefly, the complexities of the reactions of miners and the women in the community to a showing of *Niagara* at the local cinema. Here, there were at least three different versions of Monroe:

[183]

(a) The version that the men produced collectively. This was closest to the media version, as something sexually provocative and arousing. Individual men more or less had to conform to this version while in the group to avoid any suggestion of less than complete masculinity.

(b) The women's version of the men's version. This was the same as the men's collective versions except that it was cast in a somewhat critical light. The men fancy themselves but wouldn't know what to do with Marilyn Monroe should she turn up in their beds.

(c) Private versions of men and women, expressed after the film, presumably in the presence of researchers. These were much more heterogeneous but included expressions of disgust or near boredom. (Dennis *et al.* 1956.)

Thus not only are there different versions of Marilyn Monroe, but different versions for different occasions and in front of different audiences.

Since Denise Farran's analysis of a single photograph was originally published, Graham McCann's book length study of Marilyn Monroe has been produced (McCann 1988). This too recognizes the multiplicity of versions that exist of Marilyn Monroe and there are some detailed accounts of how some of these are constructed. Interestingly he raises the question of how he as a man might be entering into deep waters by conducting a study of such a prominent female icon. He is aware, to some extent, of the interplays between his interests as a sociologist and biographer and his own gender identity although he does not, perhaps, fully recognize that his desire to 'take Marilyn Monroe seriously' has some affinities with a chivalric model of a male hero rescuing a woman from her various captors. What McCann's study as well as Farran's analysis of a single photograph show, is that there is considerable scope for detailed analysis of the range of responses to popular icons, male and female. Now what do I really think about Clint Eastwood?

Conclusion

I hope that I have demonstrated that some methods, which have been identified as 'feminist', can be used by men in order to explore their own masculinities and issues of men and masculinity at a more general level. Indeed, this kind of analysis demands a constant and free, but reflexive, flow between the particular and the general. Here I follow Liz Stanley and suggest the reader use these accounts as experienced cooks use cook-books. Use them as you wish and modify them how you like and if you do not find them helpful, throw them away and try something else (Stanley 1990c: 13). The last thing that is intended is that anyone should slavishly set out to follow my or any other example.

Nevertheless, cooks have genders and men should not think that they can simply put on the apron, take up the wooden spoon and continue where women have left off. For one thing, to continue the metaphor, the cooking takes place in a world dominated by male chefs. Further, when men enter the kitchen there is often a subtle change of tone. 'If you don't like the heat, stay out of the kitchen' runs one masculinist proverb.

In more different terms, men may adopt 'feminist' methods but they do so in a context which is still patriarchal in many, if not all, of its aspects. Thus, as I have argued earlier (in Chapter 2) there is not, and cannot be, a simple parallel between women studying women (and men) and men studying men (and women). For one thing, given the continuing inequalities of power, then men's accounts with all the best will in the world may become either confessions or alibis. In both cases, the response may have the consequence of obscuring the continuing and real sources of gender inequality and power. Even if this be not the case, there is always the danger that men may become all too successful at deploying feminist methods, that they may attract research funding, set up centres, organize journals and the like.

I shall return to some of these issues in the concluding chapter. For the time being I should stress that, as a countervailing strategy, men (and the women with whom they work) should always remember the collective and shared nature of their undertaking. There must always be channels whereby these explorations are shared and criticized, not in the gladiatorial way des-

[185]

cribed earlier, but as part of a continuous exchange of ideas and experiences. The production of knowledge, even autobiographical knowledge, is never an individual enterprise and a recognition of this fact may help prevent some of the gender issues from being submerged or mystified. Similarly, and for the same reason, the developing of new ways of exploring men and masculinity cannot take place apart from a continuing critique of the institution within which the gendered knowledge is produced.

CHAPTER 9

Studying men in a patriarchal society

Introduction

Very simply, it can be said that this book has dealt with two sets of divisions. In the first place, there are divisions between men and women. In the second place, there are divisions between feminists and non-feminists. There are clearly problems with the second set of divisions for it may be reasonably argued that the world is not straightforwardly divided up into feminists and non-feminists; the often-noted 'I'm not a feminist but . . .' phenomenon is but one indication of this difficulty. Further, there are problems about the linkages between these two divisions. While today many men and most women will argue that men cannot be feminists, this was not always the case. And while all or most feminists are women, not all women are feminists. Finally, the division between men and women is not all that straightforward, either.

Nevertheless, despite all this actual or potential confusion, one thing is clear: without feminist thought and practice, the problems that this book addresses would never have been raised. I outlined this process of the impact of feminism on men within sociology (and elsewhere) in Chapter 1 and attempted to outline why the feminist critique presented difficulties for men seeking to study men and masculinity in Chapter 2. I attempted to outline various strategies which men might adopt in order to overcome some of these difficulties. The most central of these was reading or, more precisely, rereading; a critical and reflexive rereading of texts that were in practice about men and masculinities but which rarely gave recognition to this fact and often claimed to be talking about the whole of humanity. The group of *men* studied in 'Street Corner *Society*' became an example of 'The *Human* Group' in Homan's reworking of the study. Since, traditionally, work, in the sense of paid employment, has been seen as a main anchor of masculine identity, I felt that a useful point of departure might be those studies which looked at the situations of men in their places of work. However, work and occupation while often confirming or reinforcing masculine identities may also pose threats to those identities and I explored two of these potential threats: that of redundancy and unemployment and those provided when there were marked shifts in the gender composition of particular occupations, especially when women moved into work situations hitherto defined as belonging to men. I then looked at two challenges to men and masculinities specifically presented by feminism. The 'first wave' of feminism, identified with the movement for women's suffrage, presented a challenge to dominant patriarchy authority but also provided the opportunity for some men to identify with the feminist cause. The second, more recent, wave of feminism provided a comprehensive challenge to all aspects of patriarchal society and the gender order. Here, I looked at one of these, to the actual business of scientific, especially social-scientific, enquiry itself and whether men might learn something through specific debates about feminist methods and methodologies.

In so far as there has been a logic to all this it may be viewed as an interplay between three elements: the present-day feminist critique of sociological and other scholarly practices, situations where issues of men and masculinities have been put on the line, and texts, sociological or otherwise, which deal, directly or indirectly, with issues of men and masculinity. To follow through one example of this dynamic process: the feminist critique encouraged me to problematize issues of men and masculinity and this led me to reconsider these texts themselves, to ask whether they were providing straightforward 'real' statements about the situations of unemployed men or whether these texts, less consciously, were providing information about dominant constructions of men and masculinity. This triangular relationship may be found, with some variations, in all the strategies that I have explored here.

I am aware that many of my colleagues, if they have bothered to read this far, will still be sceptical. What, they might ask, is all the fuss about? Why don't I go off and do some proper sociology? I have attempted to state the problems at various points in this book, most obviously in Chapter 2 and the penultimate chapter. Very briefly it is this: if knowledge, seeing the word 'knowledge' as a process rather than a once-and-for-all accomplishment, is gendered, what problems does this present for the activities of male sociologists, especially those who wish to study issues of men and masculinity? There is another question lurking in the background, one which I have not asked directly yet partly because I am not sure whether I know the answer. This is, simply, what can men say or write about men that has not already been said by women, or could not be said by them in the future?

This last question is clearly the most difficult since, if it cannot be answered, the whole enterprise, of which this book might be seen as a part, will fall to the ground. It is a question that has been asked by some feminist women who are sceptical, to say, the least, about the developments around 'Men's Studies', even where this term has not been explicitly used (see for example Maynard 1990, especially pp. 282–5). The argument has two strands. In the first place, it is simply not true that there have been no studies of men and masculinity. On the contrary feminist writings have dealt with issues of sexual harassment and sexual violence, with patterns of discrimination in the workplace and the labour market, with the gender division of labour within the home and many other issues where men have been involved. Further, some of the key concepts, patriarchy and sexism, deal with issues of men and masculinity. In the second place, men's attempts to study themselves must always, to some extent, be suspect since it is their power that feminism has challenged. The study of men cannot, therefore, be separated from wider issues of sexual politics: 'To use words like 'compulsory', 'hierarchic' and 'hegemonic' to describe men's domination of women is to transform biology into politics. Whatever term is used, the implication is that men benefit from the subordination of women' (Brittan 1989: 128). These issues clearly affect the 'Men's Movement': 'The men's movement has one rather high credibility problem. Men are not widely oppressed; they seem to have no common passionate grievance to air' (Ingham 1984: 235). At this point, the male sociologists concerned about such matters might be tempted to go off and have a whinge. Women told us we shouldn't be studying women. Fair enough. Now they tell us that we shouldn't study men. What time do the pubs open? I shall try to avoid this response and try to provide an answer to the question as to what men can provide that women have not already provided. This may also provide further clues to questions about the gendered nature of sociological enquiry. I shall argue that, in part, the answers depend on how you understand the gender order in the first place.

Why can't a man be more like a woman?

Roughly speaking, there are two ways of speaking about gender: in terms of power and in terms of difference. These are certainly not logical or practical distinctions but they nevertheless do indicate broad tendencies in understanding the gender order. Translating this into a familiar mode of representation we have the model shown in Figure 9.1.

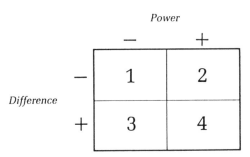

Figure 9.1 Models of the gender order

Box number 1 in the diagram is included for the sake of completeness since it is an understanding of the gender order that, in effect, denies the existence of that order. This may be to argue that gender is not that important, certainly not as compared with other modes of differentiation, or that it was important once but that this has declined in modern times. In most cases, this would seem to be an implicit view of gender, represented by an absence rather than a reasoned justification for this absence. It need hardly be added that most of the supporters of this particular model (if it may be described as such) will be men. Clearly, if this understanding were to be accepted, then there would be no need for this book.

Item 2 (Figure 9.1) is where differences of power are stressed and the major terms are 'patriarchy', 'domination', 'oppression' and 'exploitation'. Put simply, the only significant differences between women and men are in terms of the fact that the former are dominated by the latter. All other differences derive from this fundamental power difference. This includes biological differences since the point is not so much what differences exist between men and women but how they are accented and given

[190]

significance. Certainly alleged differences between 'masculine' and 'feminine' derive from differences based on power and domination and not the other way around.

In this case, knowledge is gendered in an ideological sense, that is to say it serves, directly or indirectly, to obscure the basic inequalities or oppressions within a patriarchal society. It is, clearly, here difficult for men to come to understand their role as oppressors but not impossible and there is no reason, in principle, why some men at least might not come to understand their role in a patriarchal society and seek ways of overthrowing that system. The parallel would be with members of the bourgeoisie who are prepared to give their understandings and experiences to the service of working-class movements or with whites who join the fight for colonial freedom or against racism, mainly through exposing the nature and sources of white oppression. Here, in principle, men would not have any distinctive contribution to make to the struggle against sexism or patriarchy, unless it be their greater familiarity with men's practices. Indeed, their 'insider' knowledge might be particularly valuable in alerting women to the difficulties they may expect to encounter or to weaknesses in systems dominated by men.

An approach which emphasizes power tends to be broadly liberal and rationalistic. It suggests that the significant differences between women and men are few and of declining significance, and that once women have been granted full and equal access to institutions of power and influence (full legal, political and employment rights) then such differences that remain will be of little practical importance. There have, always (as far as it is possible to tell) been understandings which have stressed real differences between women and men which cannot be removed by legislation or by wishing them away. Certainly, in the nineteenth century many of the discourses, conservative and radical, were around the nature of sexual differences and it is likely that these discussions have become accentuated in the latter part of the twentieth century. There may be several reasons for this. Intellectually, the development of psychoanalysis (in various strands) has proved to be a powerful stimulus in the exploration of sexual differences at the deepest levels. Politically, the apparent failure of legislation to bring about any far-reaching changes in all areas of the lives of men and women brought about a need for some kind of reappraisal of the very nature of sexual differences in society.

[191]

Finally, it may be noted that the developments of discourses around sexuality may have led to strengthening the links between sexuality and gender and thus accentuating the differences between women and men. While these discourses have also, clearly, had particular connotations in terms of gay and lesbian sexualities, they are of particular relevance when exploring oppositions between masculine and feminine. Thus numerous articles ask how it is possible for a woman to hold a senior managerial or professional job and still dress and appear in a way that is feminine and 'sexy'.

Hence, there have been approaches which give particular emphasis to sexual differences and which minimize questions of power (3 in Figure 9.1). Such an approach may cut across conventional distinctions between radical and conservative and between optimist and pessimist. In some versions, this emphasis upon difference may be rooted in biology, although this need not be the case. Differences in ways of perceiving and being in the world, in ways of thinking and in ways of morally evaluating human actions may be mapped on to differences between women and men. These differences may have very deep roots, in the unconscious, say, although they need not be seen as being completely fixed or inevitable.

Clearly, in this ideal-typical case there need be no problem with 'Men's Studies' and the study of men and masculinity by men. Indeed, this is what men ought to be doing. Studies by men of women, on the other hand, must always remain suspect. If men have, in the past, been inhibited from studying their own gender this may be due less to questions of power and more to fundamental gender differences. Men have been reluctant to study their own gender because masculine thought has a tendency towards universalizing and abstraction, and because men have an unwillingness to explore their own feelings and emotions. Both men and women are likely to benefit if the proper study of men were to be men.

It is clearly the fourth case which presents the most problems. Here differences and power are interdependent. Power rests upon historically constructed but deep-rooted gender and sexual differences; differences are maintained, reinforced and given solidity through power. Men, since they exercise power or enjoy the benefits of power or both, have no real motivation to subject their own practices to critical scrutiny. Further, the deep-rooted character of sexual differences means that not only are men incapable of studying or understanding women they are also, through the very nature of these differences as they apply to men, almost incapable of studying or understanding themselves. A bleak picture indeed! Even if men were capable of developing a critical study of their own practices it is doubtful whether they would be producing anything that women would want to, or be interested in hearing.

These categorizations are, of course, parodies although examples of each position are probably not all that difficult to come by. It is also likely that some version of the fourth position comes closest to characterizing the modern feminist critique. It maintains an emphasis upon power and inequality (and patriarchy still remains the preferred term even though it has been subjected to a considerable amount of critical examination) while also drawing upon and understanding themes of sexual differences, partly in order to understand the deep-rooted nature of patriarchal systems. It may be suggested, however, that there may always be some measure of tension between an understanding in terms of power and one in terms of difference and that the two cannot readily coexist in equal measure. This is because any kind of power model involves a relationship. To talk of masters and slaves, bourgeoisie and proletariat, white and black and of men and women is to talk of relationships. In the case of gender, we are talking about particular kinds of relationships that are both abstract and concrete, both structural and interpersonal. Power relationships do seem to presuppose some shared sets of understandings even if there is plenty of scope for misunderstanding and mystification as well. This must, in some measure, contradict some more extreme understandings of sexual difference.

I want to explore this notion of difference a little further, in order to discover whether any kind of mutual understanding between women and men is possible. If there are some possibilities for such understanding, if men and women do not inhabit two separate spheres, then it may not only be possible for men to study themselves but to report and discuss their findings with women, possibly to their mutual benefit.

Jardine, in her discussion of 'Men in feminism', uses the metaphor of learning a language and argues that many men, affected by feminism, are in the position of strangers who have learned all the right words, the grammar and the tenses and yet do not quite know how to put them together (Jardine 1987). They have learnt the vocabulary but are still hesitant with the syntax and intonation.

I am both attracted and puzzled by this metaphor. Perhaps many men, myself included, are a bit like Eliza Doolittle in *Pygmalion* where the carefully constructed appearance may easily be shattered by a 'not bloody likely' or where, sometimes, we speak the language a little too well, with a little too much pre-thought and preparation and not enough idiomatic fluency and spontaneity. Turning to men's writings, about themselves and about feminism and patriarchy, there is also a certain gaucherie, where the desire to please seems to override the need to analyse, explore and to understand.

Yet the metaphor is a little puzzling. Do men want, as this metaphor seems to imply, to pass as feminists? *Should* they want to pass as feminists? Or, more generally, do men want to 'pass' as women, like Dustin Hoffman in *Tootsie?* And this raises further problems as we have seen. If we accept the findings of psychologists over the past few decades, indeed the findings of biologists, we might reasonably conclude that there are very few significant differences between women and men, that the cultural factor can be said to account for some of the differences that remain and that, in any event, the overlaps between men and women, and their similarities are as impressive, probably more impressive, than any observed differences. It is only a kind of in-built bias in science to search for differences rather than to explore similarities, that has exaggerated these differences in the past. Differences between 'masculine' and 'feminine', it can be argued are cultural constructions which are routinely identified with persons labelled men and women although in practice these constructions – seen as sets or clusters of characteristic – may be found in both genders in different mixes. Certainly some of the lines of argument that I have pursued in earlier chapters have suggested that there are overlaps in the experiences of women and men, that they can work together at times and that such differences that remain cannot always be clearly spoken of in terms of straightforward constructions of men and masculinity. To argue otherwise would seem to open the way for biologism and essentialism and ultimately a kind of pessimism.

Is it the case, as this metaphor might suggest, that men and women have difficulty in understanding each other? It is certainly, even confining one's attention to sociological literature, possible to find many examples where men and women do seem to inhabit two different worlds or to operate with two different frameworks of understandings. Bernard's well known discussion of 'his' and 'her' marriage is a case in point (Bernard 1973). Yet it would also seem that men and women are together in a wide range of situations, at least in our society, in work and leisure as well as in marriage and sexual relationships and that they appear, for all practical everyday purposes, seem to understand each other reasonably well. After all, understanding in this everyday sense, does not necessarily mean approving or sharing.

Let me give a fanciful example. Let us suppose that man were able to disguise himself sufficiently in order to join a meeting of the British Sociological Association's Women's Caucus. (I stress I do not recommend this as a research strategy.) Would this man 'understand' what was going on? And in what sense of the word 'understand'? Since I have never attended any such meeting and am never likely to, I cannot answer this question with any accuracy. But, assuming that our man had a reasonable practical knowledge of British sociology, my guess is that he would have no difficulty in understanding a large part of the meeting: concerns about the gender composition of various committees, complaints about the use of sexist language in some of the sessions, some reports of sexual harassment at the bar and so on. What he might not understand might be the strength of feeling that could be expressed at some of the issues or why it was felt necessary to have a separate meeting for women in the first place.

It is here, of course, that we begin to unpack at least two senses of the word 'understand', senses which relate to Jardine's language metaphor with which this chapter began. I can begin to understand the range of meanings attached to the word 'patriarchy' or 'sexism' and I might begin to use these words in my writings or in daily discussions. There may be disagreements as to whether I am using these words correctly but these may be rectified in the usual way – 'ah yes, I see what you mean' – or there may be some recognition of difference.

On the other hand, it may well be argued, there is all the difference in the world between being able to use the word 'patriarchy' in a scholarly paper (or perhaps learning to criticize the word) and experiencing sexual harassment, feeling one's movements restricted at night or in public places, experiencing discrimination or being patronized by colleagues or by having

[195]

one's arguments marginalized through references to hormones. The same, of course, applies to the gulf between a white theoretical analysis of racism and the day-to-day experience of threat, hostility and discrimination or between the scholarly discussion of the concept of 'class' and the lived experiences of manual labour, unemployment and near poverty. As a middle-class, white male I am at least triply disadvantaged in making any attempts to understand in this more experiential meaning of the word.

Yet, even here, perhaps the gulf is not so absolute as it might at first appear. A couple of examples may begin to open up the point:

(a) A male student is employed by his local authority during the long vacation, cutting grass in some of the open spaces around his town. While the student is cutting a piece of lawn, a young man, with his arm around a young woman, approaches across the green. The young man deliberately organizes his walk so as to force the student to stop moving and to pull back his machine a little. No words or glances are exchanged.

(b) A young man is standing at a bus stop, reading a book. Another young man, well-built, looking rather like a stereotypical rugby player, is swaggering down the hill. As he passes the bus stop he gives a loud barking noise, causing the other to jump. He goes on, grinning to himself.

These two incidents actually happened to me. I was encouraged to recall them, when a couple of Australian women were discussing their surprise at the way in which young men had responded to them, when they had been walking to the shops or to the bus stop in Manchester. They concluded that these responses had little to do with sexuality and a lot to do with the exercise of power and dominance. The point that I tried to make, using these illustrations, is that while the harassment of women by men probably remains the quintessential form of this kind of dominance behaviour, it could also take place between men and between whites and blacks. I could also refer to other incidents, such as the experience as an adolescent of going to the cinema alone and having older men attempt to fondle my genitals.

My personal illustrations (which I do not think are all that unusual) are consistent with the argument that patriarchy is also about the dominance of men by men as well as the dominance of women by men or with Connell's discussion of hegemonic masculinities (Connell 1987). The point I wish to make is not to argue that the experiences of men and women are the same (there are clearly differences between these two relatively isolated incidents which occurred at a particular stage of my life-course, and the more or less continual exposure to comments, whistles or actual physical abuse that many women experience for a much larger portion of their lives) in these or in other respects, but to suggest that there are points of contact, enough to open up lines of communication and exchange.

The use of the metaphor of learning a language does rather suggest the 'two cultures' model, since different languages (actual or metaphorical) are conventionally taken as the mark of cultural difference. Even here, there are puzzles: are we talking about men in relation to women or men in relation to feminism? Either way it is puzzling. Why do men want to learn a 'feminist' or 'women's' language? Do they want to become, or at least pass as, 'feminists' or 'women'? As I shall argue later, it would seem that the first is, for the present at least, ill-advised and the second hardly possible. Thus the experience of the male–female transsexual involves much more than having a particular operation on one's genitals (Garfinkel 1967; Bogdan 1974). To learn to become a woman in this way is a long and arduous process, one which is often illuminating in the light that it throws upon routine constructions of gender and everyday sexisms but not one that can be recommended as an exemplary model.

I want to modify the metaphor slightly. It is not so much a question of learning (in the fullest sense) the language of feminism or of women. It is more the question of understanding one's own language, the language of men and masculinity. We all know that speaking and using a language on a routine day-to-day basis is a very different matter to understanding that self-same language, the way in which it works, the assumptions that it is based upon and so on. This is why people require specialized courses in order, say, to teach 'English as a foreign language'. In some ways this is as difficult as learning another language, since it involves standing back and taking a hard analytical look at one's own practices. This is what this book has attempted to do.

Another variation on the language analogy (one suggested to me by Janet Finch) might be provided by some Nordic countries such as Denmark and Sweden. Here, it may be argued, they speak

[197]

'different' languages but the languages have sufficient similarity for the members of these two countries to understand each other reasonably well for most practical purposes. There are differences but not an unbridgeable gulf. Were it not for the question of power, this might be a more exact analogy. The misunderstandings due to power are different from those due to difference. The latter are a matter of ignorance which can be rectified in ways which, while not always simple, can be recognized. The former are to do with questions of mystification and ideology and are less easily tackled.

What are the consequences of this discussion for our concern about the knowledge which men might provide about their situation which women have not already provided, and provided, moreover, without the ideological distortions? I think that this is still very much an open question, but I think that it can be answered in a way which is guardedly optimistic. One obvious area is to do with all-men institutions to which women have no access. Here men may be seen as acting as ethnographic moles, releasing information which might not otherwise be available. It may be noted that we are here talking about more areas than may first be imagined. It is not simply a question of institutions such as the Freemasons or some London clubs but other less formal masculine spaces such as work groups, drinking groups, even toilets. Similarly, men may give open access to features of their more 'inner' lives (particularly, say, around areas to do with sexuality and fatherhood) although here we must bear in mind the problems of the excessively confessional approaches discussed earlier.

However, if we accent questions of power rather than of difference, there may be more areas open not only to exploration by men but by men and women together, in exchange if not necessarily mutually. If, for example, we see (as most definitions have seen) questions of patriarchy to do with relationships between men as well as between men and women then there is clearly scope for some further explorations. The rather simple examples of men dominating men that I have provided earlier in this section may be a case in point. There are clearly hierarchies between men, fleeting and temporary, as well as structured and long-lasting. They may be in terms of strength, sexualities, wealth or class. The point is not that these practices and experiences are exactly the same as those between men and women but that they have sufficient similarities for there to be the possibilities of some cautious dialogues. Women will be able to point out where there are differences as well as similarities, and together there may be some exploration of the connection between these practices of power.

This last point raises the importance of the audience for studies of men and masculinity and the conditions of their productions. It suggests that while there may be times which are appropriate for all-men groups to discuss and share such issues, more and more of the discussions must take place in mixed audiences. And this also means that men, as well as exploring their own practices, should also continue to work for change in the institutions in which they work so that their contexts of discovery may be truly mixed.

The return of the invisible man

To begin to explore power differences between men and to use this as a basis for understanding power and differences between men and women seems to take us back to the beginning, when, as is now common practice, I argued for the importance of writing and talking about 'masculinities'. It will be remembered that I experienced difficulties when confronted with the question 'What does it feel like to be a man?'. What kind of answer was being expected? Where should I begin? Perhaps with biological or socio-sexual processes? What it feels like to have erections, or fail to have erections; what it feels like to masturbate or live in the fear of the consequences of masturbation; what it feels like to have an orgasm or fail to have an orgasm; what it feels like to hear that one has become a father or that one has failed to achieve that goal; what it feels like to be gay or to live in anxiety about one's sexuality: all these and many others, could be points of departure. Already, differences between men are being explored as well as possible overlaps with the experience of women. I could go further and ask questions about what it feels like to be trained to kill another man or to refuse to take part in such a training, what it feels like to bully or to be bullied, what it feels like to be in a shower-room full of naked men or a boardroom full of over-dressed men. The differences multiply, the answers to the original questions are continually deferred. Is it the best we can do to say that we are all different and that it is impossible to generalize?

[199]

Yet principled reasons might be offered for this kind of response. It may be associated with a kind of deconstructionism, the realization of cultural differences and differences within cultures that anthropologists find much easier to handle and to come to terms with than many sociologists writing about gender (Moore 1988). It is clearly in keeping with discussions about the pluralization of masculinities as a means of avoiding reductionism or reification. Whatever 'men' are, they are not the sum total of all the individual experiences, past and present, of those persons who have been routinely identified as 'men'. Yet it is difficult, also, to find some essence of masculinity running through all these individual exemplars. Even the pluralization of the term 'masculinities' does suggest at least some family resemblances between the different instances.

An analysis might begin to seek out the principles of some rudimentary classification (age, occupation, sexual orientation, religion, marital status and so on) while a more sophisticated analysis would seek some kind of relational or hierarchical ordering of such terms. Thus, for a given society, certain characteristics might be seen to cluster together; further, certain characteristics might be seen as of greater importance than others. In our own society this might include sexual orientation, occupation and marital status for example. Finally, it might be argued that different societies order and evaluate these characteristics in different ways, such that certain constructions and combinations of traits associated with men are more highly prized, more dominant or more privileged than others.

This is partly what Connell has in mind when he writes of hegemonic masculinities (Connell 1987). Within a given society there is an array of masculinities which are constructed out of the combination of the single trait, gender, with certain other statuses or characteristics. Thus heterosexual masculinities are generally prized over homosexual masculinities, marital ones (at least over a particular age) over single, upper status (in occupational terms) over lower status and so on. Moreover, holding these other factors and statuses constant, certain characteristics that might be used as descriptions of men are also given plus or minus signs: strong over weak, rational over emotional, active over passive and so on.

The ways in which these characteristics and statuses can be combined and ordered may still be a matter of some complexity. Moreover, the relationship between them may not always be stable; there may be contradictions of status and there may be room for challenge or negotiation. For example, it is generally assumed in Connell's account that heterosexual masculinity has priority over homosexual variations. Clearly, as he would recognize, this argument does not apply to all societies or at all times. An interesting variation comes from an account of the boys' school story, looking especially here at Alec Waugh's autobiographical novel, *The Loom of Youth* (1916): 'it is not a sign of weakness or degeneracy but of energy, strength and physical fitness. Rugger leads to it more surely than Swinburne, and the Pride of the School is likely to get the pick of the boys' (Quigly 1984: 209). Quigly argues that it was this argument which made the book so shocking when it was first published.

Another example may be provided around the word 'pompous'. My guess is that the most people on hearing the word will immediately have a mental picture of a man. The term has sometimes been used of women – Mrs Thatcher on occasions – but the probability will be that it will be seen as a masculine trait. It is clearly also not a prized trait. Yet, in order for a person to be accorded the label 'pompous', he must be of a reasonably high status to begin with: schoolmasters, local councillors and minor politicians would seem to be favourable candidates. It is associated with the exercise of power, but with its exercise in an inept or unseemly manner. Moreover, in popular culture, it is often another man who may deflate the pomposity: the clown or the thrower of a custard pie. It was a small boy who pointed out the absence of the Emperor's new clothes. Popular culture is, of course, also gendered and it is likely that women have been quietly, or less quietly, deflating men's pomposities for some centuries.

The point of these illustrations is to suggest that the ordering of masculinities according to some model of hegemony is not without its difficulties. For one thing, what are the boundaries of the 'society' of which we are speaking? What may be more or less accepted or regular with a boy's public school may not necessarily apply in a straightforward way in the world outside. Moreover, there are contradictions between different statuses and traits, at least potentially, just as there are often contradictions in individuals' evaluations of these traits. The most enthusiastic admirer of Rambo might be a little hesitant at having a whole set of Rambo clones moving in next door. The value of qualitative analysis or detailed historical and literary analysis is that it provides the opportunity to explore these complexities and dilemmas in more detail. This is certainly the kind of analysis of men and masculinity that we require in the future. Doubtless the person who asked 'What does it feel like to be a man?' as well as many feminists, will find that the analysis up to now might be more or less interesting but still does not answer the question. The implied answer 'Well it all depends what sort of man you are talking about' does not really seem to rise to the challenge. More to the point is that analysis has, up to this point, tended to consider men in isolation, in relation to each other. I have argued that this is an important aspect of the construction of masculinity and indeed of patriarchy and should be a major strand in the analysis of men and masculinities. However, we also need to consider men in relation to women. It may be argued that constructions of masculinity, senses of being a man or less than a man, come to their fore in relation to women. The point about the construction of hegemonic masculinity is, ultimately, in relation to the control and domination of women. Thus, heterosexuality may be legitimated and homosexuality stigmatized, because the former in all kinds of ways reinforces the institutions of patriarchy, while the latter might seem to threaten them, at least under certain social conditions. It may be acceptable (or at least ignored) at least in the public school setting since this can be constructed as a passing phase, and that more valuable aspects of the construction of male power are taking place at the same time. The pompous man may be a figure of fun among men because, we might speculate, he too readily shows the mechanisms and the meanings of male power. By deflating such pomposity with laughter and slapstick we remove this potential threat while keeping alive the real institutions of male domination.

I am exploring two themes in parallel here. At the more structural level I am repeating the argument that patriarchy is both about the domination of men over women and some men over some other men and about the relationships between these two sets of dominations. I do not subscribe to the arguments that relationships between men can *only* be understood in terms of the wider domination of men over women; I believe that some male practices have their relative autonomy. Thus I do not think that bullying or fighting in the playground between boys is simply a rehearsal for the exercise of power over women and I do not believe that wars, largely conducted by men, are simply to be explained in terms of the reproduction or the reinforcement of patriarchy.

At the more interactional level I am concerned about the constructions of men and women (especially of men) in relation to each other through everyday social interaction. Thus, what it feels like to be a man can only fully be answered in the context of gendered encounters, encounters where sexual or gender difference is accented. In practice this may mean almost every encounter in which men and women meet, although there may be variations in degree. Further such encounters might not be direct. A sense of masculinity may be constructed in front of a pin-up, a picture of a woman which accentuates her differences (hair, lips, breasts, buttocks) and stresses her being-for-men, a passive recipient of the male gaze. Or a boy may challenge or stand up to another boy in the course of an exchange of insults which cast doubts upon his gender or sexual orientation. Or, yet again, drill sergeants may tell new recruits that they are marching like a bunch of old women. (In the British armed services, the sewing kit that men carried about to repair uniforms and replace buttons was called a 'housewife'.)

On one level, therefore, I see masculinity as something which in part emerges out of and in part constitutes gendered encounters. As Mailer expressed it in characteristic style: 'Masculinity is not something given to you, something you're born with, but something you gain . . . and you gain it by winning small battles with honor' (Mailer, quoted in Schwenger 1984: 17). This is interesting in that, while seeming to adopt an interactionist approach to masculinity, Mailer is also, clearly, deploying one ideological version of a hegemonic masculinity. Seeing gender in the context of the family, Thompson and Walker adopt another version of a relational or interactionalist approach: 'something evoked, created and sustained day-by-day through interaction among family members' (Thompson and Walker 1989: 865). This is not to say, of course, that individuals have complete freedom as to which versions of masculinity they express or suppress in particular encounters. As we have seen, any society has a range of masculinities, historically shaped, which are hierarchically, if not always in an absolutely fixed fashion, arranged. Thus the versions of masculinity which are put on parade are doubly determined by the demands of the particular situation and by the array of masculinities that may be available and privileged. There is also some measure of historical determination when we consider the extent to which issues of masculinity are brought to the fore, held up for examination, or presented as an issue. For the most part, in many cases one may assume, it is simply not a problem. This reflects the wider structure of a patriarchal society which in the normal course of events does not call upon its men, in contrast to its women, to experience their gender as some kind of problem. Yet as we have seen, certain interactional and structural circumstances may put men and masculinities on the line. One major set of circumstances may be those associated with the rise of the feminist critique. One, doubtless unsatisfactory, answer to the question 'What does it feel like to be a man?' may then be the response 'Who's asking?'.

New Men and Post-Modern Men

It is not uncommon for the recent flood of books and articles to raise the image of something called the 'New Man'. Sometimes actual sightings are reported. Often, they are treated rather like alleged sightings of emus or pumas in the English countryside, as manifestations of a journalistic 'silly season' rather than as anything more substantial. Others, more historically inclined may suggest that the New Man is not all that new. Hodson reports that George Bernard Shaw was referring to the New Man in 1903 (Hodson 1984: 135) and a literary account of the eighteenth century not only points to one manifestation of this species but highlights some interesting ambiguities:

> Perhaps the increasing emphasis on father–daughter relations in the eighteenth century can be seen as symptomatic of the efforts of eighteenth century men to become less aggressive, more 'feminine' more gentle (in the modern sense) . . . . If the daughter is charmingly childlike in trust, devotion, submissiveness, the father is also permitted to be familiar, soft and tender. In fact, the father is to gain authority (even authority to destroy) through tenderness; a sort of emotional blackmail is substituted for more straightforward authoritarianism.
>
> (Doody 1988: 24)

Whether or not he exists in anything like sufficiently large numbers to constitute a genuine change, it is clear that this New Man is constructed out of a variety of themes. In the first place there is an emphasis on tenderness and expressiveness. The New Man is supposed to be more willing and more able to express and to share his feelings, especially with other men. He is more tender and more likely to eschew open or violent expressions of aggression; Rambo is conventionally held up as a negative role model. In terms of activities, the New Man is supposed to be more willing to take up domestic responsibilities, especially those in connection with fathering. Modern iconography has been augmented by numerous pictures of bare-chested men, clutching infants. In terms of style, again the New Man is expected to be more expressive in terms of clothing, fabrics, make-up and toiletries. Politically, the New Man is expected to attend Men's Groups and to take active steps in countering sexisms at the workplace or in public places.

It would be fair to say that most of the recent sociological accounts, as well as may of the journalistic accounts are, in fact, sceptical about this Man and his alleged sightings. Evidence as to actual changes in practices, as opposed to style, is difficult to assess, partly because of its general lack of historical depth. A Norwegian sociologist, summarizing a cross-national European study comes to a pessimistic conclusion:

> Nowhere in our data do we find signs of changes in men's activity patterns which would indicate such a transcendence of the male gender role as is indicated in the expression 'full share' – neither in the older nor the younger age group, neither in the socialist nor the capitalist countries.
>
> (Ve 1989)

This is probably fair, although it does not state how far, if at all, men have been moving in the direction of 'full share'. (For some further assessment see Morgan 1990b.) And if we go beyond the household, accounts of the New Man jostle with accounts of a 'male backlash' against feminism.

Amongst the discussions of the 'New Man' there developed a more ambiguous figure, that of 'Post-Modern Man'. One version of this would begin with the recognition that the gender order constitutes one of the central 'grand narratives' of the past and near-present but that, this too, could be challenged and fragmented in the celebration of plurality and discontinuity that is conventionally associated with post-modernity. More specifically, this has been characterized by some feminist critiques as a kind of 'critical cross-dressing' (Showalter 1987) or 'getting a bit of the other' (Moore 1988). Post-Modern Man finds it difficult to say what it feels like to be a man partly because he is spending more and more time trying to be a woman or to find out what it feels like to be a woman. This may sometimes literally involve putting on a frock or, more likely, playfully exploring a diversity of femininities and masculinities in many areas of cultural production and consumption.

There are some paradoxes with this movement. For one thing most of the writers who occupy the high ground of post-modern theorizing, as is the case with most modes of theorizing, are men. Moreover, the style of theorizing that is adopted is very much in keeping with a hegemonic masculine model: abstract, often 'difficult', detached and objective. For the more playful versions of deconstruction one often has to go to feminist writings. Certainly, this discussion of men and post-modernism has not been without its feminist critiques: 'Post-modernist thinkers are defending against the downfall of patriarchy by trying not to be male. In drag, they are aping the feminine rather than thinking their place as men in an obsolescent patriarchy' (Gallop 1988: 100). Indeed, Gallop's criticisms might be readily applied to much of the recent debate around men and masculinities. However, it would be wrong perhaps to be too dismissive. The exploration of a plurality of masculinities, both theoretically and practically, is the beginning of a critique of dominant narratives of the gender order. The dangers are obvious, particularly of a degeneration into a kind of apolitical consumerism, especially within the prevailing climate. (Similarly, something might be said of 'green consumerism'.) The gains are the beginnings of a realization of the potential diversity of human expression and experience, a diversity which is poorly served by structuring the world into masculinity and femininity.

What are we up to?

How do we describe the range of activities that men, and some women, are currently engaged in, in the critical exploration of men and masculinities? In recent years, the debate has focused on

[206]

the use of the term 'Men's Studies' especially as the term might be seen to signify new trends within the academy. In Britain, it would seem there is general disapproval of the term from men as well as from feminist women (see Hearn and Morgan 1990). The reasons for this, which have been thoroughly explored elsewhere (e.g. some of the papers in Hearn and Morgan 1990; also Maynard 1990), may be summarized briefly: there is danger that it may appropriate funds and resources, already scarce, that might otherwise have gone to feminist, women's or gender studies; there is the fear that it might, once again, marginalize the theories and writings of women, in favour of a newer and largely masculine canon; there is the fear that it might develop into yet another men's club with all the unfortunate consequences that might follow from that. All these worries and fears are justified, although to be fair, it is also the case that most of the people who have used the term 'Men's Studies' are also aware of these dangers.

If we reject the label 'Men's Studies', what are the alternatives? While some men might have a preference for the term 'feminist' or 'feminist studies' there is a recognition that this term would be even less appropriate, however appropriate it might have been in former times. 'Gender Studies' has some advocates, although perhaps lacks something of the critical edge that is implied in some of the other titles. Hearn's preference for 'The Critique of Men' probably comes closest to what men are in fact up to, although it would probably be a bit of a mouthful to translate into a course title (Hearn 1989b). Certainly, it combines a recognition that the focus is upon men and their practices and that there are clear sexual–political implications of this recognition.

Two things, to me, do seem to be clear. The first is that there is still a lot of work to be done in the exploration of men and masculinities and that this itself presents both opportunities and dangers. The opportunities have, to some extent, been explored in this book which, if it has any value, will send readers off to other texts, and to other studies as well as thinking about new pieces of research or critical investigation. The danger, perhaps, is that this quest may become too seductive. I find myself fascinated by the range of issues that these developments in gender studies have brought about, by the puzzles that are thrown up and by the myriad possibilities for further research and study. Yet, at the same time, I am not sure if I want to become too firmly identified with this kind of activity. Another part of me wants to argue that while gender, in this case masculinity, is important, it is not the whole story. It is possible that a totally effective 'critique of men' will be self-destructive and that what will be left will be sociological studies, historical studies or whatever, all of which will take account of gender as a matter of course.

The other point I wish to emphasize is that clearly something is happening around the area of gender, in theory and practice, and that most of this is to be welcomed. The fact that, in most Western countries at least, there is a growing recognition that there is not an area of human life which is not, in some way, touched by issues of gender and power in combination, is a major advance. As with all such advances it has its ambiguities and its threats, some of which have been explored in the past chapters. That nearly all of these issues have been put upon the agenda by feminist women is a matter of record; sexual harassment, violence in the family, rape in marriage, men's formal and informal exclusionary tactics and institutions and so on. This list is extensive, if not endless. But it is also the case that men have, in various ways and to varying degrees, responded to these issues. Many of the accounts have, quite rightly, dealt with the incompleteness and inadequacy of these responses. But there seems little doubt that these responses will continue and that 'the critique of men', or whatever other title one wishes to choose, will play its small part in the development of human freedom.

Bibliography

Acker, J. (1973) Women and social stratification: A case of intellectual sexism. In J. Huber (ed.), *Changing Women in a Changing Society*, pp. 174–83. Chicago: University of Chicago Press.

Aga, S. (1983) Women's attempts to break down the sex barriers in the labour market. In A. Leira (ed.), *Work and Womanhood: Norwegian Studies*, pp. 88–123. Oslo: Institute for Social Research.

Agassi, J. B. (1979) *Comparing the Work Attitudes of Women and Men.* Lexington, Mass.: Lexington Books.

Allen, J. (1987) 'Mundane Men': historians, masculinity and masculism. *Historical Studies* 22 (89): 617–28.

Allen, S., Waton, A., Purcell, K. and Wood, S. (eds) (1986) *The Experience of Unemployment.* Basingstoke: Macmillan.

Anderson, A. and Gordon, R. (1978) Witchcraft and the status of women. *British Journal of Sociology* 29: 171–84.

Bakke, E.W. (1933) *The Unemployed Man.* London: Nisbet.

Balzer, R. (1976) *Clockwise: Life In and Outside an American Factory.* New York: Doubleday.

Banks, O. (1985) *The Biographical Dictionary of British Feminists; Vol. 1 1800–1930.* Brighton: Wheatsheaf.

Barham, S. B. (1985) The phallus and the man: An analysis of male striptease. In L. Manderson (ed.) pp. 56–66. *Australian Ways.* Sydney: Allen & Unwin.

Barker, D. L. and Allen, S. (eds) (1976a) *Dependence and Exploitation in Work and Marriage.* London: Longman.

—— (1976b) *Sexual Divisions and Society: Process and Change.* London: Tavistock.

Beales, H. L. and Lambert, R. S. (eds) (1934) *Memoirs of the Unemployed.* London: Gollancz.

Berger, P. L. (1964) *The Human Shape of Work.* New York: Macmillan.

Berger, P. L. and Luckman, T. (1966) *The Social Construction of Reality.* New York: Doubleday.

Bernard, J. (1973) *The Future of Marriage.* New York: Souvenir Press.

Blauner, R. (1964) *Alienation and Freedom: The Factory Worker and His Industry.* Chicago: University of Chicago Press.

Blumstein, P. W. and Schwartz, P. (1977) Bisexuality in Men. In C. Warren (ed.) *Sexuality: Encounters, Identities and Relationships*, pp. 79–98. Beverly Hills: Sage.

Bogdan, R. (1974) *Being Different: The Autobiography of Jane Fry.* New York: Wiley.

Bologh, R. W. (1990) *Love or Greatness: Max Weber and Masculine Thinking – A Feminist Inquiry*. London: Unwin Hyman.

Booth, W. C. (1988) *The Company We Keep: An Ethics of Fiction*. Berkeley: University of California Press.

Bordo, S. (1986) The Cartesian masculinization of thought. *Signs* 2: 439–56.

Bostyn, A.-M. and Wight, D. (1987) Inside a community: values associated with money and time. In S. Fineman (ed.), *Unemployment: Personal and Social Consequences*, pp. 138–54. London: Tavistock.

Bouchier, D. (1983) *The Feminist Challenge*. Basingstoke: Macmillan.

Bourdieu, P. (1965) The sentiment and honour in Kabyle. In J. G. Peristany (ed.), *Honour and Shame*, pp. 191–242. London: Weidenfeld & Nicolson.

Bouwsma, W. J. (1988) *John Calvin: A Sixteenth-Century Portrait*. Oxford: Oxford University Press.

Brah, A. (1986) Unemployment and racism: Asian youth on the dole. In S. Allen, A. Waton, K. Purcell and S. Wood (eds), *The Experience of Unemployment*, pp. 61–78. Basingstoke: Macmillan.

Brannen, J. and Wilson, G. (eds) (1984) *Give and Take in Families*. London: Allen & Unwin.

Brittain, V. (1963) *Pethick-Lawrence: A Portrait*. London: Allen & Unwin.

Brittan, A. (1989) *Masculinity and Power*. Oxford: Blackwell.

Brod, H. (ed.) (1987) *The Making of Masculinities*. Boston, Mass.: Allen & Unwin.

Brown, R. G. S. and Stones, R. W. H. (1973) *The Male Nurse*. Occasional Papers in Social Administration, No. 5. London: Bell.

Burns, T. and Stalker, G. M. (1961) *The Management of Innovation*. London: Tavistock.

Butler, O. (ed.) (1984) *Feminist Experience in Feminist Research*. Studies in Sexual Politics, No. 2. Manchester: University of Manchester, Department of Sociology.

Callender, C. (1987) Women seeking work. In S. Fineman (ed.), *Unemployment: Personal and Social Consequences*, pp. 22–46. London: Tavistock.

Campbell, J. K. (1965) Honour and the devil. In J. G. Peristany (ed.), pp. 139–71. *Honour and Shame*. London: Weidenfeld & Nicolson.

Canaan, J. and Griffin, C. (1990). The new men's studies: part of the problem or part of the solution? In J. Hearn and D. H. J. Morgan (eds), *Men, Masculinities and Social Theory*, pp. 206–14. London: Unwin Hyman.

Chodorow, N. (1978) *The Reproduction of Mothering*. Berkeley-Los Angeles-London: University of California Press.

Cockburn, C. (1983) *Brothers: Male Dominance and Technological Change*. London: Pluto Press.

—— (1987) *Two-Track Training: Sex Inequalities in the YTS*. Basingstoke: Macmillan.

—— (1988) The gendering of jobs: workplace relations and the reproduction of sex segregation. In S. Walby (ed.), *Gender Segregation at Work*, pp. 29–42. Milton Keynes: Open University Press.

Coffield, F. (1987) From the celebration to the marginalization of youth. In G. Cohen (ed.), *Social Change and the Life Course*, pp. 87–105. London: Tavistock.

Collinson, D. L. and Collinson, M. (1989) Sexuality in the workplace: the domination of men's sexuality. In J. Hearn, D. L. Sheppard, P. Tancred-Sheriff and G. Burrell (eds), *The Sexuality of Organization*, pp. 91–109. London: Sage.

Connell, R. W. (1987) *Gender and Power*. Cambridge: Polity Press.

Cook, J. and Fonow, M. (1986) Knowledge and woman's interests: issues of epistemology and methodology in feminist sociological research. *Sociological Inquiry* 56: 2–29.

Cornwell, J. (1984) *Hard-Earned Lives*. London: Tavistock.

Corrigan, P. and Sayer, P. (1985) *The Great Arch: English State Formation and Cultural Revolution*. Oxford: Blackwell.

Coyle, A. (1984) *Redundant Women*. London: The Women's Press.

Crompton, R. and Jones, G. (1984) *White-Collar Proletariat: Deskilling and Gender in Clerical Work*. London: Macmillan.

Crowther, M. A. (1982) Family responsibility and state responsibility in Britain before the welfare state. *The Historical Journal* 25 (1): 131–45.

Cunnison, S. (1983) Participation in local union organization. School meals staff: a case study. In E. Gamarnikow, D. H. J. Morgan, J. Purvis and D. E. Taylorson (eds), *Gender, Class and Work*, pp. 77–95. London: Heinemann.

Dalley, G. (1988) *Ideologies of Caring: Rethinking Community and Collectivism*. Basingstoke: Macmillan.

Dalton, M. (1959) *Men Who Manage*. New York: John Wiley.

Darking, L. (1989) Labour of love. *Guardian*, 31 October 1989, p. 36.

Davidoff, L. (1983) Class and Gender in Victorian England: The Diaries of Arthur J. Munby and Hannah Cullwick. In J. L. Newton, M. P. Ryan and J. R. Walkowitz (eds), *Sex and Class in Women's History*. London: Routledge & Kegan Paul.

Davidoff, L. and Hall, C. (1987) *Family Fortunes*. London: Hutchinson.

Deacon, A. and Bradshaw, J. (1983) *Reserved For The Poor: The Means Test in British Social Policy*. Oxford: Basil Blackwell and Martin Robertson.

Dennis, N., Henriques, F. and Slaughter, C. (1956) *Coal is Our Life*. London: Eyre & Spottiswoode.

Dingwall, R. (1977) *The Social Organization of Health Visitor Training*. London: Croom Helm.

—— (1979) The place of men in nursing. In M. M. Colledge and D. Jones (eds), *Readings in Nursing*, pp. 199–209. Edinburgh: Churchill Livingstone.

Dinnerstein, D. (1978) *The Rocking of the Cradle and the Ruling of the World*. London: Souvenir Press.

Ditton, J. (1977) *Part-Time Crime: An Ethnology of Fiddling and Pilferage*. Basingstoke: Macmillan.

Doody, M. A. (1988) *Frances Burney: The Life in the Works*. Cambridge: Cambridge University Press.

Douglas, M. (1966) *Purity and Danger*. London: Routledge & Kegan Paul.

Dressel, P. L. and Petersen, D. M. (1982) Becoming a male stripper:

recruitment, socialization and ideological development. *Sociology of Work and Occupation* 9: 387–406.

Duroche, L. (1990) Male perception as social construct. In J. Hearn and D. Morgan (eds), *Men, Masculinities and Social Theory*, pp. 170–85. London: Unwin Hyman.

Eardley, T. (1985) Violence and sexuality. In A. Metcalf and M. Humphries (eds), *The Sexuality of Men*, pp. 86–109. London: Pluto Press.

Easlea, B. (1981) *Science and Sexual Oppression*. London: Weidenfeld & Nicolson.

Edwards, S. S. M. (1981) *Female Sexuality and the Law*. Oxford: Martin Robertson.

Ehrenreich, B. (1983) *The Hearts of Men: American Dreams and the Flight from Commitment*. London: Pluto Press.

Elshtain J. B. (1987) *Women and War*. Brighton: Harvester Press.

Emmett, I. and Morgan, D. H. J. (1982) Max Gluckman and the Manchester shopfloor ethnographies. In R. Frankenberg (ed.), *Custom and Conflict in British Society*, pp. 140–65. Manchester: Manchester University Press.

Engels, F. [1845] (1969) *The Condition of the Working Class in England*. London: Panther.

Esseveld, J. (1988) *Beyond Silence: Middle-Aged Women in the 1970s*. Lund: University of Lund, Department of Sociology.

Etzkowitz, H. (1971) The male sister: sexual separation of labour in society. *Journal of Marriage and the Family* 33: 431–4.

Evans, F. B. (1984) Women's employment – a domestic occupation? a reconsideration of women's employment, unemployment and domesticity. PhD thesis, University of Kent.

Farran, D. (1990) Analysing a photograph of Marilyn Monroe. In L. Stanley (ed.), *Feminist Praxis*, pp. 262–73. London: Routledge.

Feldberg, R. L. and Glenn, E. N. (1979) Male and female: job versus gender models in the sociology of work. *Social Problems* 26: 524–38.

Filby, M. P. (1987) The Newmarket racing lad: tradition and change in a marginal occupation. *Work, Employment and Society* 1: 205–24.

Finch, J. (1983) *Married to the job*. London: Allen & Unwin.

—— (1984) It's great to have someone to talk to: the ethics and the politics of interviewing women. In C. Bell and H. Roberts (eds), *Social Researching*, pp. 70–87. London: Routledge & Kegan Paul.

Fineman, S. (ed.) (1987a) *Unemployment: Personal and Social Consequences*. London: Tavistock.

—— (1987b) The middle class: unemployed and underemployed. In S. Fineman (ed.), *Unemployment: Personal and Social Consequences*, pp. 74–94. London: Tavistock.

Firestone, S. (1971) *The Dialectics of Sex*. St Albans: Paladin.

Floge, L. and Merrill, D. M. (1986) Tokenism reconsidered: male nurses and female physicians in a hospital setting. *Social Forces* 64: 925–47.

Ford, A. (1985) *Men*. London: Weidenfeld & Nicolson.

Fryer, D. and Ullah, P. (eds) (1987) *Unemployed People: Social and Psychological Perspectives*. Oxford: Oxford University Press.

BIBLIOGRAPHY

Gallop, J. (1988) *Thinking Through the Body*. New York: Columbia University Press.
Game, A. and Pringle, R. (1983) *Gender at Work*. Sydney: Allen & Unwin.
Gans, H. J. (1962) *The Urban Villagers*. New York: The Free Press.
Garfinkel, H. (1967) *Studies in Ethnomethodology*. Englewood Cliffs, N.J.: Prentice-Hall.
Garraty, J. A. (1978) *Unemployment in History*. New York: Harper & Row.
Gherardi, S. and Turner, B. (1987) *Real Men Don't Collect Soft Data*. Quaderno 13: Dipartimento di Politica Sociala, Universita di Trento.
Gilligan, C. (1982) *In A Different Voice*. Cambridge, Mass.: Harvard University Press.
Girouard, M. (1981) *The Return to Camelot: Chivalry and the English Gentleman*. New Haven and London: Yale University Press.
Gold, R. L. (1964) In the basement: the apartment building janitor. In P. L. Berger (ed.), *The Human Shape of Work*, pp. 1–50. New York: Macmillan.
Goldthorpe, J. H., Lockwood, D., Bechofer, F. and Platt, J. (1968) *The Affluent Worker: Industrial Attitudes and Behaviour*. Cambridge: Cambridge University Press.
Gouldner, A. W. (1955) *Patterns of Industrial Bureaucracy*. London: Routledge & Kegan Paul.
Griffiths, M. (1988) Feminism, feelings and philosophy. In M. Griffiths and M. Whitford (eds), *Feminist Perspectives in Philosophy*, pp. 90–108. Bloomington, Ind.: Indiana University Press.
Griffiths, M. and Whitford, M. (eds) (1988) *Feminist Perspectives in Philosophy*. Bloomington, Ind.: Indiana University Press.
Grimshaw, J. (1986) *Feminist Philosophers*. Brighton, Wheatsheaf.
Hamilton, R. (1977) *The Liberation of Women: A Study of Patriarchy and Capitalism*. London: Allen & Unwin.
Hanmer, J. (1990) Men, power and the exploitation of women. In J. Hearn and D. Morgan (eds), *Men, Masculinities and Social Theory*, pp. 21–42. London: Unwin Hyman.
Hannington, W. (1937) *The Problem of the Distressed Areas*. London: Gollancz.
Hansen, K. T. (1986) Household work as a man's job: sex and gender in domestic service in Zambia. *Anthropology Today* 2 (3): 18–23.
Harding, S. (ed.) (1987a) *Feminism and Methodology*. Milton Keynes: Open University Press.
—— (1987b) Is there a feminist method? In S. Harding (ed.), *Feminism and Methodology*, pp. 1–14. Milton Keynes: Open University Press.
—— (1987c) Conclusion: epistemological questions. In S. Harding (ed.), *Feminism and Methodology*, pp. 181–90. Milton Keynes: Open University Press.
Harris, C. C. (1987) *Redundancy and Recession in South Wales*. Oxford: Blackwell.
Harrison, B. H. (1978) *Separate Spheres: The Opposition to Women's Suffrage in Britain*. London: Croom Helm.

[213]

Hartstock, N. C. M. (1987). The feminist standpoint: developing ground for a specifically feminist historical materialism. In S. Harding (ed.), *Feminism and Methodology*, pp. 157–80. Milton Keynes: Open University Press.

Hearn, J. (1987) *The Gender of Oppression: Men, Masculinity and the Critique of Marxism*. Brighton: Wheatsheaf.

—— (1989a) Reviewing men and masculinities – or mostly boys' own papers. *Theory, Culture and Society* 6: 665–89.

—— (1989b) *Sociological Issues in Studying Men and Masculinities*. University of Manchester, Hollsworth Fellowship, Working Paper No. 2.

Hearn, J. and Morgan, D. (eds) (1990) *Men, Masculinity and Social Theory*. London: Unwin Hyman.

Hearn, J., Sheppard, D. L., Tancred-Sheriff, P. and Burrell, G. (eds) (1989) *The Sexuality of Organization*. London: Sage.

Henry, S. (1978) *The Hidden Economy: The Context and Control of Borderline Crime*. London: Martin Robertson.

Henwood, F. and Miles, I. (1987) The experience of unemployment and the sexual divisions of labour. In D. Fryer and P. Ullah (eds), *Unemployed People: Social and Psychological Perspectives*, pp. 94–110. Oxford: Oxford University Press.

Hepworth, M. and Turner, B. (1982) *Confession: Studies in Deviance and Religion*. London: Routledge & Kegan Paul.

Hodson, P. (1984) *Men: An Investigation into the Emotional Male*. London: BBC/Ariel Books.

Holter, H. (ed.) (1984) *Patriarchy in a Welfare Society*. Oslo: Universitetsforlaget.

Homans, G. (1950) *The Human Group*. New York: Harcourt, Brace and World.

Hughes, E. C. (1958) *Men and Their Work*. Glencoe, Ill.: The Free Press.

Hunt, F. (1986) Opportunities lost and gained: mechanization and women's work in the London bookbinding and printing trades. In A. John (ed.), *Unequal Opportunities: Women's Employment in England, 1800–1918*, pp. 71–94. Oxford: Blackwell.

Hurstfield, J. (1986) Women's unemployment in the 1930s: some comparisons with the 1980s. In S. Allen, A. Waton, K. Purcell and S. Wood (eds), *The Experience of Unemployment*, pp. 29–44. Basingstoke: Macmillan.

Ingham, M. (1984) *Men: 'The Male Myth Exposed'*. London: Century Publishing.

Jackson, D. (1990) *Unmasking Masculinity: A Critical Autobiography*. London: Unwin Hyman.

Jahoda, M., Lazarsfeld, P. and Zeisal, H. (1972) *Marienthal: The Sociography of an Unemployed Community*. London: Tavistock.

Jardine, A. (1987) Men in feminism: Odor di uomo or compagnons de route?. In A. Jardine and P. Smith (eds), *Men in Feminism*, pp. 54–61. New York: Methuen.

Kanter, R. M. (1977) *Men and Women of the Corporation*. New York: Basic Books.

—— (1988) Phases of societal and sociological inquiry in an age of discontinuity. In M. W. Riley (ed.), *Sociological Lives*, pp. 71–8. Newbury Park: Sage.

Kaufman, M. (ed.) (1987) *Beyond Patriarchy: Essays by Men on Pleasure, Power and Change.* Toronto: Oxford University Press.

Keller, E. F. (1982) Feminism and science. In N. O. Keohane, M. Z. Rosaldo and B. C. Gelpi (eds), *Feminist Theory: A Critique of Ideology*, pp. 113–26, Brighton: Harvester.

—— (1985) *Reflections on Gender and Science.* New Haven & London: Yale University Press.

Kimball, G. (1989) Egalitarian husbands. In M. S. Kimmel and M. A. Messner (eds), *Men's Lives*, pp. 550–7. New York: Macmillan.

Kimmel, M. S. (ed.) (1987a) *Changing Men: New Directions in Research on Men and Masculinity.* Newbury Park: Sage.

—— (1987b) The contemporary 'crisis' of masculinity in historical perspective. In H. Brod (ed.), *The Making of Masculinities*, pp. 121–54. Boston, Mass.: Allen & Unwin.

—— (1987c) Rethinking "Masculinity": New directions in research. In M. S. Kimmel (ed.), *Changing Men: New Directions in Research on Men and Masculinity*, pp. 9–23. Newbury Park: Sage.

Komarovsky, M. (1940) *The Unemployed Man and His Family.* New York: Dryden Press.

Land, H. (1980) The family wage. *Feminist Review* 6: 55–78.

Lang, G. E. and Lang, K. (1988) Recognition and Renown – The Survival of Artistic Reputation. *American Journal of Sociology* 94 (1): 79–109.

Leach, W. (1981) *True Love and Perfect Union: The Feminist Reform of Sex and Society.* London: Routledge & Kegan Paul.

Legge, K. (1987) Women in personal management: uphill climb or downhill slide?' In A. Spencer and D. Podmore (eds), *In A Man's World: Essays on Women in Male-Dominated Professions*, pp. 33–61. London: Tavistock.

Leira, A. (ed.) (1983) *Work and Womanhood: Norwegian Studies.* Oslo: Institute for Social Research.

Lewis, C. and O'Brien, M. (eds) (1987) *Reassessing Fatherhood: New Observations on Fathers and the Modern Family.* London: Sage.

Lewis, I. (1964) In the court of power: the advertising man. In P. Berger (ed.), *The Human Shape of Work*, pp. 113–81. New York: Macmillan.

Lewis, J. (1984) *Women in England 1870–1950.* Brighton: Wheatsheaf.

—— (1986) The working-class wife and mother and state intervention 1870–1918. In J. Lewis (ed.), *Labour and Love: Women's Experience of Home and Family 1850–1940*, pp. 99–120. Oxford: Blackwell.

Lewis, J., Clark, D. and Morgan, D. H. J. (1991) *Whom God Hath Joined Together: The Work of Marriage Guidance.* London: Routledge.

Lockwood, D. (1958) *The Blackcoated Worker: A Study in Class Consciousness.* London: Unwin University Press.

Lyons, A. (1989) *Dead Ringer.* Harpenden: No Exit Press.

McCann, G. (1988) *Marilyn Monroe. The Body in the Library.* Cambridge: Polity Press.

McKee, L. and Bell, C. (1986). His unemployment, her problem: the domestic and marital consequences of male unemployment. In S. Allen, A. Waton, K. Purcell and S. Woods (eds), *The Experience of Unemployment*, pp. 134–49. Basingstoke: Macmillan.

McKee, L. and O'Brien, M. (eds) (1982) *The Father Figure*. London: Tavistock.

McRae, S. (1986) *Cross-Class Families*. Oxford: Oxford University Press.

Marine, G. (1972) *A Male Guide to Women's Liberation*. New York: Holt, Rinehart & Winston.

Mars, G. (1982) *Cheats at Work: An Anthropology of Workplace Crime*. London: Unwin Paperbacks.

Marsden, D. (1982) *Workless*. London: Croom Helm.

Mattinson, J. (1988) *Work, Love and Marriage: The Impact of Unemployment*. London: Duckworth.

Maynard, M. (1990) The reshaping of sociology? Trends in the study of gender. *Sociology* 24: 269–90.

Merton, R. K. (1957) *Social Theory and Social Structure*, 2nd edn. Glencoe, Ill.: The Free Press.

Middleton, C. (1988) Gender divisions and wage labour in English history. In S. Walby (ed.), *Gender Segregation at Work*, pp. 55–73. Milton Keynes: Open University Press.

Miller, A. (1987) *Timebends. A Life*. London: Methuen.

Millett, K. (1977) *Sexual Politics*. London: Virago.

Millman, M. and Kanter, R. B. (1976) *Another Voice: Feminist Perspectives on Social Life and Social Science*. New York: Octagon Books.

Moore, H. L. (1988) *Feminism and Anthropology*. Cambridge: Polity Press.

Morgan, D. H. J. (1969) Theoretical and Conceptual Problems in the Study of Social Relations at Work: An Analysis of Differing Definitions of Women's Roles in a Northern Factory. PhD thesis, University of Manchester.

—— (1975) *Social Theory and the Family*. London: Routledge & Kegan Paul.

—— (1981) Men, masculinity and the process of sociological enquiry. In H. Roberts (ed.), *Doing Feminist Research*, pp. 83–113. London: Routledge & Kegan Paul.

—— (1986) Gender. In R. Burgess (ed.), *Key Variables in Social Investigation*, pp. 31–53. London: Routledge & Kegan Paul.

—— (1987) *It Will Make a Man of You: Notes on National Service, Masculinity and Autobiography*. Studies in Sexual Politics, No. 17. Manchester: University of Manchester, Department of Sociology.

—— (1990a) Masculinity, autobiography and history. *Gender and History* 2: 34–9.

—— (1990b) Issues of critical sociological theory: men in families. In J. Sprey (ed.), *Fashioning Family Theory: New Approaches*, pp. 67–106. Newbury Park: Sage.

Morgan, K. O. (1975) *Keir Hardie: Radical and Socialist*. London: Weidenfeld & Nicolson.

Morris, L. D. (1987) 'The household and the labour market' and 'Domestic circumstances'. In C. C. Harris (ed.), *Redundancy and Recession in South Wales*, pp. 127–55. Oxford: Blackwell.

Network (May 1984) *Challenging the Feminist Challenge: A Forum on Bouchier*, pp. 6–7. London British Sociological Association.

Newton, P. (1987) Who becomes an engineer? Social psychological antecedents of a non-traditional career choice. In A. Spencer and D. Podmore (eds), *In A Man's World: Essays on Women in Male Dominated Professions*, pp. 182–202. London: Tavistock.

Nichols, T. and Beynon, H. (1977) *Living with Capitalism*. London: Routledge & Kegan Paul.

Oakley, A. (1976) Wisewoman and medicine man: changes in the management of childbirth. In J. Mitchell and A. Oakley (eds), *The Rights and Wrongs of Women*, pp. 17–58. Harmondsworth: Penguin.

—— (1981) *Subject Women*. Oxford: Martin Robertson.

Pahl, R. (1984) *Divisions of Labour*. Oxford: Blackwell.

Pankhurst, E. [1914] (1985) *My Own Story*. Westport, Conn.: Greenwood Press.

Pankhurst, E. Sylvia (1911) *The Suffragette: The History of the Women's Suffrage Movement, 1905–1910*. London: Gay & Hancock.

Pateman, C. (1988) *The Sexual Contract*. Cambridge: Polity Press.

Peristany, J. G. (ed.) (1965) *Honour and Shame: The Value of Mediterranean Society*. London: Weidenfeld & Nicolson.

Pethick-Lawrence, F. W. (1942) *Fate Has Been Kind*. London: National Book Association, Hutchinson.

Pilgrim Trust (1938) *Men Without Work*. Cambridge: Cambridge University Press.

Pitt-Rivers, J. (1965) Honour and social status. In J. G. Peristany (ed.), *Honour and Shame*, pp. 19–78. London: Weidenfeld & Nicolson.

Poland, F. and Stanley, L. (1988) *Feminist Ethnography in Rochdale*. Studies in Sexual Politics, No. 22. Manchester: University of Manchester, Department of Sociology.

Pollert, A. (1981) *Girls, Wives, Factory Lives*. London: Macmillan.

Prather, J. (1971) Why can't women be more like men?: a summary of the sociopsychological factors hindering women's advancement in the professions. *American Behavioural Scientist* 15: 172–82.

Pringle, R. (1988) *Secretaries Talk*. London: Verso.

Purcell, K. (1982) Female manual workers, fatalism and the reinforcement of inequalities. In D. Robbins *et al.* (eds), *Rethinking Inequality*, pp. 43–61. Farnborough: Gower.

Quigly, I. (1984) *The Heirs of Tom Brown*. Oxford: Oxford University Press.

Rathbone, E. [1924] (1949) *Family Allowances* (original title *The Disinherited Family*). London: Allen & Unwin.

Reid, F. (1978) *Keir Hardie: The Making of a Socialist*. London: Croom Helm.

Riley, M. W. (ed.) (1988) *Sociological Lives*. Beverly Hills: Sage.

Rogers, M. W. (ed.) (1988) *Men Only: An Investigation into Men's Organizations*. London: Pandora.

Rose, P. (1985) *Parallel Lives: Five Victorian Marriages*. Harmondsworth: Penguin.

Ross, E. (1986) Labour and Love: rediscovering London's working-class mothers, 1870–1918. In J. Lewis (ed.), *Labour and Love: Women's Experience of Home and Family 1850–1940*, pp. 73–98. Oxford: Blackwell.

Rossi, A. S. (ed.) (1970) *Essays on Sex Equality: John Stuart Mill, Harriet Taylor Mill*. Chicago: University of Chicago Press.

Rowbotham, S. (1974) *Hidden from History*, 2nd edn. London: Pluto Press.

Roy, D. F. (1960) 'Banana Time': job satisfaction and informal interaction. *Human Organization* 18: 158–68.

Russ, J. (1983) *How To Suppress Women's Writings*. Austin: University of Texas Press.

Schochet, G. J. (1975) *Patriarchalism in Political Thought*. Oxford: Blackwell.

Schwenger, P. (1984) *Phallic Critiques: Masculinity and Twentieth Century Literature*. London: Routledge & Kegan Paul.

Segal, B. E. (1962) Male nurses: a case study in status contradiction and prestige loss. *Social Forces* 41: 31–8.

Segal, L. (1988) Look back in anger: men in the 50s. In R. Chapman and J. Rutherford (eds), *Male Order*, pp. 68–96. London: Lawrence & Wishart.

—— (1989) Slow change or no change? Feminism, socialism and the problem of men. *Feminist Review* 31: 5–21.

—— (1990) *Slow Motion: Changing Masculinities, Changing Men*. London: Virago.

Seidler, V. J. (1989) *Rediscovering Masculinity: Reason, Language and Sexuality*. London: Routledge.

Sennett, R. and Cobb, J. (1977) *The Hidden Injuries of Class*. Cambridge: Cambridge University Press.

Sharpe, S. (1984) *Double Identity: The Lives of Working Mothers*. Harmondsworth: Penguin.

Sherif, C. W. (1987) Bias in psychology. In S. Harding (ed.), *Feminism and Methodology*, pp. 37–56. Milton Keynes: Open University Press.

Showalter, E. (1987) Critical cross-dressing: male feminists and the woman of the year. In A. Jardine and P. Smith (eds), *Men in Feminism*, pp. 116–32. New York: Methuen.

Sinfield, A. (1981) *What Unemployment Means*. Oxford: Martin Robertson.

Skocpol, T. (1988) An 'Uppity Generation' and the revitalization of macroscopic sociology: reflections at midcareer by a woman from the 1960s. In M. W. Riley (ed.), *Sociological Lives*, pp. 145–59. Beverly Hills: Sage.

Smith, D. (1987) Woman's perspective as a radical critique of sociology. In S. Harding (ed.), *Feminism and Methodology*, pp. 84–96. Milton Keynes: Open University Press.

—— (1988) *The Everyday World as Problematic*. Milton Keynes: Open University Press.

—— (1989) Sociological theory: methods of writing patriarchy. In R. A. Wallace (ed.), *Feminism and Sociological Theory*, pp. 34–64. Newbury Park: Sage.

BIBLIOGRAPHY

Snodgrass, J. (ed.) (1977) *For Men Against Sexism: A Book of Readings.* Albion, Ca.: Times Change Press.

Spencer, A. and Podmore, D. (1987) Women lawyers – marginal members of a male-dominated profession. In A. Spencer and D. Podmore (eds), *In A Man's World*, pp. 113–33. London: Tavistock.

Spender, D. (1982) *Women of Ideas and What Men Have Done to Them.* London: Routledge & Kegan Paul.

Stanley, L. (1985a) *Accounting for the Fall of Peter Sutcliffe and the Rise of the So-called 'Yorkshire Ripper'.* Occasional Papers, No. 15. Manchester: University of Manchester, Department of Sociology.

—— (1985b) *Feminism and Friendship: Two Essays on Olive Schreiner.* Studies in Sexual Politics, No. 8. Manchester: University of Manchester, Department of Sociology.

—— (1990a) Feminist praxis and the academic mode of production: and editorial introduction. In L. Stanley (ed.), *Feminist Praxis*, pp. 3–19. London: Routledge.

—— (1990b) The impact of feminism in sociology: the last twenty years. In C. Kramarae and D. Spender (eds) *The Knowledge Explosion.* New York: Pergamon.

—— (1990c) Moments of writing: is there a feminist auto/biography?' *Gender and History* 2: 58–67.

—— (ed.) (1990d) *Feminist Praxis: Theory and Epistemology in Feminist Sociology.* London: Routledge.

Stanley, L. and Wise, S. (1990) Method, methodology and epistemology in feminist research processes. In L. Stanley (ed.), *Feminist Praxis*, pp. 20–62. London: Routledge.

Strachey, R. (1928) *'The Cause'. A Short History of the Women's Movement in Great Britain.* London: G. Bell.

Strauss, S. (1982) *'Traitors to the Masculine Cause': The Men's Campaigns for Women's Rights.* Westport, Conn.: Greenwood Press.

Sydie, R. A. (1987) *Natural Women, Cultured Men: A Feminist Perspective on Sociological Theory.* Milton Keynes: Open University Press.

Symons, A. J. A. [1934] (1966) *The Quest for Corvo: An Experiment in Autobiography.* Harmondsworth: Penguin.

Symons, J. [1950] (1986) *A. J. A. Symons: His Life and Speculations.* Oxford: Oxford University Press.

Tawney, R. H. [1926] (1938) *Religion and the Rise of Capitalism.* West Drayton: Penguin.

Taylor, L. and Walton, P. (1971) Industrial sabotage: motives and meanings. In S. Cohen (ed.), *Images of Deviance*, pp. 219–45. Harmondsworth: Penguin.

Theweleit, K. (1987) *Male Fantasies*, Vol. 1. Cambridge: Polity Press.

Thomas, A. (1990) The significance of gender politics in men's accounts of their 'gender identity'. In J. Hearn and D. Morgan (eds), *Men, Masculinities and Social Theory*, pp. 143–59. London: Unwin Hyman.

Thompson, L. and Walker, A. J. (1989) Gender in Families – Women and Men in Marriage, Work and Parenthood: A Review. *Journal of Marriage and the Family*, 51 (4): 845–71.

[219]

Todd, J. (1989) *The Sign of Angellica: Women's Writings and Fiction, 1660–1800.* London: Virago.

Ullah, P. (1987) Unemployed black youths in a northern city. In D. Fryer and P. Ullah (eds), *Unemployed People: Social and Psychological Perspectives,* pp. 111–47. Oxford: Oxford University Press.

Underwood, K. (1964) On the pinnacles of power – the business executive. In P. Berger (ed.), *The Human Shape of Work,* pp. 181–210. New York: Macmillan.

Ve, H. (1989) The male gender role and responsibility for children. In Boh, K. *et al.* (eds), *Changing Patterns of European Family Life,* pp. 249–63. London: Routledge.

Walby, S. (1983) Patriarchal structures: the case of unemployment. In E. Gamarnikow, D. H. J. Morgan, S. Purvis and D. E. Taylorson (eds), *Gender, Class and Work,* pp. 149–66. London: Heinemann.

—— (1986) *Patriarchy at Work.* Cambridge: Polity Press.

—— (ed.) (1988) *Gender Segregation at Work.* Milton Keynes: Open University Press.

Walczak, Y. (1988) *He and She: Men in the Eighties.* London: Routledge.

Walker, C. R. and Guest, R. H. (1952) *The Man on the Assembly Line.* Cambridge, Mass.: Harvard University Press.

Walkowitz, J. R. (1980) *Prostitution in Victorian Society: Women, Class and the State.* Cambridge: Cambridge University Press.

Wallace, C. and Pahl, R. (1986) Polarization, unemployment and all forms of work. In S. Allen, J. Waton, K. Purcell and S. Wood (eds), *The Experience of Unemployment,* pp. 116–33. Basingstoke: Macmillan.

Ward, K. and Grant, L. (1985) The feminist critique and a decade of published research in sociological journals. *Sociological Quarterly* 26: 139–57.

Weber, Marianne [1926] (1988) *Max Weber: A Biography.* New Brunswick and Oxford: Transaction Books.

Weber, M. [1904–5] (1930) *The Protestant Ethic and the Spirit of Capitalism.* London: Allen & Unwin.

—— [1921] (1968) *Economy and Society: An Outline of Interpretive Sociology.* New York: Bedminster Press.

West, C. and Zimmerman, D. (1977) Women's place in everyday talk: reflections on parent–child interaction. *Social Problems* 24: 521–9.

Westergaard, J., Noble, I. and Walker, A. (1989) *After Redundancy.* London: Routledge.

Westwood, S. (1984) *All Day, Every Day.* London: Pluto Press.

Wheelock, J. (1990) *Husbands at Home: The Domestic Economy in a Post-Industrial Society.* London: Routledge.

White, A. (1989) *Poles Apart: The Experience of Gender.* London: J. M. Dent.

Whyte, W. F. (1955) *Street Corner Society.* Chicago: University of Chicago Press.

Williams, C. (1981) *Opencut: The Working Class in an Australian Mining Town.* Sydney: Allen & Unwin.

Wise, S. (1987) A framework for discussing ethical issues in feminist research: a review of the literature. In *Writing Feminist Biography 2,*

Studies in Sexual Politics, No. 19, pp. 47–88. Manchester: University of Manchester, Department of Sociology.

—— (1990) From butch god to teddy bear? Some thoughts on my relationship with Elvis Presley. In L. Stanley (ed.), *Feminist Praxis*, pp. 134–44. London: Routledge.

Woodhouse, A. (1989) *Fantastic Women: Sex, Gender and Transvestism*. Basingstoke: Macmillan.

Zimmeck, M. (1986) Jobs for the girls: the expansion of clerical work for women, 1850–1914. In A. V. John (ed.), *Unequal Opportunities: Women's Employment in England 1800–1918*, pp. 153–78. Oxford: Blackwell.

Name index

Subject index